Around the

Opry Table

▪▫▪▫▪▫▪▫▪▫▪▫▪▫▪▫▪▫▪▫▪▫▪▫▪▫▪▫▪▫▪▫▪▫▪▫

Also by the
Grand Ole Opry:

The Grand Ole Opry: The Making of an American Icon

Around the
Opry Table

A FEAST OF RECIPES AND STORIES
FROM THE GRAND OLE OPRY®

KAY WEST

CENTER STREET®

NEW YORK   BOSTON   NASHVILLE

Center Street
Hachette Book Group USA
237 Park Avenue
New York, NY 10017

Visit our Web site at www.centerstreet.com.

Center Street is a division of Hachette Book Group USA, Inc.
The Center Street name and logo is a trademark of Hachette Book Group USA, Inc.

Printed in the United States of America

First Edition: October 2007
10 9 8 7 6 5 4 3 2 1

Library of Congress Cataloging-in-Publication Data
West, Kay, 1955–
Around the Opry table : a feast of recipes and stories from the Grand Ole Opry / Kay West.
p.   cm.
Includes bibliographical references.
ISBN-13: 978-1-931722-87-2
ISBN-10: 1-931722-87-0
1. Cookery, American.   2. Country musicians—United States.
3. Grand ole opry (Radio program)   I. Title.

TX715.W5284 2007
641.5973—dc22   2007001460

For my mother and father,
Joyce and Jay,

and my daughter and son,
Joy and Harry

Contents

Acknowledgments

My thanks to Gaylord Entertainment's Steve Buchanan and Melissa Fraley, who during this endeavor became Melissa Fraley Agguini and a mother to boot. One can get married *and* birth a baby in the time it takes to write a book. They invited me to do this project, and I am immeasurably grateful for that opportunity. For invaluable assistance behind the scenes and access to the inner sanctum of the Grand Ole Opry, I thank Pete Fisher, Gina Keltner, Brenda Colladay, Dan Rogers, Tim Thompson, Jo Walker, Becky Sanders, Tommy Huff, and Sally Smith. For his razor-sharp memory and irreverent humor, Jerry Strobel. For infinite patience and encouragement, editor Christina Boys. For their scholarly knowledge of and deep affection for the Opry, John Rumble with the Country Music Hall of Fame Library, and Ronnie Pugh of The Nashville Room at the Nashville Public Library.

My thanks to all the Opry members who generously shared their time, stories, and recipes with me; it was an honor to be in their presence. Appreciation as well to managers, tour managers, agents, lawyers, label executives, and publicists—the hardest-working people in show business—for their logistical aid.

Though I spent countless hours in solitary confinement and social quarantine working on this project, it did not happen in a vacuum. For being there, in thought, word, and deed: my family and especially my children, for their good nature and generous hearts; Mother's Resource Group: Janet, Pat, Bridgett, Michelle, Barbara, Joanne, Claire, Christine, Tracy, Jill, and Monica; League of Beleaguered Women: Liz, Christine, Susan, and Carrington; Nashville Heat Baseball Moms: Betsy, Sue, Felice, Katie, Anne, Nancy, Mary Ellen, Susan, Rosanne, Jill, and Ellen; and in a league of his own, Gentleman John. The *Nashville Scene*'s Liz, Jack, and for the longest time, Jonathan; *Nashville Lifestyles'* rooster in the henhouse, Bill; spiritual advisors Becca and Charlie; Wacky Jayne, Kimmie, Susie Q, Amanda Carol, Caroline, Hunter, and always Gay; Nashville Sounds Baseball and Tracy; Mirror Restaurant's

Colleen, Michael, Stephanie, Albert, OMB, Hal, and Kim; Nashville Fire Department Station 9 for the willingness to test recipes and their brutally honest critiques; RRT, for the safety net; and finally, because if he can't be first, he wants to be last, Wayne Halper. This would not have happened without you. There's a pie with your name on it.

Introduction

In the early days of the Opry, touring was far from the comfortable experience it is today. Entire bands were crammed into a single car, suitcases stuffed in the trunk and instruments strapped on the roof, driving miles and miles from one small town to the next—an arduous journey unbroken by convenience marts or roadside restaurants. It was not at all unusual for fans to invite the performers who had been broadcast into their lives every Saturday night via WSM radio to come into their homes, sit at their table, and share a meal before a show. Nor was it uncommon for food to be used as commerce, meaning Opry members literally sang for their supper. Porter Wagoner, whose membership in the Opry dates back a half century, had friendships with some of the earliest members, like Roy Acuff, who said there were many times that if people didn't have the cash for a ticket, they would bring food to the box office instead. "Maybe a slab of bacon, or some ham. If it was a big family, they might bring three dozen eggs!"

Fan clubs could be counted on to put on a mighty fine feed when the objects of their affection came to town. Bill Anderson recalls summers touring a circuit of outdoor parks in the Northeast, and the good eating they enjoyed thanks to the friendly competition between local ladies who took pride in their cooking skills.

We used to play two shows at those parks, and members of the fan club in the area where we were playing would get together and plan a picnic for us between shows. They'd set up big long tables end to end, and lay out the most incredible spreads of the best home cooking. These ladies would have cooked for days. There might be six different hams, fourteen bowls of potato salad, a dozen plates of deviled eggs, and pies as far as you could see. All the ladies would be making sure you tried their ham, and they'd want a picture of you eating it to prove it. They'd come over with a plate of ham and their Instamatic camera and you'd try to tell them you had already had some ham and how good it was, but they'd say, "That was Mabel's *ham. I want a picture of you eating* my *ham." God help you if you fussed over one ham more than another! I have fans that have been coming to see me for forty years, and they rarely come empty-handed. They are genuinely fans and friends, and that's one of the most lasting treasures of this business.*

On the road, artists know that certain towns mean certain foods from certain folks will find their way to the bus: bratwurst in Milwaukee, Key lime pie in Florida, country ham in Kentucky, and tamales in New Mexico.

At home, the backstage desk at the Grand Ole Opry House is the receiving department for tomatoes, potatoes, pies, and pickles. One year, nearly thirty cakes arrived to celebrate Vince Gill's birthday. As one fan explained, "They give us so much with their music, we just want to give them something back to show them how much we love them."

More than any other institution in America, with the possible exception of organized religion, the Grand Ole Opry serves as an extended family; many would argue that the Opry *is* a religion. After all, two of its ancestral homes have been churches.

Sixty-five current cast members are the immediate family who fill the sacred circle at the center of the stage of the Opry House; the spirit of more than 250 singers, musicians, dancers, comediennes, and entertainers who preceded them hover in the rafters above; and the Opry's countless friends and fans stand in the wings, completing the circle.

Since its inception in 1925 the Opry has been a guest in their homes, thanks to radio, television, and in the twenty-first century, the Internet. Opry members have come to their cities and towns, performed in their schoolhouses and roadhouses, dance halls and concert halls, in theaters and amphitheaters. Millions of the faithful have made the pilgrimage from their homes to the home of the Grand Ole Opry, smack dab in the middle of Tennessee. They've claimed a spot in the crowded hallway outside the first WSM studio in the National Life and Accident Insurance Company building in downtown Nashville, or settled into a cushioned pew in the climate-controlled comfort of the spacious 4,400-seat Grand Ole Opry House.

For more than eighty years, the Grand Ole Opry has generously shared its weekly repast of music, comedy, showmanship, culture, and characters with this extended family. *Around the Opry Table* serves up a feast of another type: memorable meals, appetizing anecdotes, favorite foods, and treasured recipes from its storied past and abiding present.

Off the stage, cast members and staff come together for meals, whether at a restaurant to grab a bite to eat between shows, at formal dinners, or at casual potlucks. Spending so much time on the road, time around the table with their *own* families enjoying the foods that say "welcome home" becomes especially precious.

Interviews with cast members, Grand Ole Opry staff, and fans, Opry archives and old cookbooks have yielded a collection of recipes, stories, and songs from family, friends, and fans that span the history of the Opry, from Uncle Dave Macon's passion for good old-fashioned country ham to the thoroughly modern Tennessee paella served at Dierks Bentley's Opry induction party. There are mama recipes and great-grandma recipes, one from Aunt Floy and one from Aunt Margaret; there are recipes from way back in the hills, up north, down south, out west, back east, and a couple from the old country. *Around the Opry Table* serves up a banquet of meals and memories that speak of friendship, gratitude, generosity, and love, spanning miles and years, slow cooked by place and time.

Around the

Opry Table

Uncle Dave Macon with Opry announcer George D. Hay.

Uncle Dave Macon

Joined the Opry cast in 1925

(1870–1952)

A handbill promoting a schoolhouse show—a typical venue in small towns—in June 1930, touts the headliner, Uncle Dave Macon, as "the greatest trick comical banjo player in the South." Whether or not trick comical banjo playing was a highly competitive field at the time is not known, but there is no doubt that Uncle Dave—who was fifty-five years old when he joined the Opry—was a consummate showman and a larger-than-life personality.

Born in 1870 in Smart Station, Tennessee, he spent the first thirteen years of his life on a farm in Rutherford County. In 1883, his father—a Confederate war captain—purchased the Broadway Hotel in downtown Nashville, relocating his wife and ten children from country to city. The Broadway was the road home for many traveling entertainers and musicians, and young Dave took advantage of their presence in the lobby of his father's hotel to learn banjo at the feet of the masters.

When his father was murdered in 1885, his mother moved the family back to rural Tennessee, where she operated a country inn and raised her brood. Macon married Matilda Richardson in 1899, sired seven children, and operated his own horse-drawn wagon company in the Kittrell community of Rutherford County, Tennessee. He indulged his love of the spotlight by providing "pass the hat" entertainment at area schools, introducing himself as Uncle Dave to put children at ease. In 1918, when the automobile burst out of its starting gate with more horsepower than his stable could hope to muster, he parked his wagons and decided to take a stab at making music his livelihood. His ebullient stage persona and mastery of the banjo captivated audiences, and for the next seven years, Uncle Dave barnstormed the South, making regular appearances for the Loews theater chain. In December 1925, he was invited to join the cast of WSM's Barn Dance by announcer George D. Hay, known as the Solemn Ole

Judge, or simply Judge Hay, after a stint writing a humor column titled "Howdy, Judge" for the *Commercial Appeal* newspaper in Memphis. Uncle Dave's membership predated even the name Grand Ole Opry, which was bestowed by the judge. Hay, who prided himself on dispensing catchy nicknames, introduced the entertainer as the Dixie Dewdrop.

Having performed his singing, banjo-picking, joke-telling act professionally since an early age, and with several recordings for Vocalion and vaudeville tours under his belt, Uncle Dave Macon was the first bona fide star of the Grand Ole Opry cast. The sheer energy of his performances and his folksy, conversational introductions to his songs leapt through rapt home listeners' radios, and tremendous crowds turned out for his traveling shows.

In 1939, Republic Studios in Hollywood expressed an interest in making a movie of the growing national phenomenon of the Grand Ole Opry, and sent one of their executives to Nashville to catch the show. WSM executives decided to take full advantage of Uncle Dave's charismatic personality and gracious Southern hospitality and asked if he would entertain the gentleman at his farm in Cannon County. Uncle Dave enthusiastically accepted, and directed his cook to prepare a "real, sho-nuf Tennessee dinner with all the trimmings." Opry announcer and program director Judge Hay, who was part of the party, was so impressed that he wrote about it in his column, "A Story of the Grand Ole Opry," which ran in Minnie Pearl's *Grinder's Switch Gazette.*

"After Uncle Dave asked the blessing, we were served a dinner which is not for sale anywhere in these United States . . . rich country ham, fried chicken, six or seven vegetables done to a Tennessee turn, jelly, preserves, pickles, hot corn bread and white bread. Then came the cake. . . ."

On the drive back to Nashville, according to Judge Hay, the man from Hollywood turned to him and said, "I have never met a more natural man in my life. He prays at the right time and he cusses at the right time and his jokes are as clever as the dickens."

Not surprisingly, Uncle Dave was chosen to be one of the stars of the film *Grand Ole Opry,* along with Roy Acuff and His Smoky Mountain Boys, and Judge Hay, in 1940. When it came time for production to begin, Judge Hay and Uncle Dave took the train to Hollywood while Acuff and his group drove Acuff's Ford limousine touring car. According to Acuff biographer Elizabeth Schlappi, Acuff carried along a rather unusual piece of luggage in the trunk.

Knowing that it was highly unlikely there would be any country ham on the West Coast, Uncle Dave had prevailed upon Roy Boy—as he had dubbed him—to tote one with him in a wooden crate. Acuff agreed, and as he recounted to Schlappi in *Roy Acuff: The Smoky Mountain Boy,* "I put it in my car and started off with it. We soon found that the border guards were checking everything at each state line. I guess they were looking for fruit flies or whiskey or something. Well, anyway, everywhere we stopped, we'd have to undo that ham box, knock the slats off, and let them examine the ham."

By the time filming was completed, Uncle Dave had polished off the ham. He asked Acuff to take the box back so he could use it as a hen's nest. The easygoing fiddler agreed.

Uncle Dave Macon not only ate ham every chance he got, he sang an ode to it in his stage show, adapting a late nineteenth-century black minstrel tune, "Ham Beats All Meat," as the basic recipe for "Country Ham and Red Gravy."

Country Ham and Red Gravy
Uncle Dave Macon

Rich folks go to market house to buy that mutton and lamb
I am going to the country store to get that good sweet ham

Oh, how them people yell, when they heard the dinner bell
Oh, how them onions smelled, three miles away

Uncle Dave continued performing at the Grand Ole Opry until three weeks before his death in 1952; in 1966, he was posthumously inducted into the Country Music Hall of Fame. Every summer in Rutherford County, Uncle Dave Macon Days, founded in 1977, honors and celebrates one of the county's most famous sons. The family-oriented event draws nearly fifty thousand people to Murfreesboro for one of the few old-time music competitions in the country, and a purse totaling sixty-one hundred dollars is awarded during the music and dance contests. The three-day event concludes with that fine old bluegrass festival tradition, a gospel sing and a stirring rendition of "Will the Circle Be Unbroken."

Pee Wee King.

Pee Wee King

Joined the Opry cast in 1937

(1914–2000)

It's no wonder that this songwriter, musician, bandleader, television entertainer, and recording artist adopted the nickname Pee Wee; born Julius Frank Anthony Kuczynski into a working-class Polish-German family on February 18, 1914, he grew up in Wisconsin where he was simply called Frank. He joined his father's polka band as a teenager, playing the accordion, then formed his own band in high school, taking the name Frank King (in tribute to polka bandleader Wayne King). In 1933, he joined the Badger State Barn Dance and soon had his own radio show on WJRN in Racine. In 1934, he moved to Louisville at promoter J. L. Frank's encouragement, backing up Gene Autry for a time. It was Autry who gave his five-foot-six accordionist and fiddler the nickname that stuck for life. When Autry moved to Hollywood, King stayed in Louisville, marrying Frank's stepdaughter Lydia in 1936.

In 1937, he moved to Knoxville, where he formed the Golden West Cowboys, which he took along with him to Nashville, beginning a ten-year run on the Grand Ole Opry. King and the Golden West Cowboys took Minnie Pearl along as part of the Camel Caravan, a WSM touring company that performed at military installations in the United States and Central America in 1941 and 1942. King caused quite a stir when he used an amplified electric guitar onstage at the Opry in 1940, and introduced drums to the Ryman stage in 1947. He and his band were among the first Opry members to sport flashy costumes made by Hollywood tailor Nudie. King appeared in several Westerns playing himself as a bandleader; the first was 1938's *Gold Mine in the Sky,* starring his old friend Gene Autry.

For a short time, while a member of the Opry, he even had a restaurant about seven miles from downtown Nashville on Dickerson Pike, called Pee Wee King's

Hitchin' Post. Photos of King and his many friends from throughout his career decorated the walls, red-checked cloths covered the tables, and the old-fashioned country cooking made it a favorite dining spot for Opry members.

King left the Grand Ole Opry to move back to Louisville to work on WAVE radio and television, hosting his own TV show, which ran for the next ten years.

In 1969, King retired from live performing and returned to Nashville, where he worked for the Country Music Hall of Fame, at one time serving as its director. He was elected to the Country Music Hall of Fame in 1974, and was also a member of the Nashville Songwriters Hall of Fame.

The following recipe from Pee Wee King's wife appeared in the February 1945 edition of *The Grinder's Switch Gazette*.

Mrs. Pee Wee King's Favorite Cake Recipe

1 cup sugar
½ cup shortening
2 eggs
2 cups flour
2 teaspoons baking powder
Dash of salt
¾ cup milk

1 teaspoon vanilla
1 cup sliced apples or other seasonal
     fruit, or 1 cup canned fruit, drained
½ tablespoon sugar
½ teaspoon cinnamon
1 cup chopped nuts (optional)

Cream together the sugar and shortening. Add the whole eggs and stir together thoroughly. Sift together the dry ingredients and add ½ cup at a time, alternating with a little milk, to the sugar mixture. After all the flour and the milk have been added and stirred well, add the vanilla.

Place in a greased 9-inch pan, either round or square, cover the top with sliced apples or canned prunes, plums, or peaches. Stir together sugar and cinnamon, and sprinkle on top of fruit. Chopped nut meats may be added to the dough and sprinkled on top if desired. Bake in a moderate oven [350°] for 30 to 40 minutes or until done.

THE GRINDER'S SWITCH GAZETTE

Among her many occupations, Minnie Pearl was the chief writer and editor of *The Grinder's Switch Gazette*, a tabloid sheet published with the assistance of the WSM publicity department from 1944 through 1946. Much of the content was Opry-related news, including announcements of tour dates, recordings, appearances, and a copy of a Grand Ole Opry program with performance times, artists, and sponsors. Minnie covered comedy and Grinder's Switch gossip, with guest columns from other entertainers and sometimes Opry announcer George D. Hay. There were also illustrations and photos, as well as recipes contributed by fans and Opry members or, more likely, their wives.

Curly Fox and Texas Ruby.

Curly Fox and Texas Ruby

Joined the Opry cast in 1937

(Texas Ruby, 1908–1963; Curly Fox, 1910–1995)

In the Grand Ole Opry's early days, colorful nicknames frequently chosen by announcer George D. Hay were the norm—Bashful Brother Oswald, Stringbean, Little Jimmy Dickens, Grandpa Jones, Uncle Dave Macon, Pee Wee King, the Duke of Paducah, Fiddlin' Sid, just to name a few. Musician Arnim LeRoy Fox and singer Ruby Agnes Owen established themselves as Curly Fox and Texas Ruby. While the catchy name didn't guarantee them a spot on the Opry stage, it certainly didn't hurt.

Fox learned to cut hair and play fiddle from his father, the town barber in Graysville, Tennessee. An impromptu performance by the flashy Skillet Lickers in his dad's barbershop while the band was passing through town inspired Fox to hit the road himself, heading for big-city Atlanta. He started a band, the Tennessee Firecrackers, and acquired the nickname Curly, an obvious choice from photos that show him the proud possessor of a wavy pompadour. In the midforties, he traveled about with different groups, recording some songs for Decca, and taking part in fiddling competitions.

Meanwhile, Ruby Agnes Owen was seeking her own share of the spotlight in her home state of Texas, where she grew up on a ranch, belting out Western classics to the cowboys when she was just three years old. In 1930, she went to Fort Worth with her father and brothers on a cattle drive. While Mr. Owen was taking care of business, Ruby and her brothers amused themselves by singing and harmonizing out by the wagon. One of the more appreciative members of their audience was a cattle buyer, who also happened to be a stockholder in KMBC radio station in Kansas City, and he lassoed Ruby a job at the station. Over the next few years, she sang at stations in Philadelphia, Detroit, and Cincinnati, where she teamed up with Zeke

Clements and his Bronco Busters band, with whom she made her first appearances on the Grand Ole Opry. Missing home, she talked Clements into heading back west, but a pit stop in Des Moines led to a two-year layover thanks to a job on WHO's popular barn dance. The emcee of Ruby and Zeke's show was an aspiring actor named Ronald "Dutch" Reagan. Ruby, who was hardly a shrinking violet, took a disliking to the future president, and after one particularly profane tirade from the strong-willed singer, Reagan took off for California. Eventually, the big-voiced gal's short fuse and affection for a drink or two precipitated a breakup with Clements, but Ruby wasn't on her own for long.

Curly Fox and Texas Ruby met in 1937 when they were both performing for the Texas centennial; they teamed up as an act and appeared regularly on the Grand Ole Opry from 1937 to 1939, when they married. As one of the preeminent husband-wife touring acts of the time, they moved from one big station to another, coming back to Nashville and the Grand Ole Opry in 1944, and staying until they relocated to Houston in 1948. They spent the next fourteen years performing on local television in Texas, before bouncing back to Nashville again in 1962. Fox returned to the Opry, though Ruby, whose health was failing, made only sporadic performances. On March 29, 1963, returning from a Friday night show at the Opry, Fox found their mobile home in flames. Ruby tragically perished in the fire, which was suspected to have started when she fell asleep smoking in bed. Fox continued a solo career for some time, then moved to his hometown in Graysville, where he lived with a sister until his death in 1995.

It's hard to imagine this notoriously hard-drinking, cigarette-smoking, good-time gal in the kitchen wearing an apron, but nonetheless, she offered Minnie Pearl this recipe and it was published in the November 1945 *Grinder's Switch Gazette*. Can sizes and other measurements were based on standards of that time; the contemporary equivalent is added.

Texas Ruby's Favorite Recipe for Hawaiian Yams

Courtesy of The Grinder's Switch Gazette, *November 1945*

1 No. 2 can [*20 ounces*] yams or 4 medium-sized yams, cooked, peeled, and sliced
8 slices pineapple
3 sliced bananas
One 16-ounce bag large marshmallows
6 tablespoons butter
1 cup brown sugar

Place in baking dish—a layer of yams, layer of pineapple, layer of bananas, and a layer of marshmallows, repeating until baking dish is full. Melt the butter and the sugar and pour over the mixture and bake in a moderate oven [*350°*] until brown.

Roy Acuff.

Roy Acuff

Joined the Opry cast in 1938

(1903–1992)

Backstage at the Grand Ole Opry House, there are seventeen dressing rooms, numbered 1 through 18; superstition omits number 13. Only one has a name on the door, though its original occupant passed away in 1992. Dressing room number 1 belonged to Roy Acuff from the night of the first performance there on March 16, 1974, when he christened the brand-new 4,400-seat Grand Ole Opry House with a rafter-lifting performance of "Wabash Cannonball." It was a memorable night: President Richard Nixon made his Opry debut, leading the audience in singing "Happy Birthday" to his wife, First Lady Pat Nixon. He performed less successfully on the yo-yo, in spite of having yo-yo expert Acuff as his teacher. The president did not attempt the fiddle.

While the instrument was practically an extension of Acuff's left arm, the King of Country Music only began playing because his original plan—to play baseball for the New York Yankees—ended after a series of sunstrokes while playing semi-professional ball in his midtwenties took him off the field. While recuperating at his parents' home in East Tennessee, he picked up his father's fiddle and learned to play well enough to join a traveling medicine show in 1932, one year shy of his thirtieth birthday. Not only did he hone his fiddling skills and start singing, he also soaked up lessons in entertaining an audience with humor and showmanship from the eclectic repertoire of performers.

Acuff formed his own band, the Tennessee Crackerjacks, which were later renamed the Crazy Tennesseans. Though they were regulars on WROL in Knoxville, they were not making much of an impact outside of the region, but that all changed with one song. "The Great Speckled Bird" was a gospel tune that Acuff and his band began performing in their live show to good response, and they were invited to come to Chicago to record it on the ARC label. The group cut several songs during that session in 1936, including another that would become an Acuff standard, "Wabash Cannonball."

Acuff and his band made a guest appearance on the Opry in 1937, but it wasn't until February 5, 1938, that Acuff's performance of "The Great Speckled Bird" in more "hillbilly fashion" earned him membership in the Opry cast, though not before he agreed to change the name of his band to the Smoky Mountain Boys.

A string of hits in the forties, tireless touring, and regular appearances on the Grand Ole Opry made Roy Acuff one of country music's first superstars. Tagged the King of Country Music, backstage at the Ryman and later at the Grand Ole Opry House he was simply Roy, or to up-and-coming artists and employees, Mr. Acuff. His kindness, gentle manner, and generosity with his time made him one of the most beloved Opry members of all time; to many, Roy Acuff *was* the Grand Ole Opry. Dressing room number 1 was the heart of the show on Saturday nights, where he received VIPs, guests, fans, and fellow members with his trademark graciousness and good humor. Rooms number 1 and number 14 (recog-

Roy and Mildred Acuff with son Roy Neill and the family dog Brownie, 1940s.

nized today as Porter Wagoner's) were the only two of the seventeen to be outfitted with kitchenettes—a sink, mini-refrigerator, a couple of cabinets, a three-burner electric stove, and a small oven—and a private bath complete with a shower stall. During his twenty-two-year residency in number 1, Acuff hung a sign from WSM Radio over the door leading to his bath; when the lights were turned on inside, the sign above the door lit up with the words "On the Air."

Throughout his career, Acuff was honored with countless awards, among them entry into the Country Music Hall of Fame in 1962, their first living member; a Lifetime Achievement Award from the National Academy of Recording Arts and Sciences; and in 1991, a National Medal of the Arts from President George H.W. Bush.

His wife, Mildred, died in 1981; several of his longtime band members also passed away in the eighties, and in 1987, he released his final charting record, "The Precious Jewel," an inspirational duet with Charlie Louvin, fellow member of the Opry. With his health failing, he took up residence in the late eighties in a home built especially for him on the grounds of what was then the Opryland Themepark, just a short walk from the Opry House. Acuff became a goodwill ambassador for the compound, often taking strolls on the grounds to meet and greet park visitors, or waving to fans from his balcony.

Tommy Huff, who has shared backstage hospitality duties with Sallie Smith since 2003, met Acuff when he started working weekends at the Opry in 1988. "When I came to work there, I didn't really know much about country music," Huff, a Nashville native, admits. "But being around it, hearing it every weekend, made me a fan, and I came to love it all, the legends and the new artists being inducted back then. I used to love to watch Roy Acuff and Minnie Pearl together, the way they talked to each other. They were so close, they would finish each other's sentences, and make each other laugh so much. They had such chemistry on and off the Opry stage, they truly loved each other. Mr. Acuff was my favorite of all the Opry members. He was so nice to everyone. It didn't matter who you were; he treated everyone the same. In the summer, he would say to the people who worked at the Opry, 'I'm going to throw a barbecue for you guys.' And we'd get there one weekend out of the blue, and there'd be a spread of barbecue, corn, beans, and watermelon that he arranged for just us regular people. That meant a lot to us, and everyone loved him."

The following recipe from Roy Acuff's wife was originally published in December 1944 in *The Grinder's Switch Gazette.*

Mrs. Roy Acuff's Favorite Recipe for Hot Rolls

1 large-sized potato, peeled
1 cup sugar
1 cup milk
1 cup shortening
1 tablespoon salt
1 cake yeast (or 1 package active dry yeast)
2 eggs
8 cups flour (approximately)

Cook the potato till soft. Put aside 1 cup of potato water to cool. In the meantime, put into a saucepan the sugar, milk, and shortening and heat until all dissolved. Set this aside to cool. While the potato water and sugar mixture are cooling, force the potato through a sieve with a fork. Add the salt to the potato. When the potato water has cooled, dissolve in the yeast cake, then mix with the potato. Add to this the cooled sugar mixture and the 2 well-beaten eggs. Mix well.

Sift 8 cups of flour. Add to the above mixture 1 or 2 cups at a time. Stir after each addition, and continue to add the flour, 1 or 2 cupfuls at a time, until you have a good workable dough.

Roll out and shape three or four before you intend to cook them. Brush with melted butter before they rise, and brush again with melted butter before putting in the oven. Cover with waxed paper while rising. Cook in moderate oven [*350° to 400°*] for 20 minutes or until done. This dough will keep in the icebox very nicely for several days.

In a Pickle

Roy Acuff was a member of the prestigious Masons, the oldest and largest fraternal organization in the world. Thirteen signers of the Constitution and fourteen presidents of the United States, including George Washington, were Masons, but the organization points out that its more than two million North American members represent a tremendous breadth of occupations and professions, as well as religious beliefs and creeds. When he moved to Nashville, Roy was initiated as an Entered Apprentice at the East Nashville Masonic Lodge in 1943, was raised to Master Mason in 1944, and was made a Thirty-third Degree Mason in 1985. It was their common membership in the Masons that laid the groundwork for a friendship between Acuff and seven men from Warsaw, North Carolina—a relationship that has reaped lasting benefits for nearly everyone associated with the Grand Ole Opry.

Among all the fans who have shown their appreciation to the Opry with gifts of food, the Pickle Boys from North Carolina particularly ingratiated themselves to members and staff. Spokesman for the band of seven is Colonel James Strickland, a World War II veteran now in his eighties, who has been an Opry fan since he was a child. When he and some of his buddies began taking trips together to Nashville more than fifty years ago, the Opry was still at the Ryman, which is where they first met fellow Mason Roy Acuff. From then on, every time they came to Nashville, they were guests of his backstage, and came to know and develop friendships with other Opry members. Thanks in part to the limited space at the Ryman, it wasn't until the Opry moved to its new home on Briley Parkway that they began bringing pickles from their hometown, where Cates Family Pickles were made. Now sold as Peter Piper Pickles, jars of bread and butter chips, baby dills, dill spears and chips, and relish are as likely to be in every Opry member's and employee's home or bus refrigerator as a carton of milk and a tub of butter.

The group comes to Nashville several times a year and when they visit the Opry,

Colonel Strickland, H. C. Allen, Charles Taylor, Max Grice, Alan Brown, J. B. Herring, and Dr. Ben Cooper all wear a jacket and tie out of respect for the institution, and identical black fisherman hats so they are recognized. "Hey, Pickle Boy!" is the common greeting thrown at them as they visit in the halls and greenroom.

"They're real good pickles and we just wanted to bring something to say thank you for everything the Opry has done for us, and meant to us, over the years," explains Strickland. "They have been so nice to a bunch of old country boys. In the beginning, we just carried a few jars, but that didn't seem right, so we tried to find out what kind everyone likes and bring those. Charlie Walker likes bread and butter, Norah Lee Allen likes dill. Last time we came up, we brought seventeen cases of pickles. We think of ourselves as pickle ambassadors. Minnie Pearl always wrote a thank-you note to us and to the company. She was such a wonderful lady."

At any given time, there are more than two million pickles in the Peter Piper Pickles warehouse in Turkey, North Carolina, but just a few miles away in Warsaw—home of the company's manufacturing facility—Jewel Taylor, wife of one of the Opry's Pickle Boys, prefers to make her own. Every other year, she puts up five gallons of them, and then distributes them to family and friends as gifts. Not only are these good on their own, she says they make a world of difference in homemade chicken, tuna, and potato salads.

Pickle Boys' Sweet Pickles

Cucumbers
Salt (1 cup per gallon)
Alum (1 cup per gallon)

1 gallon white vinegar
Pickling spices
Sugar

This is a multistepped, two-week process, so allow time to finish. Make as small or as large a batch as you like, but cucumbers must be covered in water bath, which should be measured in gallon increments, with 1 cup of salt (day 1) or 1 cup of alum (day 2) per gallon. Jewel Taylor says any kind of cucumber is fine, but not too young and not so old that their seeds are large.

Day 1: Scrub your cucumbers with a vegetable brush and place in a container large enough to hold them with water. Bring 1 gallon (or more as needed) water to a boil; add 1 cup of salt per gallon of water, mix thoroughly. Pour salt water over cucumbers, let stand 24 hours.

Day 2: Drain salt water from cucumbers. Bring 1 gallon (or more) of water to a boil, add 1 cup of alum per gallon of water, mix thoroughly. Pour over cucumbers, let stand 24 hours.

Day 3: Drain alum water from cucumbers. Rinse cucumbers. Boil plain water and pour over cucumbers. Let stand 24 hours.

Day 4: Drain water from cucumbers. Bring to boil 1 gallon of white vinegar (or more if needed). Place pickling spices as desired in cheesecloth bag, tie shut, and place in boiling vinegar. Pour over cucumbers. Let stand 7 days.

Day 11: Drain vinegar and remove cucumbers from container. Slice for pickles as desired, in rounds for chips or lengthwise for spears. Place thick layer of sliced cucumbers in bottom of container, cover with sugar; repeat layering until all cucumbers are used, finishing with sugar on top. Cover. Add more sugar each day until juice covers cucumbers. This will take about 2 days. Refrigerate, or place in other containers and distribute to friends and family.

GooGoo Clusters

Opry Sponsor

GooGoos are a Nashville-invented and -manufactured confection, and for many years, they were only available for sale regionally, yet once they came on board as a Grand Ole Opry sponsor, their fame spread from coast to coast. Contrary to local legend, GooGoo was not an acronym for Grand Ole Opry; the candy bar predates the radio show by thirteen years, and in fact, the famous jingle was not sung on the Opry stage until sometime in the 1960s.

The gooey cluster of peanuts, caramel, and marshmallow covered in milk chocolate was developed in 1912 by Howell Campbell, the youthful owner of the Standard Candy Company on First Avenue in downtown Nashville. Howell was the first confectioner to make a candy bar with multiple ingredients. The candy, initially sold unwrapped in big glass candy jars, actually went nameless for a while, even as its popularity grew. People loved it, but didn't know how to ask for it. One day, on the streetcar on his way to work, Campbell discussed his dilemma with a fellow passenger. A schoolteacher, she remarked that the candy was "so good, people would ask for it from birth." Thinking about the sound his newborn son made—goo goo—Campbell was struck by an aha moment, and named his candy GooGoo.

A partnership with the Grand Ole Opry seemed written in stone, but it would be more than forty years before the 7:30 segment of the Saturday night show became known as the GooGoo Grand Ole Opry. Other Nashville Standard Candy Company products like King Leo peppermint stick candy were featured over the years, but none developed such a fan base as GooGoo's. Maybe it was the segment's opening jingle, sung to the tune of "Shave and a Haircut": "Go Get a GooGoo, it's Good!" Roy Acuff hosted the segment for many years, and dubbed announcing team Hairl Hensley and Harold Weakley the GooGoo Twins.

Bill Monroe

Joined the Opry cast in 1939

(1911–1996)

During his lifetime, Bill Monroe received some of the most prestigious honors an artist could hope for. He was inducted into the Country Music Hall of Fame in 1970, the Nashville Songwriters Hall of Fame in 1971, was an inaugural inductee of the International Bluegrass Music Hall of Honor in 1991, earned the Grammy's Lifetime Achievement Award in 1993, and in 1995, was bestowed the National Medal of Honor by President Bill Clinton at a White House ceremony. But it was after his death that the fifty-seven-year member of the Grand Ole Opry was recognized in a manner that had some folks scratching their heads. On May 6, 1997, Bill Monroe, the pride of Rosine, Kentucky, was inducted into the Rock and Roll Hall of Fame at the institution's twelfth annual ceremony. He would have been proud to know that his presenters were Ricky Skaggs and Emmylou Harris, just two of the legion of artists who owe some significant part of their career to the legendary Father of Bluegrass.

Monroe is among those rare artists who can be credited with creating a style of music that had a reach, impact, and influence well beyond its core audience. Before Bill Monroe came barreling out of the Bluegrass State, mandolin in hand, singing "high and lonesome" in a manner that came to define the genre's vocal style, there simply was no category called bluegrass.

Monroe was the youngest of eight children raised on a farm on Jerusalem Ridge in a well-off family headed by father James and mother Malissa, who played fiddle, accordion, and harmonica and who sang old British-American folk songs for her children. Two of his older brothers played fiddle, and another brother and a sister played guitar, so when he was nine, Monroe learned to play the mandolin, which no one else in the family had bothered with. His mother's brother, Pendleton Vandiver, a fiddler, was a tremendous influence on Monroe and was later immortalized in one of Monroe's most well-known tunes, "Uncle Pen." By the time he was sixteen, both James and Malissa Monroe had passed away, and Bill Monroe lived for some time with Uncle Pen before joining brothers Charlie and Birch in Chicago. They formed a trio, which not long afterwards became a duo when Birch left; Bill and Charlie, committed to pursuing music full-time as the Monroe Brothers, performed on radio stations in Iowa and Nebraska.

Like many entertainers of the time, they hooked up with a traveling medicine show, and in North Carolina, they caught on at Charlotte's WBT, becoming popular enough to merit several recordings on RCA's

Bill Monroe.

Bluebird label in 1936. Two years later, the Monroe Brothers split up, and Bill formed his first band, The Kentuckians, which he renamed the Blue Grass Boys before heading to Nashville to audition for Opry founder and announcer George D. Hay.

On October 28, 1939, the twenty-eight-year-old singer was brought onstage as the newest member of the Grand Ole Opry, and introduced himself to the audience with such a rousing performance of the Jimmie Rodgers hit "Muleskinner Blues" that he got three encores that first night at the War Memorial Auditorium. It did not escape his attention that he—William Smith Monroe—shared the same initials as the Opry's broadcast parent, WSM.

Monroe's guest appearances on the NBC network portion of the show boosted his national popularity so much that he was soon grossing as much as two hundred thousand dollars a year on the road, where he produced his own tent show, featuring other Opry members, with a format based upon the traveling medicine troupes that combined music and comedy.

Monroe continued to develop the style of music that was not formally identified as bluegrass until the 1950s. To the foundation of bass-fiddle-mandolin-guitar, he added banjo—first played by Dave Akeman, better known as Stringbean—and then, in a musical milestone, the three-finger banjo picking of Earl Scruggs. In 1948, Scruggs and Blue Grass Boys guitarist Lester Flatt left Monroe and formed the Foggy Mountain Boys. In the fifties, other bluegrass bands came together and other talents stepped into the spotlight, but Monroe's strong personality, songwriting prowess, unique voice, innovative musicianship, and visionary leadership kept him in the forefront even as rockabilly, rock and roll, and the Nashville Sound took over the radio and charts.

In the 1960s, Monroe was rediscovered by a new generation thanks to the emergence of folk festivals on college campuses, which were receptive to the purity, soulfulness, and acoustic artistry of bluegrass music. In 1967, at the suggestion of promoter Carlton Haney, Monroe started a bluegrass festival on property he owned in Bean Blossom, Indiana. The oldest continuous-running bluegrass festival in the world, now named the Bill Monroe Memorial Bean Blossom Bluegrass Festival, celebrated its fortieth year in 2006 with eight days of nonstop music performed by the musical children, grandchildren, and great-grandchildren of the Father of Bluegrass.

"Sugar Coated Love," written by Audrey Butler, was recorded in 1951 with Carter Stanley when the Stanley Brothers had temporarily disbanded. It is included in the box set *The Music of Bill Monroe, 1936–1994,* a four-CD collection of nearly one hundred of Monroe's recordings.

Sugar Coated Love
As Performed By Bill Monroe

Sugar coated love, you gave me on a plate
I took a bite and then I looked to see what I had ate
I found I had a cinder all covered up in white
That old sugar coated love is something I can't bite

You say you are leaving me for another man
He has all the wealth and charm and not my kind of brand
Baby, I fell down on my knees a-pleading for your love
Can't understand what I saw in a sugar coated love

You called me your sugar plum, your baby, and your pet
Said I was your Romeo and you my Juliet
I thought you were my angel, my little sugar dove
You sure had me fooled, babe, with that sugar coated love

Minnie Pearl

Joined the Opry cast in 1940

(1912–1996)

The Grand Ole Opry traces its roots back to one of the most significant contributors to Nashville's economy and growth in the early twentieth century, the National Life and Accident Insurance Company, the principals of which went on to establish themselves as formative and powerful members of Nashville society. Ironically, the radio station that was begun as a marketing tool for the insurance company—its call letters, WSM, touting the company motto, We Shield Millions—gained its first national fame as the home of hillbilly music. While that relationship proved to be lucrative for both parties, it did not exactly endear the two partners to one another in their own hometown. For many years, well into the era of modern country music, there existed a wide divide between the Athens of the South, as Nashville was known in some circles, and Music City USA, as the city was known in others. Blue-blooded members of the country club set had little in common with the rural folk and mountain people who comprised the audience and cast of the Grand Ole Opry. In fact, most members of the former prided themselves in some elitist fashion in never once listening to, much less attending, a performance of the country's most famous radio program. The two factions seldom if ever socialized, mixed, or even crossed paths.

The exception to that unwritten rule was found in the endearing character of a naïve, scatterbrained, but ebullient hillbilly girl from an imaginary backwater town named Grinder's Switch. Minnie Pearl made her debut on the Opry stage in November 1940, drawing more than three hundred cards and letters. Over the years, Minnie, with her price-tag-adorned hat, her gingham dresses, her unabashed flirting, and her signature greeting—"Howdeeee!"—became one of the Grand Ole Opry's most beloved and visible members, as recognized and revered as Roy Acuff, her good friend and colleague.

Minnie Pearl.

Though millions of listeners around the world knew her as Minnie Pearl, in Nashville, she was equally famous as Sarah Cannon. She came to Nashville in the midthirties from Centerville, Tennessee, as Sarah Ophelia Colley, the daughter of a prosperous lumberman who had lost his money in the Depression, to attend Ward-Belmont College for Women as a theater major. After college, she barnstormed the country for the Wayne P. Sewell Company, producing local theater for Lions Clubs and civic groups in small towns throughout the Southeast. It was during that time that she developed the routine of a small-town girl named Minnie Pearl. Returning to Centerville to care for her ill mother, she pulled out the character for a banker's convention attended by some WSM executives, who suggested she audition for the Opry. The Minnie Pearl name first appeared as a cast member on the Opry program dated December 7, 1940.

It was as Sarah Cannon—she and Henry Cannon, a pilot, married in 1947—that she ingratiated herself into the Nashville community at large. A voracious reader, an excellent cook, a skilled tennis and bridge player, a gracious hostess with impeccable taste, and a tireless volunteer and spokeswoman for countless charities and organizations, Sarah Cannon moved effortlessly between worlds. As one intimate put it, "Minnie had one foot in the Grand Ole Opry and one foot in Belle Meade, and she didn't treat one any different than the other, though different sides of her personality came out in each."

Susie Quick was a feature writer for Nashville's afternoon newspaper, the *Banner*, in the mid- to late 1980s. As she recalls it, *Banner* publisher Irby Simpkins was having a dinner party at his home, and Sarah and

Henry Cannon were among the guests. "Minnie always ended up holding court at those kinds of things," says Quick. "She was so charming, funny, and fun, so well-read and informed on just about everything. She was just a natural, wonderful storyteller. Irby was transfixed by her, and thought it would be a great idea for her to put some of those stories into print, to create a column for the paper. He got together with her later and proposed the idea, telling her he could team her up with one of his writers, and asking if she had any preference. She knew me because I had written a story about her struggle with breast cancer not too long before that, so she asked him if that nice young lady who had written the story about her was available. That was how it started, and how I came to know her."

"Minnie's Memories" ran in the *Banner* for a couple of years in the mideighties, transcribed from tapes Quick made during meetings at Minnie's contemporary, California-style home next door to the Governor's Mansion on Curtiswood Lane. The two would get together in the mornings, often over a breakfast of cold Pepsi and hot Krispy Kreme doughnuts that Quick would pick up on the way over.

Twenty-five at the time, Quick remembered the challenge of keeping up with one of country music's most popular personalities, and one of the most in-demand members of the Nashville community, then in her mid-seventies. In addition to appearing on the Grand Ole Opry, she donated her time to her favorite causes, visited her museum on Music Row daily, played bridge at the Belle Meade Country Club, and played tennis at least three times a week. She and Henry entertained frequently, and Minnie did her shopping at the locally owned Green Hills Market, where she had an account and knew each employee by name. By eight every morning that she was at home, Minnie was well into her day, sitting in her yellow and green study, answering calls and correspondence, and tending to her schedule. "The phone rang constantly," Quick remembers. "She could work the phones like nobody's business, always selling Minnie Pearl. She did a lot of speaking engagements. She would ask, 'Do you want the full costume or just the hat?' But she also spoke before many groups as Sarah Cannon, for breast cancer research in particular. Though everyone, including her sisters, called her Minnie, she didn't want the Minnie character associated with breast cancer, so when speaking on behalf of that cause, it was always as Sarah Cannon." One of Nashville's preeminent medical centers for breast cancer treatment and research, the Sarah Cannon Cancer Center, was founded and named in her honor.

The newspaper column, says Suzie, usually wrote itself, as Minnie was an inveterate storyteller. After typing it up, she took it to Minnie for her approval, often between Opry performances. As Minnie's eyesight began to fail, Susie became her part-time chauffer, driving Miss Minnie in her yellow Eldorado to the Opry and around town.

Of vital assistance to Minnie and her husband, Henry Cannon, was their longtime housekeeper, Mary Cannon (no relation), who had been with them since they were married. "Mary and Minnie were like sisters. Mary came every day, and eventually, as Mary became more feeble, they had to hire another woman to help Mary!" According to Quick, both Minnie and Mary were incredible cooks. Minnie's 1970 cookbook, *Min-*

Mary Cannon and Minnie Pearl.

nie Pearl Cooks, is full of great Southern classics, most of them taken from Minnie's own recipes, which either she or Mary would cook, as well as several contributions from Mary Cannon, such as the hot-water corn

cakes. The beef stew with corn and lima beans was Mary's, but when Minnie made it, she added a secret ingredient—a healthy dose of Maker's Mark, Minnie's cocktail of choice, served on the rocks. Quick says that the beef stew was more of a family meal, a comfort food during Nashville's cold, gray winters. Minnie was very proud of her homemade Roquefort dressing, and though she and Mary Cannon worked side by side in the kitchen of the Curtiswood Lane home, it is one thing that Minnie always insisted on making herself. She enjoyed having guests for lunch and dinner, and the Fabulous Salad with this Roquefort dressing made frequent appearances on her table.

In 1990, Susie Quick moved to New York City, though she made regular trips back to Nashville, and always made a habit of going over to Curtiswood Lane to drive Miss Minnie to the Opry. One evening, in the yellow Eldorado, she turned to Susie and admitted, "That's where I would have gone at your age. To *Broadway*. But I couldn't get the Nashville dust off my shoes."

Minnie Pearl performed her last show in Joliet, Illinois, on June 15, 1991; two days later she suffered a serious stroke that left her virtually bedridden in a Nashville nursing home for the next five years. When she died following a final series of strokes in 1996, it seemed that all of Nashville—Belle Meade and Music Row—filled the church for the services, then motored under a heavy and sad gray sky in a caravan of cars to her final resting place at Mt. Hope Cemetery in Franklin, Tennessee.

The following recipes were originally published in *Minnie Pearl Cooks*.

Fabulous Salad

"My friends refer to this as Minnie's fabulous salad. I think the flavor of anyone's salad is improved by the choice of greens and other ingredients. For instance, I like all sorts of different ingredients like raw spinach, raw cauliflower, and artichokes. I take great pleasure in experimenting with different dressings and different salad ingredients. Of course, the secret of any good salad is to have greens washed, dried, and chilled ahead of time, and to toss the salad at the last minute so it doesn't get soggy."—Minnie Pearl

  Lettuce—Bibb, Boston, or leaf
  Raw spinach
  Cucumber
  Avocado
  Spring green onions
  Marinated artichokes
  Tomatoes (optional)

Wash all vegetables. Pat dry and chill. Just before serving, break salad greens into bite-sized pieces. Peel and slice cucumber, avocado, and onions. Add artichoke. Pour Roquefort or Bleu cheese dressing over salad. Toss and serve immediately.

Roquefort or Bleu Cheese Dressing

"The reason my Roquefort dressing tastes different is because I make it fresh. Homemade Roquefort dressing left on the shelf or in the refrigerator for 4–5 days may lose its delicious flavor and may become slightly rancid. That's the reason the Roquefort Dressing on the grocer's shelf is not as good as freshly made.

"I use an old time garlic muller to make a paste of the garlic and seasonings. It's a little wooden bowl with a little wooden pestle.

"I've used Roquefort cheese and Bleu cheese. My friends can't tell the difference. Bleu cheese is a lot less expensive. However, we have some purists. If I say bleu cheese, they won't try the recipe. The amount of cheese you use is a personal matter. I sometimes like to crumble bleu cheese over the salad as well. Mix slowly. This 'marries' the ingredients as they say—and you know how I am about marryin'!"—Minnie Pearl

    1 small, minced clove garlic
    1 teaspoon salt
    2 or 3 turns freshly ground black pepper
    1 teaspoon dry mustard
    ¼ teaspoon paprika
    ¾ cup cooking oil
    ¼ cup vinegar
    3 ounces (more or less) Roquefort or bleu cheese
    Juice of 2 lemons

Using garlic muller, mull all garlic and seasonings. (If muller is not available, use small bowl and wooden spoon to mash garlic and work in seasonings.) Place paste in small bowl. Combine oil and vinegar, mix well. Add oil and vinegar to paste, a little at a time, until well mixed. Combine in cheese. Squeeze lemon juice into garlic muller, mull to remove all paste from muller, then pour juice into dressing.

Beef Stew

2 tablespoons cooking oil

2 pounds beef chuck, cut into cubes

2 tablespoons salt

Pepper to taste

1 tablespoon oregano

1 medium onion, chopped

1 cup corn

1 cup lima beans

3 carrots, sliced

5 medium potatoes, quartered

One 16-ounce can tomatoes

Heat oil in heavy saucepan or Dutch oven. Brown meat on all sides. Add 4 cups water, salt, and pepper. Cook slowly for about 2 hours. Stir occasionally to prevent sticking. Add oregano and vegetables. Continue cooking until vegetables are tender. Makes 6 to 8 servings.

Whitey Ford, the Duke of Paducah, at the Opry microphone.

Whitey Ford, the Duke of Paducah

Joined the Opry cast in 1942

(1901–1986)

S ince its inception, comedy has been an integral part of the Grand Ole Opry, whether contributed as asides by band members assigned the role of crack-up, or as full-blown routines performed by such legendary Opry funnymen and women as Rod Brasfield, Lonzo and Oscar, Sarie and Sallie, Stringbean, Minnie Pearl, Archie Campbell, and Jerry Clower. One of the most enduring of the Opry comedians was Whitey Ford, the Duke of Paducah.

Born Benjamin Francis Ford in De Soto, Missouri, in 1901, he earned the nickname Whitey as a child, thanks to his blond hair. Lacking a formal education—he was only schooled through the third grade—he enlisted in the navy for four years in 1918. After his discharge, the budding banjoist joined a Dixieland jazz band, knocking around the Midwest until coming to WLS's National Barn Dance in Chicago around 1929. It was during his stint at KWK in St. Louis in the mid-1930s that he acquired his stage name, began compiling an enormous catalogue of jokes, and developed his country bumpkin character. He spent several years touring on the NBC network radio show Plantation Party out of Cincinnati and Chicago; that relationship led to his move to Nashville in 1942 to star on the NBC radio network's segment of the Grand Ole Opry. He was replaced in 1947 by Rod Brasfield, but kept working at the Opry, recording and syndicating a series of radio shows, and touring through the mid-1950s. In the late fifties, he hosted a Nashville television program called *Country Junction.* After his retirement from the Opry, his humor reached an even greater audience thanks to the library of four hundred thousand jokes he sold in the seventies to the producers of the long-running hit show *Hee Haw.* But only the Duke of Paducah could deliver the tagline that closed every one of his shows: "I'm goin' back to the wagon, boys, these shoes are killin' me!" Four months after his death in June 1986, he was elected to the Country Music Hall of Fame.

Whitey Ford often contributed humor and stories to Minnie Pearl's *Grinder's Switch Gazette.* The following story included a bonus recipe for an Italian dish that must have seemed rather exotic to country cooks of the time. Note his allowance for a substitution of olive oil, which would be considered nearly heretical in Mediterranean cooking, and the use of what Ford refers to in his notes as "an Italian mixture of herbs"; contemporary cooks know it as simply oregano.

The Duke's Recipe for Spaghetti and Meatballs
Courtesy of The Grinder's Switch Gazette, *August 1945*

Dear Readers:

On the front cover of Minnie Pearl's Gazette *you see a picture of me cooking. The picture was made while I was living in Chicago by an NBC photographer who happened to pay me a visit and caught me making Italian spaghetti and meatballs. Minnie has heard me brag so many times about my recipe that she thought it might be a good idea if I passed it along to you; so here we go. This recipe was given me by the chef in a famous Italian restaurant in Elizabeth, New Jersey. I was playing there with the late Johnny Marvin, and it was just a few steps from the stage door to the back door of this restaurant. Almost every show, this Italian chef would come and catch my act. After every show, we would go over to the restaurant and have meatballs and spaghetti. Before the week was out, we had gotten on such friendly terms that I got enough nerve to ask him for the recipe. Much to my surprise, he gave it to me. He claims that this is the style spaghetti and meatballs that Caruso, the great opera singer, liked so well.*

Sauce

1 medium onion	One 6-ounce can tomato paste
2 medium green peppers	One 28-ounce can Italian plum tomatoes
2 ribs celery	Dried oregano
Olive oil	Fresh parsley (optional)
1 clove garlic	One 4-ounce can mushrooms (optional)
Salt	Parmesan cheese (optional)

Meatballs

1 pound ground beef	1 rib celery
½ pound ground pork	1 clove garlic

½ pound ground veal
1 small onion
1 small green pepper
1 rib celery
1 clove garlic

Olive oil
Salt and pepper
1 to 2 eggs
Flour for binding meats

To make good spaghetti sauce, you must have the following ingredients: tomato paste, tomatoes, onion, garlic, green pepper, a little celery, olive oil, and if possible, an Italian mixture of herbs known as oregano. Dice up 1 medium-sized onion, 2 medium-sized peppers, a few pieces of celery and put them in a hot skillet containing about ⅛ inch of olive oil. (If you don't like olive oil, your favorite cooking oil may be substituted.) Sauté the onion, pepper, and celery in this hot grease until they are very soft. Do not let your fire get too hot or let the ingredients burn or fry brown. If it starts to cook dry, add enough water to keep moist and steaming. Dice 1 clove of garlic in very small pieces. Cover it with about 1 teaspoon of salt, enough for your entire pan of sauce. Take a case knife [*table knife*] and mash it to a pulp. After you have it completely pulverized, add it to your ingredients in the pan. After the ingredients in your pan have fried down until they are entirely done, add a can of tomato paste and stir it until it is entirely mixed. Rinse the can out several times, adding the water to the sauce. This completes the main body of the sauce, but many things can be added as you desire. Add a can of tomatoes, mashed, and some water; let it cook on a slow fire for several hours. If you want a quick sauce, add only water or tomato juice to the ingredients you have in your pan. About 30 minutes is the usual time for cooking this. The Italian herbs [*oregano*] should be added to suit your taste. One teaspoonful to a good-sized pan of sauce is sufficient. Another thing that makes this sauce delicious is to add a cup of chopped parsley and a can of mushrooms about 10 minutes before serving. Do like I do, folks. When we are having a houseful of company, I make the plain sauce; but when I cook it just for me and my big, fat wife, I add all the fancy things—chopped parsley, mushrooms, and sometimes I grate some Italian cheese and fold it in the sauce just before serving.

Italian meatballs are very easily made, but you must have the right ingredients. If you were going to make about 2 pounds of meatballs, you would need 1 pound of ground beef, ½ pound of ground pork, and ½ pound of ground veal. These should be run through the grinder several times [*or purchase ground meats from market*]. These proportions hold good whether you make more or less. Dice 1 small onion, 1 small pepper, and 1 rib of celery. Also mash up 1 small clove of garlic with salt as instructed before. Sauté these ingredients in olive oil or other shortening until they are thoroughly done but not brown. Put your meat in a large mixing bowl, add the desired amount of salt and pepper to it. Mix in the sautéed ingredients of your pan, using 1 or 2 eggs with enough flour to hold it together. After thoroughly mixing, make into small round balls and fry. After they are thoroughly done, drop them in your pan of sauce about 10 minutes before serving them. It will give them a delicious flavor and absorbs very little of your sauce. I have been eating this recipe for about twelve years and it hasn't hurt me yet; so try it, neighbors.

My secretary has just reminded me that I have forgotten to tell you how to cook spaghetti. I buy the real Italian spaghetti, the kind with a hole in it the size of a lead pencil. [*This type of pasta is now typically available in imported specialty markets, usually of Greek origin.*] I particularly like this kind because it gives the sauce a chance to go through the spaghetti. Your water should be boiling before you put the spaghetti in, and it will cook in 10 to 15 minutes. Be sure to add salt to your water before boiling. When you take it off the stove, pour it into a colander in the sink and let all of the hot water drain off. Then put it under the hot water faucet and rinse thoroughly. This may cool it off a little, but if you keep your sauce real hot, it will heat up when you serve it.

MRS. WHITEY FORD'S, THE DUCHESS OF PADUCAH, **FAVORITE SWEET POTATO RECIPE**

Courtesy of The Grinder's Switch Gazette, *January 1945*

4 large sweet potatoes, boiled, peeled, and mashed
1½ cups butter
2 eggs
1 cup sugar (white, light brown, or maple)
1 cup sherry wine
1½ cups heavy cream
½ teaspoon salt
1 cup finely chopped nuts, pecans preferred

Mash the potatoes, add the butter, and blend well together. Beat the eggs with the sugar; add the sherry and cream. Combine all the ingredients, reserving enough of the chopped nuts to go on top. Place the mixture in a buttered baking dish, sprinkle the top with the remaining chopped nuts and bake in 375° oven until lightly browned, about 30 minutes.

Backstage at the Ryman

From 1943 until March 1974, the Grand Ole Opry was staged at the Ryman Auditorium, built in downtown Nashville in 1892 by riverboat captain Thomas Ryman as the Union Gospel Tabernacle. Thanks to its original function, as well as its soaring ceilings, beautiful stained glass windows, and the pews that provide the seating, once it began hosting the Opry, the Ryman was nicknamed the Mother Church of Country Music. Though the building was regarded with all the reverence accorded a house of worship, the Ryman was not designed to accommodate a hundred musicians, square dancers, cloggers, announcers, sponsors, and stage crew within the cramped confines of its backstage. On one side of the stage were two dressing rooms for male entertainers, and a restroom so small Tex Ritter used to say that in order to use it, you had to drop your drawers first, then back in. The women had it even worse; a small ladies' restroom on the other side of the stage did double duty as their dressing room.

Cast members, announcers, and staff who spent time at the Ryman remember it fondly for the stellar acoustics and camaraderie it nurtured, but for the most part, were thrilled to move to the spacious, beautifully outfitted, and climate-controlled Grand Ole Opry House. The Ryman sat deteriorating for many years, until in 1996 it was gorgeously restored and modernized. It now has eight dressing rooms spread over three floors, though the backstage area on the main floor is still as tight as a ship's quarters.

Often for several months in the winter, the Grand Ole Opry returns to the Ryman, and travels back through time. Musicians walk down the same narrow, pothole-pocked alley that runs between the back door of the Ryman and the rear entrances of some of the most infamous honky-tonks of Lower Broad, places like Tootsies Orchid Lounge, Robert's Western Wear, the Stage, and Layla's Bluegrass Inn. At the short but steep stone staircase that winds to the backstage door, Metro Nashville Police officers are posted, ready to offer a helping hand with the heavy door as musicians struggle with their instruments. Barely one foot from there, in a

The Ryman Auditorium.

vestibule tucked between the long curving staircase that leads to the second floor and the door to the backstage hallway, is a battered desk, the post for Miss Jo or Miss Becky, who alternate weekends at the backstage door. Jo Walker and Becky Sanders both began their jobs as Opry ticket takers in 1969 while working at Nashville Life and Accident Insurance Company, the Nashville company that started WSM Radio and the Grand Ole Opry. "Where you got us?" is the question posed countless times to Becky or Jo by cast members arriving for the show and looking for their assigned dressing room.

Members also come to their desk for the menus kept in the upper-left-hand drawer from nearby restaurants that fill to-go orders. Jack's Bar-B-Que, Rippy's, and Bailey's are all there, but the one most often studied is the grease-stained red sheet from Robert's Western Wear, a bar and live music venue whose back door scoots right up to the Ryman. The Carol Lee Singers, who are on duty from the time the show begins at 6:30 until it signs off at midnight, know the menu by heart. Typically, Norah Lee Allen places the order from the backstage phone, and bass singer Rod Fletcher makes the run across the alley to pick up the boxes. "We think Robert's has the best burgers in town," Allen vows. "They cook them on one of those old flat-top grills, and they come with lettuce, tomato, pickle, and onions, but we don't do onions. You can't do that when you're working as close together as we do."

Most of the Opry performers have time between the first and second show to grab a bite in a downtown restaurant. Demos' and Big River Grille are quick and inexpensive, and the Palm can rustle up a steak in a hurry, for a pretty penny.

Announcer Hairl Hensley came to the Opry in 1972, when the Ryman was still its year-round home, and he remembers it fondly. "I enjoyed the closeness of the Ryman, everyone was on top of everyone else. People were always going out to eat together before or after their segments. It was very convenient to walk somewhere. There were three or four places we liked; a joint up on Commerce and Fifth, and the Linebaugh's on Broadway. They're gone now. Of course, Tootsies was always popular, it was so close. Most of the entertainers would hang out in the upstairs room that you entered from the alley. Opry managers knew just where to find them."

Ernest Tubb.

Ernest Tubb

Joined the Opry cast in 1943

(1914–1984)

Ernest Tubb's break into country music might never have happened had it not been for the support of Carrie Rodgers, the widow of his idol Jimmie Rodgers. But his legacy and enduring influence owes much to the tonsillectomy he had when he was twenty-five, an operation which revealed a voice slightly flawed, yet so true and distinctive that it overcame its shortcomings.

Ernest Dale Tubb was born in 1914 on a cotton farm where his father was foreman, in Ellis County, Texas, about forty miles south of Dallas. The family moved several times throughout his youth, and his parents divorced when he was just twelve. He remained with his mother when she moved to her brother's farm, and to help out, started working various jobs at the expense of his education.

When Ernest was fourteen years old his sister brought home a Jimmie Rodgers record, an experience that would change his life. He bought Rodgers' records whenever he had a bit of extra money, emulating his hero as best he could. As a young adult, working on road crews around Benjamin, he met Merwynn Buffington, a guitarist who encouraged him to learn to play. Tubb bought a guitar from a pawnshop, and learned enough chords to accompany himself and his imitative efforts at yodeling. In 1934, he married Lois Elaine Cook, and the following year took a job with the Works Progress Administration in San Antonio, where Buffington was playing on Radio KONO. Tubb made some guest vocalist appearances, and as a result was offered his own twice-weekly, fifteen-minute early-morning show.

Still fervent in his admiration of Jimmie Rodgers—who had passed away in 1933—Tubb knew the singer and his wife had last lived in San Antonio. He found Carrie's phone number in the city directory and rang her up. The widow graciously invited him to visit, and a friendship took seed. Not long afterwards, she arranged a recording session for him with Victor, her late husband's company. The first songs were tributes to Rodgers written by Carrie's sister; the other four were written by Tubb, but sung in the style of his idol. Carrie not only lent him one of her husband's guitars for the sessions, she suited him up in one of his tuxedos for a photo. In spite of those lucky charms, none of the records was a success, and Victor dropped him.

In 1939, surgery to remove his tonsils took his ability to yodel as well. The nasal twang that emerged was compelling enough to earn him a recording contract with Decca in 1940, and score a fairly successful debut single, "Blue Eyed Elaine." His next sessions, backed by electric guitar, a bass, and his own rhythm guitar, produced a song he had written that propelled him to stardom: "Walking the Floor Over You" became a massive hit and ushered in honky-tonk music, marking Tubb as the pioneer of that genre.

The success of that song sent him off with a calling card to Nashville in 1942, wife and children in tow. His arrival coincided with a recorders' strike, and studios were shut down; in the interim, he joined the Grand Ole Opry in 1943, and toured extensively with fellow members Pee Wee King and Roy Acuff, eventually forming his own band, the Texas Troubadours. When the strike ended in 1944, Tubb recorded and released "Try Me One More Time," which went to number 2, followed by his first country chart topper, "Soldier's Last Letter." From then on, Tubb had a nearly unbroken fifteen-year streak of Top 10 singles, becoming one of the first country acts to record in Nashville with his own band. In 1949, he charted thirteen hit singles in the course of one year, an unprecedented accomplishment never matched since.

In 1947, exhibiting a remarkable acumen for marketing, Tubb opened the Ernest Tubb Record Shop on Lower Broadway in Nashville, just one block from the Ryman Auditorium. A year later, Tubb began the Midnite Jamboree, a valuable showcase for young, emerging artists to introduce themselves to country audiences, which aired on WSM immediately after the Grand Ole Opry signed off for the evening.

Tubb and Elaine divorced in 1948; a year later, he married Olene Adams Carter, and they remained together until his death in 1984. Through that period, Tubb's career flourished, in the studio and on the road, with him performing as many as three hundred dates a year, and legend has it, logging two million miles on his tour bus, Green Hornet Number One. Green Hornet Number Two ate up more road, even after he was diagnosed with emphysema in 1966 and told by doctors to slow down. During the last days of his final tours, Tubb had to take oxygen and rest on a backstage cot between shows, and he was finally forced to retire in 1984. The sixth member of the Country Music Hall of Fame passed away on September 6, 1984, but his legacy endures to this day, thanks to the Midnite Jamboree, WSM's second-longest-running radio broadcast, behind only the Grand Ole Opry, and fond memories from the folks fortunate to have worked with him.

Hairl Hensley came on the Opry in 1972, and remembers that his first night was the 8:30 segment sponsored by W.E. Stephens Work Clothes. "Ernest Tubb was the host that night, and he kind of walked me through it," he recalls. "I had done live radio before, so I wasn't totally unfamiliar, but nothing of the stature of the Grand Ole Opry. He was such a pro, so easygoing about it."

Keith Bilbrey came by his announcer's job on the Grand Ole Opry through Ernest Tubb's Midnite Jamboree.

Hairl Hensley was doing the Opry, and also doing the Jamboree at that time, he had taken it over from Grant Turner. Hairl got tired of doing it, and asked me if I would like to. I jumped at the chance, that show was right up there with the Opry in terms of longevity and legends. I was the last person doing that show who actually got to work with Ernest Tubb. He was so nice to me, so nice to everyone he met. He really enjoyed people, and he liked helping newcomers in the business. Elvis Presley's first appearance at the Opry didn't go so well, and Elvis felt pretty bad, so Ernest invited him to come over after the Opry and do the Jamboree, and he had a great time and was very well received.

I went to see Ernest at Baptist Hospital the afternoon before he died. Jack Greene and I had planned to go together, but he couldn't get there so I went alone. He seemed to be doing pretty well. I've heard that sometimes people who are terminally ill rally right before their death. He sat up in his bed and took his oxygen mask off so we could speak. The Troubadours went that night, they were all there, visiting and talking. I would love to have been a fly on that wall! On the one-year anniversary of his death, we all went down to the record store, put our chairs in a big circle, and told stories. He was one of a kind. There's not been another like him.

This recipe, which appeared in *The Grinder's Switch Gazette,* May 1945, would have been from the first Mrs. Tubb, given to Minnie Pearl three years before Ernest and Lois Elaine Tubb divorced.

Mrs. Ernest Tubb's Recipe for Macaroni Salad

½ 16-ounce box macaroni
1 medium-sized onion, chopped
½ cup celery, chopped (2 to 3 stalks)
1 sweet pepper, chopped

1 hard-boiled egg, chopped
1 teaspoon salt
¾ cup Miracle Whip salad dressing

Cover the macaroni with boiling water and cook until tender. Drain off water. Add the chopped onion, celery, pepper, and egg. Then add the salt and the salad dressing. Mix well, chill and serve on lettuce leaves or other greens.

The Cackle Sisters

Joined the Opry cast in 1944

(Mary Jane DeZurick, 1917–1981; Carolyn DeZurick, 1919–)

In the midthirties, the success of the Girls of the Golden West—sisters Dolly and Millie Good, who were from St. Louis and not Muleshoe, Texas, as WLS fictitiously claimed—set the standard for sister acts in country music. The Girls' success led to the creation of several more sister duos, who donned cowgirl outfits and took the stage at other barn dances around the country. One act stood out from the rest, though, thanks to their incredibly unique and inimitable singing style. The DeZurick sisters, Mary Jane and Carolyn, grew up with their four sisters and one brother on a farm near Royalton, Minnesota. Doing the daily chores required of farm children, they heard nature's music in the sounds of the barnyard animals that they tended, and turned them into an astounding repertoire of vocal gymnastics and complex yodeling. In October 1936, they happened to perform at a Minnesota county fair that had also booked a group of entertainers from the National Barn Dance; an executive with the station's Artists Bureau invited them to appear on the program, and one month later they were signed to a contract. The DeZurick sisters, as they were known, were immediate fan favorites, injecting their songs with crowd-pleasers like a Hawaiian yodel and the cackle trill, later perfecting the triple-tongue yodel when joined by another DeZurick sister.

In 1937, after two representatives of Purina Mills attended the Saturday night show and heard the sisters sing "My Little Rooster," they were hired to appear on the transcribed *Checkerboard Time* radio show that advertised Checkerboard chicken feed and other Purina products. Tying into the poultry theme, the DeZurick Sisters performed on that show as the Cackle Sisters.

Their exposure on WLS led not only to a recording contract, but a trip to Hollywood to star and sing in the Republic Pictures movie *Barnyard Follies.* "Poppin' the

Corn" and "Listen to the Mockingbird" were among the featured songs that provided a perfect vehicle for their distinctive talents.

In 1940, the sisters—married and expecting their first children—retired temporarily from showbiz. Over the next few years, Carolyn did some work on her own, including a two-season stint in the Sonja Henie Hollywood Ice Revue, opening the show in the spotlight with a yodel.

In 1944, Purina Mills coaxed Mary Jane out of retirement to perform again with Carolyn as the Cackle Sisters, with a new young artist, Eddy Arnold, on the road, appearing onstage, and on the Grand Ole Opry in Nashville. The sisters continued living in Chicago, taking the train between the Windy City and Music City to star in the Purina-

The Cackle Sisters; Carolyn and Mary Jane DeZurick.

sponsored segment of the Opry, and became the first women to achieve stardom on both the National Barn Dance and the Grand Ole Opry.

This spiced dark bread comes from the DeZurick family recipe box, and appeared in *The Grinder's Switch Gazette* in June 1945.

The Cackle Sisters' Favorite Recipe for Molasses Nut Cake

½ cup shortening
½ cup sugar
2 eggs
2½ cups flour
½ teaspoon salt
½ teaspoon cloves

I teaspoon ginger
I teaspoon cinnamon
I½ teaspoons baking soda
I cup molasses
I cup chopped nuts (or dates)

Cream the shortening until light and fluffy. Add the sugar, and cream again. Add well-beaten eggs. Measure and sift together all the dry ingredients. Mix the molasses and 1 cup hot water, then cool to room temperature. Add dry ingredients alternately with the liquid to the shortening. Beat after each addition. Add nuts (may use dates instead). Bake in two 9-inch paper-lined cake tins in a moderate oven [*350°*] for 25 to 30 minutes.

Lew Childre.

Lew Childre

Joined the Opry cast in 1945

(1901–1961)

Unlike many Opry members, Lew Childre was not fresh off the farm, escaping a hardscrabble childhood, determined to avoid a lifetime of backbreaking field work. Born in 1901, he was the son of a judge, raised in an upper-middle-class family in Opp, Alabama. As Childre saw it, Opp offered little in the way of opportunity for an aspiring entertainer, who—to his family's chagrin—started buck dancing for change on downtown street corners before he was out of short pants. In high school, he threw himself into theater and played drums in the school band. Though he acquiesced to his father's decree that he attend premed at the University of Alabama, his heart wasn't in it. After putting in his four years, instead of going to medical school, he took off with the Milt Tolbert Show, a traveling tent show for which he was presumptuously billed as "Milt Tolbert's Most Popular Song and Dance Artist." A versatile entertainer, he played drums in the band he formed next, the Alabama Cotton Pickers, which featured accordionist Lawrence Welk.

Intrigued by the hillbilly music that was gaining popularity in the midtwenties, he bought a guitar and taught himself to play, devising a peculiar style that used Hawaiian steel methods to play Spanish guitar. With his emerging knack for marketing, he dubbed his solo act "Poop Deck Lew and his two-chord guitar." He developed a regional audience doing tent shows, then moved into the broadcast arena with radio stations in Texas and Arkansas before settling for a few years in New Orleans at WWL.

Through radio, recording for American Record Company in Chicago and touring, he began building a successful career. In the late thirties, he was spending his winters at border station XERA in Del Rio, Texas. He also took advantage of a technology introduced in the thirties known as "electrical transcription," an early form of syndication that employed twelve- or sixteen-inch discs containing fifteen minutes of programming each, which were then mailed to different radio stations. Childre became adept at producing his own transcriptions, and by 1943 he had a national daily show on Blue Network, as well as three daily shows over WAGA in Atlanta. A role on Wheeling, West Virginia's famous WWVA Jamboree, where he honed his knack for shilling products, immediately preceded his arrival at the Grand Ole Opry in 1945. He was installed as host for the opening portion of the show, sponsored by the Warren Paint Company. Attired in a painter's cap and jacket—which became his official stage outfit for that portion of the Opry—he asked announcer Grant Turner, "Hey, Grant, what time is it?" Grant's reply, "It's Warren Paint Time," signaled that portion of the Opry was under way from the late forties into the early fifties. Childre retired from the Opry in 1959 and moved to Foley, Alabama, where he lived until his death.

Though Childre died more than ten years before announcer Hairl Hensley came on board in 1972, Hensley collected a storehouse of old stories shooting the breeze backstage at the Ryman. One of his favorite anecdotes about the early Opry involved Lew Childre. "Back then, it wasn't at all unusual for fans to invite entertainers traveling through their towns to come by their homes before or after a show for a good home-cooked meal." He remembers that Lew Childre often took matters into his own hands. "Back then, there were no interstates, so they'd be traveling on old country roads. It would get to be about four or five o'clock, and Lew would start getting hungry for dinner. He'd look for a house by the side of the road with smoke coming out of a chimney, and would pull the car up to the house, knock on the door, and grandly announce, 'Hello, I'm Dr. Lew Childre from the Grand Ole Opry!' Then he might ask if he could trouble them for some water. Almost always, the people would be so impressed with a Grand Ole Opry star at their front door that they insisted he come in and have dinner. He didn't go hungry very often."

Martha White

Opry Sponsor

Martha White became a brand name years before that advertising phrase was ever coined, and can proudly boast that the name belongs to a real person. Richard Lindsey, owner of Royal Flour Mill, named the company's finest flour in 1899 for his then three-year-old daughter, Martha White Lindsey. In 1941, the mill was acquired by Cohen E. Williams, who changed the name of the company to match its best-selling product, and coined the signature phrase "Goodness Gracious, It's Good!®" Not only was Williams a savvy businessman, he was a shrewd promoter and a genuine fan of country music. Having observed the effect commercial partnerships had on a Texas radio program featuring Pappy Lee O'Daniel and his product, Hillbilly Flour, Cohen looked no farther than his own backyard to initiate a relationship with WSM and the Grand Ole Opry.

He first sponsored a fifteen-minute morning country music show, *Martha White Biscuit and Cornbread Time,* which went on the air at 5:45 A.M. and featured a group called Milton Estes, the Old Flour Peddler and His Musical Millers. In 1948, Cohen bought a fifteen-minute segment of the Opry, which makes Martha White not only the Opry's most tenured advertiser, but ranks as the longest-running sponsorship of any live radio show in the country. A portion of the historic Martha White logo backdrop used on the Opry stage during their portion of the show is part of the permanent collection at the Country Music Hall of Fame.

In 1953, Martha White hired an up and coming bluegrass band to barnstorm the South, promoting its flour and cornmeal. MARTHA WHITE was painted on their tour bus above and in larger letters than the names of the musicians, Lester Flatt, Earl Scruggs, and the Foggy Mountain Boys. The partnership led Flatt and Scruggs to superstar status in the bluegrass world, recording signature songs like "Foggy Mountain Breakdown" and "The Ballad of Jed Clampett," the theme song for the television show *The Beverly Hillbillies.*

During their fourteen years as the World's Greatest Flour Peddlers, they became as well known for singing the Martha White theme song as one of their hits. Written in the early 1950s for just one hundred dollars by the late Pat Twitty of Nashville, the song was a popular audience request. In fact, during Flatt and Scruggs' appearance at New York's prestigious Carnegie Hall, which was being recorded for a live album, someone in the audience began hollering, "Play the Martha White song!" The duo finally did it just to quiet the man down, though his voice can be clearly heard on the album. A few years later, the same thing happened again in Tokyo, where an audience member had heard the Martha White theme song on the Carnegie Hall album.

The lyric has been slightly modified through the years to reflect new products in the Martha White line. This is the twenty-first-century version of "The Martha White Theme Song," but the tune remains pure bluegrass.

The Martha White Theme Song

Now you bake right
With Martha White
Goodness gracious, good and light
Martha White

For the finest biscuits ever wuz
Get Martha White Self-Rising Flour
The one all-purpose flour
Martha White Self-Rising Flour
With Hot Rize Plus

Lester Flatt and Earl Scruggs promoted Martha White until 1969, when they disbanded. In 1972, Tennessee Ernie Ford became the company spokesman, and though he was never a member of the Grand Ole Opry, he made frequent guest appearances in the Martha White segment. In 1988, he made one of his last performances in honor of Martha White's fortieth anniversary as a Grand Ole Opry sponsor.

Flatt and Scruggs' tour bus, 1960s.

Martha White turned again to the bluegrass community in 1996 when they sponsored Alison Krauss' tour. In 2001, Rhonda Vincent, who has won the International Bluegrass Music Association's Female Vocalist of the Year honor many times as well as Entertainer of the Year, took the wheel of a brand-new red, white, and blue Martha White Bluegrass Express bus to carry on the great tradition begun more than a half century before.

In 2005, Martha White and the Grand Ole Opry further solidified their commitment to one another when the company became the first partner sponsor in Opry history. Fittingly, the ceremony took place on-stage at the Ryman, where the relationship had begun fifty-seven years before; the fifteen-minute segment purchased back then for just twenty-five dollars turned out to be priceless.

"Hot Rize®" Biscuits
Courtesy of Martha White®

2 cups Martha White® Self-Rising Flour
¼ cup shortening (we recommend Crisco®)
¾ cup milk

Heat oven to 450°. Lightly grease cookie sheet. Place flour in large bowl. With pastry blender or fork, cut in shortening until mixture resembles coarse crumbs. Add milk; stir with fork until soft dough forms and mixture begins to pull away from sides of the bowl.

On lightly floured surface, knead dough just until smooth. Roll out dough to ½-inch thickness. Cut with floured 2-inch round cutter. Place biscuits with sides touching on greased cookie sheet.

Bake at 450° for 10 to 12 minutes or until golden brown. Serve warm.

Crisco® is a trademark of the J.M. Smucker Company.

Blueberry Skillet Cake

Courtesy of Martha White®

Cake

1 cup sour cream
½ cup milk
2 tablespoons sugar
2 (7 ounce) packages Martha White® Blueberry Muffin Mix

Topping

½ cup sugar
⅓ cup Martha White® All-Purpose Flour
¼ cup cold butter, cut into pieces

Blueberry Sauce

¼ cup blueberry preserves (we recommend Smucker's®)

Heat oven to 350°. Grease 10-inch cast-iron skillet. In large bowl, combine sour cream, milk, and sugar; mix well. Add muffin mix; stir to blend. Spread batter in greased skillet. In a small bowl, stir together sugar and flour. With pastry blender or fork, cut in butter until crumbly. Sprinkle over batter.

Bake for 35 to 40 minutes or until golden brown and cake begins to pull away from sides of pan. Cool for 15 minutes. In microwave-safe bowl, microwave preserves 30 seconds or until just melted. Cut cake into wedges; spoon preserves over each serving. 8 servings.

Little Jimmy Dickens practices his casting skills with a fishing pole on the Opry stage as Brad Paisley performs.

Little Jimmy Dickens

Joined the Opry cast in 1948

In August 2006, Little Jimmy Dickens celebrated his fifty-eighth year with the Grand Ole Opry, the longest-tenured member of the longest-running live radio show in the world. "When I came to the Grand Ole Opry, you had to have something going on for you as far as records were concerned," says the diminutive entertainer, just four feet eleven inches from the heels of his custom-made cowboy boots to the top of his hat. "I didn't have the records, but I was friends with Mr. Acuff, and he invited me to appear."

The oldest of thirteen children from Bolt, West Virginia, Little Jimmy started singing on radio station WOLS in nearby Beckley while attending the University of West Virginia, walking to and from the station for his appearances. Shortly after getting his first regular radio job, he left school and began singing on other radio shows in Indiana, Ohio, and Michigan under the name Jimmy the Kid. It was on one such show that he met Roy Acuff, who invited him to Nashville to sing on the Grand Ole Opry. "Mr. Acuff treated everyone the same; he was such a gentleman and kind to all. I learned so much from him."

Shortly after, he signed a recording contract with Columbia and released his first single, "Take an Old Cold Tater (and Wait)." Not only did it become a Top 10 hit, it earned him the nickname—bestowed by none other than Hank Williams—that he is affectionately called to this day: Tater.

The song was the first of a series of novelty hits. "I kind of got branded as a novelty singer right at the start of my career. I had been doing other kinds of songs, ballads, gospel, but once 'Tater' hit the Top 10, I had to follow that up with another one like it, so I did 'A-Sleeping at the Foot of the Bed.' From then on, I always put a ballad on the B side of a single, but they got overlooked. It didn't bother me. The novelty songs were how radio knew me, but I have always done ballads in my show."

The most well-known of those novelty songs was 1965's "May the Bird of Paradise Fly Up Your Nose," a number 1 country hit that crossed over and climbed all the way to number 15 on pop charts.

Thanks to his extensive touring, in 1964 he became the first country artist to completely circle the globe on a world tour, and he has performed in Europe thirteen times. For more than half a century he has been one of the most beloved members and regularly scheduled performers on the Opry. Yet, among his peers, he is just as famous for his skills as a fisherman.

"I've loved to fish ever since I was a kid. I do it every chance I get. I do it three or four times a week in the spring or summer. But only when the weather is pretty; I'm a fair-weather fisherman. I don't golf; if I'm gonna walk, I'd better be going someplace. It's a relaxing time. I'm away from the phone; I can be off by myself."

Dickens has some favorite fishing holes, and some favorite fishing partners as well.

"I sold my boat a while ago because so many of my friends have boats, mine just sat there at the house. If we go out to a lake, we'll go to Center Hill Lake or Percy Priest. I might go out with Jerry Reed or Bobby Bare. I like fishing with Bare; he's so laid-back you have to wake him up when he's got a bite. My fishing is kind of built in for me. Stonewall Jackson has a lake on his place stocked with bass. And George Jones has two ponds at his place; one has catfish, and the other has bass and crappie. I fish from the banks when I fish there. The biggest freshwater fish I ever caught was a nine-pound bass I got in Florida; it's on my wall. The biggest saltwater fish I caught was a twenty-five-pound salmon off the coast of Washington State."

It was fishing that cemented Dickens' friendship with one of the newest members of the Opry, Brad Paisley. "Brad is a good fisherman. My wife and I went to the Christmas party he throws for his band and his staff. There were about a hundred people there. He got up to speak and he told everybody that in honor of my eighty-fifth birthday he had a present for me. He brought out a painting that he had done himself; it's two people on the banks of a pond with fishing poles. He calls it *Fishing Buddies* and it's supposed to be him and me. That really meant a lot to me."

His relationship with Paisley introduced Dickens to a whole new generation of country fans, thanks to his guest spots in the young singer's videos, as well as featured spots on his tours. "The first one was 'I'm Gonna Miss Her (The Fishin' Song)' and I've been in most of them since. They're a lot of fun 'cause you never know what to expect. Am I going to have to put a lamp shade on my head? On his concerts, he has two large screens on either side of the stage, and on one of them there's a bunch of cartoon characters dancing around and under that it says, 'Little Jimmy Dickens and Friends.' He sent a crew to my house one time to interview me, and during his show, he'll say, 'We're gonna go live by satellite to Little Jimmy Dickens' living room.' It shows me answering all these questions like I'm right there live. It's pretty silly. Mona and I like to visit him at his house when he's off the road. On his front porch he has a couple of rocking chairs he bought at Cracker Barrel. One is regular size, and one is a child's rocker. That's mine; it has my name on the back of it."

As he has been for many years, Dickens was a member of the Opry Duck Hunt that for the past few years has gone to Greenwood, Mississippi. "I didn't go to hunt. I just went for the fellowship. A couple of guys there wanted to take me fishing so I said sure. We went out in the morning and again that afternoon. We caught a couple hundred crappie. They cleaned and filleted them, then froze them so I could bring them back to Nashville. A few months later, we went over to Jim Ed Brown's house and had a fish fry. Becky was there, of course, and Jan Howard, Carl Smith, Jeanne Pruett, and Eddie. Jim Ed fried up the fish and made hush puppies. There was coleslaw, potatoes; Mona brought some baked beans. It was a real feast."

For his eighty-fifth birthday, Mona—his wife of thirty-five years—and Connie Nelson (one of Willie's ex's) threw Dickens a surprise party. Given the time of year—December—an outdoor celebration by his favorite fishing hole would have been a bit chilly, but the milestone was marked at the next best place: Bass Pro Shop at Opry Mills. "I was never so surprised in my whole life! They had part of the store curtained off and decorated real nice. There were about two hundred people there: Opry members, friends, and fishing buddies. They loaded me down with so much fishing stuff my house looked like Bass Pro Shop the next day."

And what kind of cake could mark such an auspicious occasion and feed such a crowd? A big old ten-pounder of course, shaped and decorated to look just like a fish.

Little Jimmy Dickens doesn't cook. "Oh no, Mona doesn't let me stay in the kitchen. I just get in the way. But she's a wonderful cook. She's from South Indiana, so she's a good Southern cook. When we go to the Eatin' Meetin's at the Browns', or anyplace that you're supposed to bring something, she makes her special ribs. Everybody loves them, and has asked for the recipe, but she won't give it out to anyone."

Here is one that she will share, one of Little Jimmy's favorites.

Mona Dickens' Chicken Casserole

1 box Club crackers
1 cup (2 sticks) butter, melted, divided
2½ cups cooked, boneless chicken, torn or cut up
2 cans cream of chicken soup or cream of mushroom soup
½ pint sour cream
½ cup cornflakes

Place ¾ box of crackers in zip-lock bag and roll with rolling pin to crush. Mix in a bowl with 1⅓ sticks butter. Line a round casserole with butter-cracker mixture. Mix chicken with soup and sour cream, and pour into lined casserole. Roll remaining crackers and cornflakes into crumbs, add remaining melted butter. Sprinkle on top of chicken mixture. Bake at 350° for 25 minutes or until bubbly hot.

George Morgan

Joined the Opry cast in 1948

(1924–1975)

George Morgan was the Candy Kid, thanks to his biggest hit, "Candy Kisses." It became the country crooner's signature song and an Opry audience favorite for nearly three decades.

Morgan was born in Tennessee, but grew up in Ohio, listening to the Opry every Saturday night. He learned to play guitar when he was just eleven years old, and formed a band in the forties, making some appearances on radio stations in Akron and Wooster. "Candy Kisses," which he wrote, punched his ticket to the WWVA Jamboree in Wheeling, West Virginia, even before it was recorded and released as a single.

In 1948, when Eddy Arnold decided to leave the Opry, Morgan—whose smooth singing style was similar to the Tennessee Plowboy's—stepped into that niche on the show, though he had yet to score a hit record. Columbia had signed him to their label just days before his Opry debut, but a musicians strike kept him out of the studio until it was resolved in January 1949. "Candy Kisses" was the first release from his first recording session, and the first of six singles that hit the Top 10 before 1949 ended, an unprecedented accomplishment. In *Billboard*'s April 30, 1949, issue, Morgan had three of the magazine's Top 10 country singles: "Candy Kisses" was number 2, "Rainbow in My Heart" was number 8, and "Please, Don't Let Me Love You" was number 9. Before the year was out, he had three more singles hit the Top 10, and "Room Full of Roses" crossed over to the pop charts as well.

It would be another three years before Morgan had another hit—"Almost" went number 2 in 1952—but he remained an Opry favorite, a Saturday night regular until he left in 1956 to host a television show on WLAC in Nashville. He came back in 1959, the same year his daughter, Loretta Lynn Morgan, was born. Thirteen

years later, the proud papa introduced her when she made her Opry debut on the stage of the Ryman, singing "Paper Roses."

While George and Lorrie are the Morgan names applauded by Opry fans, Anna Morgan—wife and mother—was immensely popular behind

Candy Kisses
George Morgan

Candy kisses wrapped in paper mean more to you than any of mine
Candy kisses wrapped in paper you'd rather have them any old
*   time*
You don't mean it when you whisper those sweet love words in
*   my ear*
Candy kisses wrapped in paper mean more to you than mine do,
*   dear*

I build a castle out of dreams, dear, I thought that you were
*   building too*
Now my castles all have fallen and I am left alone and blue
Once my heart was filled with gladness, now there's sadness only
*   tears*
Candy kisses wrapped in paper mean more to you than mine do,
*   dear*

the scenes, particularly at strawberry-pickin' time in Tennessee. Though she never released a record, her strawberry shortcake was a big hit backstage, especially loved by Opry manager Bud Wendell, who used to drop not-so-subtle hints to George that he sure would love some of Anna's good strawberry shortcake.

Lorrie Morgan remembers her father frequently calling home and asking his wife if she had any strawberries. "He'd say, 'Why don't you run out and get some and make up a strawberry shortcake to bring to the Opry?' She would always do it. My father loved her cooking so much, and he wanted to show it off to everyone."

Anna Morgan's Strawberry Shortcake

2 quarts berries, washed, sliced
¼ cup sugar
2½ cups Bisquick
3 tablespoons sugar or sugar substitute
½ cup milk
3 tablespoons butter, melted, plus 1 tablespoon more

Wash and slice berries. Place in bowl and stir in ¼ cup sugar. Cover and allow to sit for at least 1 hour to juice.

Stir together Bisquick, 3 tablespoons sugar, milk, and 3 tablespoons melted butter until moist and soft. Divide dough in half. Press one-half into a greased 8-inch round cake pan, brush top with 1 tablespoon melted butter. Press the rest of the dough on a board and flatten just enough to cover dough in pan, place gently atop bottom layer. Bake at 400° for 12 minutes or until golden brown. Cook cake, then separate the layers. Put one layer on a plate and cover with half the berries and juice, put second layer on top, and cover with remaining berries and juice and let all soak before serving. When ready to eat, cut into slices and add whipped cream on top.

Hank Williams

Joined the Opry cast in 1949

(1923–1953)

If there was ever a Phantom of the Opry, it would undoubtedly be Hank Williams. Inducted into the Grand Ole Opry in 1949, he was fired in August 1952 and died four months later at just twenty-nine years old. Like many tormented geniuses, it was in death that he became larger than life. Though his membership in the Grand Ole Opry lasted barely three years, his songs are performed to this day by cast members who were born long after he died.

Born in Mount Olive, Alabama—about midway between Mobile and Montgomery—Williams was slight and fragile due to a spinal deformity which was not so severe that he would be confined to bed, but caused chronic pain his entire life. His father, a World War I veteran, was hospitalized most of Williams' youth, so he was primarily raised by his mother, Lilly, forced by circumstances to be both caregiver and breadwinner. She gave him his first guitar when he was just eight, and much of his musical education came from a black street musician he met when the family lived in Georgiana, Alabama. Rufus Payne, known as Tee-Tot, is considered by music historians to be largely responsible for the blues influence in Williams' music. In 1937, Lilly moved the family to Montgomery, where she ran a boarding house. Williams' formal education came to an end when he dropped out of school at sixteen; by then, he had already made appearances on local radio stations and formed his first band, the Drifting Cowboys.

His spinal condition made Williams ineligible for military service during the war, but he worked the shipyards of Mobile while building a music career out of Montgomery; Lilly chauffeured, and collected money at the beer joints and dance halls where he and the band appeared. Even as word of the young singer was spreading beyond Alabama, his drinking and subsequent erratic behavior was establishing

Hank Williams.

a self-destructive pattern that would compromise his talent the rest of his life.

In 1943, Williams met single mother Audrey Mae Sheppard, and they were married in 1944. She learned to play stand-up bass well enough to join the band, and supplanted Lilly not only as manager, but as the driving female force in Williams' life.

In 1947, the two made a trip to Nashville and met powerful music industry executive Fred Rose, partner with Roy Acuff in the publishing company Acuff-Rose. At first, Rose was primarily interested in his songwriting, but positive public response to some songs Williams cut for Sterling Records prompted the publisher to place the singer on MGM Records. His first release for that label, "Move It on Over," was a hit, charting on *Billboard,* as was his next, "Honky Tonkin'," but his drinking had gotten so out of control that even Audrey seemed to give up, filing for divorce in 1948. Characteristic of their tumultuous relationship, the Williamses reconciled and Hank's growing popularity helped Rose secure him a slot on a new radio jamboree, the Louisiana Hayride, broadcast on KWKH in Shreveport.

Surprisingly, even the exposure a fifty-thousand-watt station afforded did not help Williams' next several record releases, which fell so flat that "Mansion on a Hill" did not even make it to the Top 10. But Williams was convinced an old Tin Pan Alley tune he had been performing on his live show could do better, and in February 1949, "Lovesick Blues" was released. By May, it was not only number 1, but it stayed atop the charts for sixteen weeks. Despite lingering concerns about his reliability, the Grand Ole Opry could no longer ignore the phenomenon of Hank Williams, and in 1949, he and Audrey moved to Nashville and he joined the cast of the show, becoming the Opry's biggest star, but ultimately, one of their most painful and frustrating heartaches.

Beginning in 1950, with the release and success of his "Long Gone Lonesome Blues," Williams recorded his own compositions, building a body of work that includes the classics "Cold Cold Heart," "I Can't Help It (If I'm Still in Love with You)," and "Hey Good Lookin'," that were not only country hits, but also rocketed up the pop charts when recorded by the likes of Tony Bennett. As his fame soared, his alcoholism—fueled in part by the crippling back pain he endured—worsened. Surgery performed in late 1951 was not successful, and at the end of that year, he disbanded the Drifting Cowboys. When he was released from the hospital, Audrey kicked him out of their home and he went to live with Ray Price, who became a member of the Opry in January 1952. In August, after repeatedly missing shows or being too drunk to perform at curtain time, Williams was fired from the Opry, and Audrey again filed for divorce. He left Nashville for Montgomery, then Shreveport when Fred Rose was able to get him back on the Louisiana Hayride. In October of 1952 he married Billie Jean Jones Eshliman, whom he had met in Nashville, despite the fact that his girlfriend, Bobbie Jett, was pregnant with his daughter. Born after his death, Jett Williams was adopted by Hank's mother, Lilly, in 1954, and grew up to be a country musician in her own right.

Outside of the Hayride appearances, Williams' tour dates were right back to where they had started, beer joints and dance halls, but even as his life spiraled out of control, "Jambalaya" became another number 1 hit record. On December 30, after a weeklong break in Montgomery, Williams and a driver set out in a rented Cadillac for bookings in Charleston, West Virginia, and Canton, Ohio. He made neither one, but is believed to have died in the backseat on December 31. His death certificate was signed on January 1, 1953, in Oak Hill, West Virginia.

In *Mother Maybelle's Cookbook,* Opry member and author June Carter Cash wrote:

For a while, the closest we ever came as a family to knowing about Cajun cooking was singing "Jambalaya" with Hank Williams and eating a new dish of Momma's by the same name. Of course, we let

Hank have the lead as he had written that song about "jambalaya, crawfish pie and file gumbo." Cajun cooking at our house was simple and heavily spiced. Momma threw all the ingredients into one pot and their aroma made you remember hunting, trapping and fishing. We leaned toward seafood—shrimp, crab and other shellfish from the Gulf of Mexico, instead of meats that were left over from the day before or crawfish.

If Hank or Audrey Williams ever made jambalaya, there is no record of it, but June Carter Cash included her mother's recipe for the Cajun dish in *Mother Maybelle's Cookbook: A Kitchen Visit with America's First Family of Country Song.*

Jambalaya

2 tablespoons salad oil	1 cup smoked Polish sausage
1 tablespoon flour	2½ cups fresh tomatoes
1½ large onions, chopped	2½ cups chicken broth
1 cup chopped green pepper	1½ cups uncooked rice
2 cloves garlic, chopped	1 tablespoon chopped parsley
4 chicken thighs, meat chopped	½ teaspoon salt
1 cup shrimp, de-veined	½ teaspoon Tabasco sauce
1 cup ham	1 tablespoon sugar

Heat oil and flour in large saucepan, and brown to roux, stirring constantly. Sauté onions, peppers, and garlic until tender. Add meat and remaining ingredients. Cover and reduce heat. Cook until rice is done and the liquid is absorbed. Pour into one big bowl. Serves at least 8 to 10. Serve with hot corn bread—pour jambalaya over bread. Give everyone a harmony part and sing "Jambalaya."

Jambalaya
Hank Williams

Good-bye, Joe, me gotta go, me oh my oh
Me gotta go pole the pirogue down the bayou
My Yvonne, the sweetest one, me oh my oh
Son of a gun, we'll have big fun on the bayou

[Chorus]
Jambalaya and a crawfish pie and filet gumbo
'Cause tonight I'm gonna see my ma chère ami-o
Pick guitar, fill fruit jar, and be gay-o
Son of gun, we'll have big fun on the bayou

Thibodaux, Fontaineaux, the place is buzzin'
Kinfolk come to see Yvonne by the dozen
Dress in style and go hog wild, me oh my oh
Son of a gun, we'll have big fun on the bayou

[Repeat chorus]

Settle down far from town, get me a pirogue
And I'll catch all the fish in the bayou
Swap my mon to buy Yvonne what she need-o
Son of a gun, we'll have big fun on the bayou

Mother Maybelle Carter and the Carter Sisters

Joined the Opry cast in 1950

(Maybelle, 1909–1978; Helen, 1927–1998; June, 1929–2003; Anita, 1933–1999)

Before Roy Acuff was crowned the King of Country Music and before Kitty Wells the Queen of Country Music, the Carter Family was the First Family of Country Music. The act that is regarded as country music's first star group came together through two marriages between three long-established, musically inclined families in southwestern Virginia in the early twentieth century. First, A. P. Carter married Sara Dougherty in 1915, one month before her seventeenth birthday. Sara's six-year-old cousin Maybelle Addington was at the wedding, as was the groom's brother, Ezra. Ten years later, the two met again at Sara and A. P. Carter's house when Maybelle was there to do a show with them at a nearby schoolhouse. A courtship ensued, and in 1926, when Maybelle was two months shy of her seventeenth birthday, she and Ezra eloped.

One year later, A.P. formed the Carter Family, a trio that consisted of himself, his wife, and his new sister-in-law, Maybelle. He and Sara, with three children under the age of ten, were struggling financially. He knew record companies would pay the princely sum of fifty dollars for a recording, though he and Sara had been unsuccessful in their first audition. The addition of Maybelle's harmonies and her unique and innovative "scratch-style" guitar playing was key to landing a record deal, and the trio recorded their first songs in the summer of 1927 for Victor Records. They were released in November—just before the birth of Maybelle and Ezra's first girl, Helen—and along with songs by Jimmie Rodgers, became the first nationally popular recordings of old-time rural music.

The success of those records led to many more, 250 were made in all during their fifteen years as an act. The Carter Family made live appearances—for fairly low pay—in the standard venue of that day, old schoolhouses. They also had contracts with several radio stations along the Texas-Mexico border, and their performances there reached a tremendous broadcast audience. Sara and A.P.'s marriage grew more troubled as time went by, and they separated in 1933; in 1939, she took the unprecedented step for a woman of that time of getting a divorce. Nonetheless, they continued recording and performing together until 1943, when Sara decided to retire, and moved to California with her new husband, A.P.'s cousin.

It wasn't in Maybelle Carter's blood to be a full-time housewife, and with her three teenage daughters, Helen, June, and Anita, they formed a new act, Mother Maybelle Carter and the Carter Sisters. Mother Maybelle was on guitar of course, Helen played accordion, June autoharp, and Anita bass. Their path to the Grand Ole Opry began at WRVA's Old Dominion Barn Dance in Richmond, Virginia, in 1946; two years later, they moved on to the Tennessee Barn Dance on WNOX in Knoxville, then the Ozark Jubilee in Springfield, Missouri. Recordings for Victor and Columbia brought them more exposure, and in 1950, Mother Maybelle Carter and the Carter Sisters joined the Grand Ole Opry and settled in Nashville.

Mother Maybelle Carter and the Carter Sisters; Maybelle, June, Anita, and Helen.

Among the girls, Helen was considered the best musician and Anita the best singer; she recorded two Top 10 hits with Hank Snow shortly after they joined the Opry, two well-received solo albums of folk songs in 1963 and 1964, and scored another Top 10 hit with Waylon Jennings in 1968.

June Carter was the showman of the three, and her charismatic personality and stunning good looks caught the eye and captured the heart of new Grand Ole Opry member and rising star Johnny Cash in 1956. He was married to Vivian Liberto at the time, and June was breaking up with her first husband, honky-tonk star Carl Smith. Mother Maybelle and the Carter Sisters joined Cash's touring show in 1961, and the attraction between the two remained, though June was married again, to contractor Edwin Nix. Both were divorced in 1966, Johnny's marriage and career increasingly affected by his drug abuse. June and Mother Maybelle helped Cash kick his addictions and in 1968, he proposed to June onstage in London, Ontario; they were wed one week later in a small church in Franklin, Kentucky. The marriage lasted thirty-five years, until their deaths four months apart in 2003. Their remarkable love story was told in the award-winning 2005 film *Walk the Line.*

Though Mother Maybelle retired from touring, she remained a revered influence and contributing artist on folk, bluegrass, and country projects nearly until her death. She issued solo albums, performed on the historic *Will the Circle Be Unbroken* collection of 1972, and was an important contributor to many of her son-in-law Johnny Cash's recordings. In 1970, the original Carter Family was inducted into the Country Music Hall of Fame. Her playing ability was affected by arthritis, then a form of Parkinson's disease, and she passed away in October 1978.

While it would hardly seem that Mother Maybelle spent much time in the kitchen between touring and recording, in 1989, June Carter Cash compiled a cookbook of recipes from her mother, sisters, and friends they met along the way. The dishes range from rudimentary to internationally influenced creations. As with much country cooking, mason jars are a vital piece of equipment.

Momma's Basic Flour Dredge

4 cups all-purpose flour

½ cup salt

2 tablespoons ground pepper

2 tablespoons dried English mustard

1½ tablespoons paprika

1 teaspoon dried basil

1 teaspoon dried thyme

1 teaspoon parsley flakes

Sift all ingredients together. Store in a tightly sealed mason jar and use whenever seasoned flour is called for. (Take out only what you need.)

Stock

Take chicken bones, veal bones, or beef bones and split them with a cleaver. Be sure to raise your hand high and whale them good. It gets the gelatin jarred loose and ready to reach the boiling pot of water. Place the bones in a large pot and cover with water. Cover the pot. Bring to a boil; boil until there is film rising and you are sure the vitamins are released into the stock. Cool. Strain the stock through cheesecloth. Put in mason jars and seal. Look for a mountain spring to keep them cool until you have a hardworking crew from good mountain "stock" to feed.

According to June, "Momma would put them in the trough of cool water by the sweet milk until she needed the stock to make her great soups glisten and glow with the strength they needed. Fresh vegetables added to this special stock made the difference in all of us. Helen, Anita, and I grew stronger because Momma knew how to make good stock."

French-Style Green Beans or Snaps

Not long after the Carter Family moved to Stop 9, Petersburg Pike, Richmond, VA, Ezra Carter planted a garden with squash, tomatoes, cucumbers, beans, and other vegetables. One time, when Mother Maybelle and the girls were on the road, the neighbors, thinking they would help, picked about two bushels of beans and set them inside the kitchen door. Mother Maybelle didn't know what to make of it; the beans had been picked so early, there were no beans inside, just long, skinny pods. Helen told the rest of the family, "That's the way they eat them here."

"You mean they eat the sticks?" asked June.

"No, they don't let them get full, they call them snaps." With a paring knife, Momma Carter cut off the string of each side of the shell, then cooked them up this way.

3 pounds snap beans, ends snapped off and cut in halves lengthwise
1½ teaspoons salt
1½ teaspoons sugar
4 to 6 pieces uncooked bacon or salt pork, or ⅛ cup vegetable oil
Pinch of red pepper
Fresh basil

Wash beans, then cover with cold water. Add salt, sugar, bacon or salt pork, and red pepper; bring to a boil. Lower heat and cook until tender. Don't overcook. Drain, place in serving dish, and sprinkle fresh basil over beans.

Kitty Wells

Joined the Opry cast in 1952

Before Patsy, before Loretta, before Tammy, before Jean, Jeannie, and Jeanne, there was Kitty, a modest, soft-spoken mother of three who favored gingham over rhinestones, who neither drank nor smoked, and whose early repertoire consisted of gospel and old-time tunes. Yet, it was Kitty Wells who in 1952 vaulted to stardom on the strength of a song that was considered so controversial she was not permitted to perform it on the Grand Ole Opry. "It Wasn't God Who Made Honky Tonk Angels," an answer song to Hank Thompson's "Wild Side of Life," blamed unfaithful men for creating unfaithful women, expressing in no uncertain terms a sentiment that hit such a nerve the record sold one million copies as it soared to number 1, making Kitty Wells the first female in country music to claim either achievement. It set the stage for a career that saw her named the top female country performer by trade publications for fourteen consecutive years, chart seventy singles—including twenty-three that went Top 10—and earn the undisputed and lifelong title the Queen of Country Music.

By the time Wells recorded "Honky Tonk Angels," she had been performing professionally for sixteen years. Born and raised in Nashville, Muriel Ellen Deason learned to play guitar from her father, a brakeman for the Tennessee Central Railroad who also played banjo. Her mother, who sang gospel, encouraged her daughters to sing in church, and the entire family listened together to the Grand Ole Opry on Saturday nights. In 1936, Muriel, her sisters Jewel and Mae, and their cousin Bessie Choate formed the Deason Sisters and began appearing on an early-morning show on WSIX radio. Muriel also worked days at Washington Manufacturing Company—an Opry sponsor—ironing shirts.

She met her husband-to-be, a musician and cabinetmaker, through his sister Louise, who lived next door to the Deasons. In 1937, at eighteen years old, Muriel married Johnnie Wright, and with Louise, they formed Johnnie Wright and the

Kitty Wells.

Harmony Girls. Two years later, Louise's husband, Jack Anglin, made the trio a quartet called the Tennessee Hillbillies. When Anglin was drafted in 1942, Johnnie and Muriel continued to perform at radio stations in the Southeast; in 1943, Muriel became Kitty Wells, a name Johnnie took from an old folk song, "Sweet Kitty Wells." When the war ended, Wright and Anglin formed a new duo, Johnnie and Jack, and they performed fairly regularly on the Opry in 1946 and 1947, with Kitty making occasional appearances when her busy schedule as a young mother would allow. When Johnnie and Jack joined the Louisiana Hayride in 1948, she took a more active role, and in 1949 and 1950, recorded some unsuccessfully received gospel songs for RCA.

In January 1952, Johnnie and Jack were invited back to join the Grand Ole Opry cast, and Kitty decided that her place was in the home. She was talked into the studio one more time by Decca Records executive Paul Cohen, who promised her a $125 session fee to sing a few songs for the label. In May 1952, she cut "It Wasn't God Who Made Honky Tonk Angels" (written by J. D. Miller) in Owen Bradley's studio; by July, it was in *Billboard*'s Top 10, and did not stop climbing until it reached number 1, staying on the charts for sixteen weeks. In spite of that, the song was banned from the NBC radio network, and she was not permitted to perform it on the Opry, but the exposure it brought the unlikely trailblazer did earn her membership in the Grand Ole Opry cast, and opened doors for female singers of that era.

In 1953, she answered Webb Pierce's "Back Street Affair" with "Paying for That Back Street Affair," then recorded a succession of country classics, among them "Release Me," "Makin' Believe," and "I Can't Stop

Loving You." Though Kitty's success eclipsed her husband's—she became a member of the Country Music Hall of Fame in 1974, and in 1991 received a Grammy Lifetime Achievement Award—it was Johnnie who chose her songs, who steered her career, and who managed the Kitty Wells/Johnnie Wright Show. It was truly a family affair, with children Ruby, Bobby, and Carol Sue an integral part of the production. In 2001, she officially retired with a farewell performance in Nashville.

One of Kitty Wells' proudest roles was homemaker, and she was known among family, friends, and colleagues for her skills in the kitchen. Responding to requests for her recipes, she compiled a couple of cookbooks, written in her warm, down-home style. The cover of *The Kitty Wells Country Kitchen Cookbook,* published in 1964 by Kitty's Cook Book Company in Madison, Tennessee, was dressed in red-and-white checked gingham, just like its author. These recipes come right from Miss Kitty's kitchen.

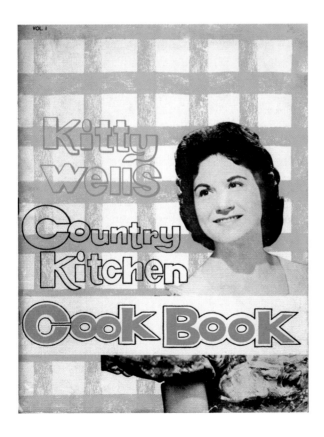

Chicken Croquettes

A good way to use leftover baked chicken or a nice meal when the chicken is cooked especially for this dish.

4 tablespoons butter
4 tablespoons flour
1 cup milk
2 cups cooked, chopped white-meat chicken
Day-old biscuits crumbled into crumbs
Two beaten eggs
Cooking oil

In a saucepan over low heat, blend butter with flour to make paste, add milk, stirring constantly to make thick white sauce. Add salt to taste. Stir chicken into sauce and mix well. Drop by tablespoon onto a sheet of waxed paper laid atop a cookie sheet. Place in refrigerator to chill. Roll each portion in fine bread crumbs made from biscuits, then in slightly beaten egg, then in crumbs again. Return to refrigerator to chill again before cooking by dropping into deep, hot fat. Cook until crispy on outside and golden brown. Good served with a thick gravy made with chicken broth.

Pink Quickie

Freeze some strawberry-flavored "soda pop" in your ice cube trays. When frozen, put the cubes into a plastic freezer bag. When you serve lemonade, pop one strawberry cube in each glass. Mighty pretty—and different, too.

Hard-Cooked Egg Cobbler

This is a perfect dish for persons who have an abundance of eggs or who can buy them at most reasonable prices. And it seems very appropriate for an Easter dessert since eggs play such a prominent part in Easter foods the world over.

12 whole eggs

2 cups sugar

½ cup (1 stick) butter

Fresh, grated nutmeg

2 pastry shells

Hard cook 12 whole eggs: Place the eggs in a saucepan and cover them with cold water. This is then placed over high heat and quickly heated to the boiling point. Once the water begins to boil watch carefully, and when they have boiled exactly 8 minutes, take them off the stove and drain them with cold water. Quickly remove the shells and slice eggs directly into a pastry-lined shallow casserole dish (8-by-12-inch is fine).

Sprinkle 2 cups sugar over the eggs, dot this with 1 stick of butter and sprinkle generously with nutmeg. Have ready 2 cups of boiling water and pour this over the egg, butter, and sugar combination. Place a top pastry over all and place in a medium-hot oven [*400°*] and cook until the top crust is nicely browned and the syrup formed has bubbled up around the edges. Serve warm or set aside and serve cold. It's good either way.

Marty Robbins.

Marty Robbins

Joined the Opry cast in 1953

(1925–1982)

Marty Robbins—singer, songwriter, actor, author, showman, stock car racer, husband, and father—was inarguably one of the most dynamic performers and versatile talents to ever grace the Grand Ole Opry stage. His tragically short time on earth—he was just fifty-seven when he died—belies the enduring impact his remarkable gifts had not just on country music, but on a vastly eclectic repertoire of musical genres.

Martin David Robinson was born in 1925 in Glendale, Arizona, just outside of Phoenix; he and his twin sister, Marnie, were raised in poverty, and his youth was difficult. The music and stories of the Old West—as told to him by his grandfather "Texas Bob" Heckle—inspired him, and one of his most influential childhood heroes was Gene Autry. After dropping out of high school, he joined the navy; during his three years in the service, he saw action in the Pacific theater in World War II. After his discharge, he took on a series of odd jobs before acing the audition to be KOY-Phoenix's cowboy singer; from there he graduated to the larger KHPO in the same town. It was during this time that he not only became Marty Robbins, but married Marizona Baldwin, whose unusual name combined Arizona and Maricopa County, where Phoenix is located. As Marty was expanding his local exposure through KHPO's new television station, the couple had two children, Ronny and Janet.

Two people who admired his work at KHPO—station manager and former WSM-Opry executive Harry Stone and Opry member Little Jimmy Dickens—were instrumental in bringing Marty to the attention of Columbia Records and the Grand Ole Opry. He signed a recording contract with the former on May 25, 1951, and not long after, made his debut as a guest on the Grand Ole Opry.

January 1953 was a milestone in Robbins' still-young career: He scored his first number 1 with "I'll Go on Alone," was inducted into the Opry on January 19, and moved to Nashville. As son Ronny—who was about three and a half years old at the time—remembers, they first lived in a small place in the blue-collar Woodbine neighborhood, three houses away from the Wilburn Brothers, who became Opry members in October of that year. "I remember other people coming over all the time and playing music. I was little, but I knew he must have hit it big when he got a little Jaguar and painted on the trunk was "That's All Right Mama." Not long after that, Ronny Robbins says, they moved to a bigger house off Franklin Road, and Jeanne Pruett and her then-husband, Jack—Marty's guitar player—moved into the Woodbine home.

"That's All Right Mama" was Robbins' country version of the Elvis Presley pop hit, recorded in 1955. Robbins continued to dabble in rock and roll; at the same time, as host of the Prince Albert–sponsored segment of the Opry, he was required to feature a gospel song during the show. Some blues-flavored country hits that followed, "Singing the Blues" and "Knee Deep in the Blues," crossed over to the pop charts. "White Sports Coat (and a Pink Carnation)," which he wrote, vaulted him to pop stardom and teen-theme infamy in 1957. But it was a move back to the Western sound he loved as a youth that produced his signature song, "El Paso," in 1959. The self-penned tune was the biggest-selling record of his career, earning a Grammy and topping both the country and pop charts.

Cowboy music wasn't the only passion Robbins carried with him from Arizona to Tennessee, as Ronny Robbins will tell you.

Growing up in Phoenix, Dad loved Mexican food, and every time we went back to Phoenix, we went to eat at his favorite restaurant, La Perla, back in Glendale. It was just a little, family-owned place. It's still there now. I can remember as a little kid standing on the seats of the red booths. There were no Mexican restaurants at the time in Nashville, so he would go to the markets in Phoenix and bring back what he needed to cook it at home. When we moved to Brentwood, friends would come over to eat; he would cook up some Mexican food, and they were crazy about it. Eddy Arnold, Dottie West, Brenda Lee. I was in love with Brenda Lee. I thought that because she was my size, she was my age. The first time she brought Ronnie Shacklett over and introduced him as her fiancé, my heart was broken, I cried and cried! Daddy would cook up a big dinner every couple months, I can remember coming home and smelling those great smells and knowing company was coming. Sometimes he made flour tortillas from scratch, or you could buy them canned. They had this big old tin top that you'd pull off with a key. He figured out a way to make a taco shell mold out of them. He took one of those lids, bent it in half, and welded a little hook on top. He would fold the tortilla inside that, then put it in a deep fryer and make taco shells. It was pretty ingenious. I still have those old molds.

In the fifties, the singer began indulging another interest, racing micro-midget cars, and Ronny remembers going to a little track on Ewing Lane in Nashville, right around the time "El Paso" hit. Not long after, Marty bought some property southeast of Nashville in Smyrna, and built his own track there.

There was an old Dairy Queen building nearby, and he decided that if he couldn't get Mexican food in Nashville, he'd open his own restaurant. So he turned that into Rosa's Cantina, after "El Paso." He got some of the band members' wives to work there, and brought his brother up from Arizona to help out. That was before interstates, and Rosa's Cantina was on U.S. 41, a main highway and truck route that ran up to Nashville. The restaurant did well, but nobody realized how much work it would be, so they shut it down not too much later.

Luckily, Nashville's first Mexican restaurant soon opened close by the channel 8 studio where *The Marty Robbins Show* was taped. "We'd run over to La Fiesta between tapings to eat. It was really good; he really enjoyed the people who owned it and they loved him."

Robbins had an especially close relationship with his fans, who called themselves Marty's Army. Like many country stars of that time, he stayed long after the show was over to visit, sign autographs, and pose for photos. He was equally popular at the race track, racing modified stock cars at the Nashville Speedway in the sixties, which is when he began performing on

the last segment of the Opry, coming directly from the track. Preacher Hamilton, NASCAR Winston Cup Series star Bobby Hamilton's grandfather, built many of the singer's modifieds; Devil Woman was the first in a long line of purple and yellow cars he had. In 1966, he entered his first NASCAR Grand National stock car race, as much a career achievement to him as a hit record.

In August 1969, just before his forty-fourth birthday, Robbins had a heart attack, and in January, he underwent bypass surgery. Though the technique was still in the experimental stages, it was a success, and by April, he was able to receive the Man of the Decade Award from the Academy of Country Music in person. Even more importantly, he passed his physical and was back on a NASCAR track that October. Three wrecks in 1974 and 1975 caused him to temporarily give it up, but he returned to the sport in 1977; his last race took place in November 1982.

That year was tremendously successful for Marty Robbins in many ways. His song "Some Memories Just Won't Die"—which proved to be a statement on the artist's career and vibrant personality—went Top 10 on the country charts, and that October, he received the Artist Resurgence Award from *Billboard* magazine. On October 11, he was inducted into the Country Music Hall of Fame, just a couple weeks after his fifty-seventh birthday. On December 2, he suffered another heart attack, and died on December 8, 1982.

> *My father didn't take us to the Opry much; he tried to keep his professional life separate from his personal life. But I have great memories of other members of the Opry, his friends that loved coming to the house to eat his Mexican food. He didn't have any recipes. He just cooked what he knew, and what he liked. As long as it had lots of cilantro, onions, and peppers, and was really hot, it was good. Like everything else he did, he put a lot of himself into it, a lot of love.*

In the South, when a baby is born, when a new family moves onto the street, when someone is ill, or when tragedy strikes, a parade of homemade casseroles, preserved foods, and sweet desserts ensues, cooked and delivered by thoughtful friends and neighbors. When Marty Robbins suffered a heart attack in August 1969, it sent shock waves through the country music industry and Marty's Army, his legion of fans. It sent his good friend, fellow performer, and highly regarded home cook Jeanne Pruett straight to her kitchen.

"When Marty had his first heart attack, I baked this cake and took it to the hospital a couple of days later," she says. "As I recall, it was one of his favorite desserts, so when you bake it, please remember Marty."

Her recipe originally appeared in Jeanne Pruett's *Feedin' Friends* cookbook, volume one.

Marty Robbins' Favorite Carrot Cake

2 cups all-purpose flour
1 teaspoon salt
2 teaspoons baking soda
1 teaspoon cinnamon
2 cups sugar

1½ cups Wesson oil
4 eggs
½ cup pecans, chopped
3 cups grated carrots

Sift flour, salt, baking soda, and cinnamon together. Cream sugar and Wesson oil in separate bowl, then add eggs. Add flour mixture and pecans. Add grated carrots last. Bake in sheet pan or two rounds for 35 to 40 minutes in 350° oven.

Frosting

½ cup (1 stick) butter, softened
3 ounces cream cheese, softened
1 box confectioners' sugar

2 teaspoons vanilla
½ cup grated, sweetened coconut

Cream butter and cream cheese together. Add sugar and vanilla, mix well. Add coconut last. If frosting is too thick, add a little milk until it reaches desired consistency. Frost cake when fully cooled.

The Louvin Brothers

Joined the Opry cast in 1955

(Ira Louvin, 1924–1965)

The Louvin Brothers' career began on the Fourth of July, 1940, when they were paid three dollars a piece to provide background music for a merry-go-round at a county fair. Compared to the backbreaking work the brothers were accustomed to, singing for their supper was a walk in the park, or a ride on the carousel as the case may be.

Born in Section, Alabama, and raised in the Sand Mountain region of the state, Ira Lonnie and his younger brother Charlie Elzer Loudermilk toiled as field hands on the family farm, and in the local cotton mills. Working side by side, and influenced by the entertainers they heard on the Grand Ole Opry radio show, they developed a distinctive style of harmonizing, a blending of notes called "shape note singing," based on the gospel harmonies that formed the musical bed of their Sunday morning church services.

Not long after their Independence Day professional debut, they won a talent contest in Chattanooga, with the first prize of an appearance on station WDEF. The Loudermilks—as they were still known—were so well received that in late 1942, they got their own program, appearing as the Radio Twins. That led to shows with the Foggy Mountain Boys and the Happy Valley Boys, and in 1947, they changed their stage name to the Louvin Brothers.

In the late forties Charlie Louvin joined the service, which stymied their commercial development as a duo, though they remained committed to songwriting, signing a publishing contract with Acuff-Rose in 1948. Their catalogue eventually contained more than five hundred songs, and led to their membership years later in the Songwriters Hall of Fame. They made some recordings for Decca and MGM in the late forties, but it wasn't until Charlie got out of the service that they were truly able to devote themselves to their act.

The Louvin Brothers.

In 1952, they signed with Capitol Records and released "The Family That Prays Together." Its success was their entrée into gospel music, where they excelled, as well as to the Grand Ole Opry, which they joined in 1955 when they moved to Nashville. Seeking more mainstream success, they recorded and released their own composition, "When I Stop Dreaming," a Top 10 hit that stayed on the charts for thirteen weeks. They followed that up with their first number 1, "I Don't Believe You've Met My Baby," and other chart toppers like "Hoping That You're Helping" and "You're Running Wild." From the midfifties through the early sixties, the Louvin Brothers had over twenty songs on *Billboard*'s country charts, and the rich harmonies that distinguished their records influenced later artists like Gram Parsons, Emmylou Harris, and the Byrds.

Unfortunately, Ira's alcoholism caused a rift between the brothers and they performed for the last time together on August 18, 1963, in Watseka, Illinois, on a bill with Ray Price. Charlie Louvin scored Top 10 hits with "I Don't Love You Anymore" in 1964 and "See the Big Man Cry" in 1965; that year, Ira was killed in an automobile accident. Charlie Louvin carried on, exploring new collaborations such as one with Melba Montgomery that produced several charting duets in 1970 and 1971.

In 2001, the Louvin Brothers—Ira posthumously—were inducted into the Country Music Hall of Fame.

Recognizing the brothers' significant impact on classic and contemporary country music, Universal South Records produced a critically acclaimed album in 2003, *Livin', Lovin', Losin': Songs of the Louvin Brothers*. The collaboration of Louvin Brothers songs cut by artists including Dierks Bentley, Del McCoury, Terri Clark, Ronnie Dunn, Rhonda Vincent, and Joe

Nichols was brought to the Opry stage on December 13, 2003, for a memorable one-hour segment of *Grand Ole Opry Live* on GAC. The album won a Grammy for Best Country Album in 2004.

Thanks to Charlie Louvin, every spring Opry members look forward to a very special delivery of a famous Southern delicacy, Vidalia onions. Joe Evans grew up listening to the Opry on a battery-operated radio in Sylvania, Georgia— the area of the state where the onions are sanctioned to be grown—and made his first pilgrimage to the Ryman Auditorium in 1955, the same year the Louvin Brothers joined. Evans, a tremendous fan of brothers Ira and Charlie, continued to follow Charlie Louvin's solo career after Ira's death. From 1983 through 1993, Louvin produced a bluegrass festival at his home place on Sand Mountain, Alabama, which Evans attended

Charlie Louvin performing at the Grand Ole Opry in 2005.

faithfully. It was to May on the Mountain that Evans began bringing Louvin the famous onions as a gift. "I had gotten to know him a little bit," says Evans, "and one time I brought him a cassette of a little bluegrass group from our area who called themselves Vidalia. Charlie looked at the name on the cassette and said, 'I'm not sure about the group, but I sure do like those Vidalia onions.' Well, the next year the onions come off just in time for me to carry some up to the mountain for him, and we brought them every year after that. Vidalias are harvested from the end of April into June, so it was pretty good timing for his festival."

Joe and his wife, Mary Nell, developed a real friendship with Betty and Charlie Louvin, who have been to visit the couple at their Georgia home several times. Returning the favor, Charlie Louvin brought the Evanses backstage of the Opry and introduced them to fellow members in 1996.

The baskets of Vidalia onions the Evanses brought along with them that trip as edible calling cards made quite the impression, and the couple have been known ever since as the Onion People. Their annual springtime visits—usually Mother's Day weekend—are highly anticipated by Opry members.

"It's a big day in our house when the Vidalias arrive," says Too Slim of Riders in the Sky. Jeannie Seely is another fan of the couple and their onions: "The Evanses would always have some bags specifically for some members—Dickens and Porter, Billy Walker, and of course Charlie; then they'd have a big basketful of onions that people could just take what they wanted. The first time I came in and saw a package with my name on it, I felt like I had made it! I went to the greenroom to thank them, and found them there giving out some recipes for the onions. Charlie Louvin told them he knew how to cook an onion and didn't need a recipe to do it, but I told them I needed all the help I can get!"

The onions were first grown in Thombs County, Georgia, on a farm owned by Mose Coleman; touting their unusually mild, sweet flavor, the savvy salesman was able to command the princely sum of three dollars and fifty cents for a fifty-pound bag. Other farmers in the area sensed the potential of the product and began dedicating acreage to the distinct onion. In the 1940s, a state-owned farmers' market was built in Vidalia, centrally located at the juncture of some of southern Georgia's most widely traveled state highways. Customers who came from nearby counties to buy fresh produce there were the ones who dubbed the sweet onions they purchased there Vidalia onions. Georgia takes its onions so seriously that in 1986, the state legislature passed the "Vidalia Onion Act," which authorized a trademark for them, and limited the area from which a Vidalia could genuinely brag the name to twenty counties. In 1989, the United States Department of Agriculture made it federally official, and in 1990, the Vidalia was named Georgia's official state vegetable.

Vidalia onions are highly perishable, so unless you eat yours up right away, it is recommended they be stored in a cool, dry place, inserted one by one into the legs of pantyhose, knotted between each onion. As the need arises, cut an onion off above the knot. Joe Evans says that Jean Shepard eats a Vidalia onion like an apple, but if that doesn't appeal, he offers these tried-and-true recipes.

Hot and Sweet Vidalia Onion Dip

2 cups Vidalia onions, chopped
2 cups low-fat mayonnaise
2 cups grated Swiss cheese
½ cup chopped ham or seafood (optional)

Combine chopped onions with mayonnaise and cheese. Place in glass cooking dish. May add ¼ cup chopped ham or seafood. Cook at 350° for 30 to 35 minutes. Serve with chips or crackers.

Vidalia Onion Layered Salad

Salad
3 cups thinly sliced Vidalia onions
1 large head lettuce, washed and torn in bite-sized pieces
8 hard-boiled eggs, sliced

Dressing
½ cup yellow mustard
½ cup mayonnaise
Onion salt to taste
⅛ teaspoon lemon pepper seasoning salt
2 teaspoons white vinegar

Mix all dressing ingredients together thoroughly and set aside. Make layers of salad by starting with half of lettuce, half of onion, and half of eggs. Pour half of dressing over that layer, then repeat. Cover and chill for 2 hours. Very good with grilled steak and potatoes.

Cheesy Vidalia Onion Bake

4 jumbo Vidalia onions, thinly sliced
⅓ cup butter or margarine
¼ cup all-purpose flour
2 cups milk
2 cups shredded cheddar cheese, sharp or mild as desired
½ teaspoon salt

Place sliced Vidalia onions in greased 2-quart casserole dish and set aside. Melt butter in heavy saucepan over low heat. Add flour, stirring well until smooth. Cook for 1 minute, stirring constantly. Gradually add milk. Cook over medium heat while stirring until it thickens and becomes bubbly. Add cheese and salt, stirring until cheese melts and sauce is smooth. Pour over Vidalias and bake uncovered at 350° for 1 hour.

Jean Shepard

Joined the Opry cast in 1955

On November 21, 2005, Jean Shepard celebrated three milestones: her birthday, her wedding anniversary, and her fiftieth year as a member of the Grand Ole Opry.

"It is wonderful to have the distinction of being the longest-tenured female member of the Opry," she said between shows on a Saturday night at the Ryman Auditorium one month later. "I've been around since water! I feel very fortunate to have come up when I did, when traditional country music was at its peak. Those artists taught me so much. Lefty Frizzell was my favorite. I met Hank Williams, Sr. He was sort of skeptical about women making it as country singers. There weren't many female entertainers on the Opry then; we were 'girl singers.' We didn't even have a dressing room; we used the ladies' room to get ready. There were two stalls, one sink, and one mirror. I wouldn't take a million dollars for those memories."

Though Shepard allows that the Opry House, now in its third decade, is "nice and roomy," the last night the show was broadcast from the Ryman on March 15, 1974, was heartbreaking for her. "I cried onstage," she admits. "A reporter that was there to cover the last night wrote that the only tears he saw came from Jean Shepard and that he went next door to Tootsies to have a beer in my honor. That was nice. Some people used to complain about the old Ryman, how hot it was in the summer and how cold in the winter; that it was too crowded. I never noticed that. I was just so happy to be there."

On an extremely cold December night, she was happy to be back in the grand, old, nicely heated building, where the Grand Ole Opry is staged for a couple of months every winter. No one looks more at home there than Jean Shepard, particularly on the weekend before Christmas when she and her band, the Second Fiddles, set out their traditional holiday spread. Ironically, though the casual buffet was set up in a production room for the television broadcast crew, Shepard noted that be-

Jean Shepard.

fore the Ryman was refurbished, this was exactly where the women's restroom had been, and where she, Kitty Wells, Patsy Cline, and Minnie Pearl had jostled elbows for mirror position. Now it was sausage balls and deviled eggs claiming shelf space.

Shepard made the three hundred sausage balls the night before, as well as all the ham and biscuit sandwiches. As each band member arrived that night, they toted in dips, chips, cheese plates, cookies, pies, cakes, paper products, and soft drinks, which they kept in the dressing room Shepard was sharing with Porter Wagoner until the television broadcast was over. When that crew left, band members and friends began setting out the food under Shepard's direction, an appetite-whetting process that had stage workers, singers, musicians, and cloggers milling about that end of the hall, waiting for a cue. Finally, when Hal Ketchum poked his head in the door and said, "I'll trade a fiddle for a biscuit," Shepard smiled and pointed him to the stack of paper plates.

"We've done this for about fifteen or sixteen years. About three times a year we do a potluck backstage mostly for ourselves, but this one at Christmas has just grown every year, and pretty much everyone here that night comes by for a plate of food. All my guys cook, except for my husband," she adds with a smile.

Drummer Gregg Hutchins has actually published his own cookbook, *Cooking with Gregg,* and has a nationally syndicated radio show broadcast five mornings a week on over one hundred stations. Though he is renowned for his pies, particularly his Aunt Floy's Butterscotch Pie, he brought two different kinds of cookies to the 2005 Grand Ole Opry

Christmas Dinner, which disappeared nearly as quickly as the lids were removed from the tins.

Making an encore appearance from holiday spreads past was bass player Rick Francis' sausage cheese dip, served out of a Crock-Pot, which was scraped clean by the hungry horde.

Aunt Floy's Butterscotch Pie
Contributed by Gregg Hutchins

- 2 regular pie shells, prebaked until light brown
- 4 eggs, separated (whites to be used for topping)
- 2 cups brown sugar
- 4 tablespoons self-rising flour
- 2 cans evaporated milk
- 2 tablespoons butter or margarine
- 2 teaspoons vanilla extract
- Pinch of salt
- 4 teaspoons granulated sugar
- ½ teaspoon cream of tartar

Combine all ingredients in a sauce pot except egg whites, granulated sugar, and cream of tartar; bring to a boil, stirring constantly (it scorches easily). Keep cooking until mixture is of a thick, pudding consistency. Pour into pie shells.

In a nonreactive bowl (stainless steel, glass, enamel, or glazed ceramic), sprinkle granulated sugar and cream of tartar into egg whites. Beat with a mixer on high until fluffy. Spread on top of pies. Turn oven to broil, put pies in oven on lower rack until brown, less than 5 minutes, watch carefully. Take pies out of oven and allow to cool 30 minutes, refrigerate at least 2 hours before serving.

Rick Francis' Sausage Cheese Dip

1 pound mild sausage (I use Tennessee Pride)
½ pound ground chuck
2 pounds Velveeta
Two 10-ounce cans Ro-Tel brand diced tomatoes (mild)
Two 10-ounce cans cream of mushroom soup (I use Campbell's)

Brown sausage and drain. Brown ground chuck and drain. Cut the Velveeta into small cubes so that it melts quicker, and add it and the meat to a Crock-Pot set on high. Stir often so cheese doesn't stick. Once the Velveeta has melted, add Ro-Tel and soup, stir until blended and heated through, then turn to low heat.

Serve with your favorite chips.

Johnny Cash

Joined the Opry cast in 1956

(1932–2003)

Country music is fortunate to call Johnny Cash one of its own. He could have made a career in gospel, folk, pop, or rock and roll. He could have devoted himself entirely to writing, or to acting, or to teaching, or even to the ministry. He did all of those in some fashion, but few figures loom larger in country music than Johnny Cash, or brought more attention and respect to the genre. His career spanned nearly a half century, and not even his death in 2003 could stop the music that poured from the heart and soul of this icon. On July 4, 2006, Cash's *American V: A Hundred Highways* was released, and less than a week later it debuted at number 1 on not only *Billboard*'s Top Country Albums chart but on their all-genre Top 200 albums chart as well. The fifth installment of Cash's critically acclaimed American Recordings series, *American V,* was completed months before his passing on September 12, 2003. Reviews of the new record were unanimous in their praise, while bemoaning afresh the loss of this American treasure.

J. R. Cash—as was recorded on his birth certificate—was born to Ray and Carrie Cash in 1932 in Kingsland, Arkansas, one of six children. A government resettlement program instituted by President Roosevelt to help pull the country out of the Depression brought the Cash family to Dyess Colony in northeast Arkansas, where they farmed twenty acres of cotton and other crops. Music was a part of everyday life—work songs in the fields and nearby railroad yards, folk songs and hymns his mother loved, and country music on the family's battery-run radio. After graduating high school in 1950, Cash moved to Detroit to find work, and was briefly employed at an auto plant in Pontiac before enlisting in the air force. It was during basic training in Texas that he met his first wife, Vivian, though they did not marry until he returned from his four-year hitch in Germany. While stationed in

Johnny Cash.

Landsberg, he started his first band, the Landsberg Barbarians, and also began writing, penning "Hey Porter" and "Folsom Prison Blues" during that time. Discharged in 1954, he and Vivian married and moved to Memphis, where Cash found work as an appliance salesman.

He also found Sun Studio, just as Elvis Presley had in 1953, and auditioned unsuccessfully as a solo artist for Sam Phillips' Sun Records. The following year he came back with his new band, the Tennessee Three—guitarist Luther Perkins, Marshall Grant on bass, and Red Kernodle on pedal steel. By the time Cash recorded "Hey Porter," the Three were Two, when Kernodle didn't show up for the session. That song didn't chart, but the follow-up, "Cry! Cry! Cry!," fared much better, and the next releases, "Folsom Prison Blues" and "I Walk the Line" among them, established Johnny Cash as a dominant new presence in country music. On July 7, 1956, he joined the cast of the Grand Ole Opry.

Through the remainder of the fifties and into the sixties, the hits kept coming on Columbia Records, and with them invitations to appear on national television programs and at as many as three hundred live performances a year. The grueling schedule took its toll, and Cash increasingly sought help from pills. By the midsixties his dependence and drug-induced rampages had ended his marriage and were affecting his career. With the strong support and tough love of Mother Maybelle Carter and her middle daughter, June—with whom John had become smitten nearly ten years earlier—Cash kicked his addiction.

He and June married on March 1, 1968, and with his personal life at peace and his demons at bay, Cash's career burgeoned again. His live concert recording that year at Folsom Prison was a tremendous success, as was the next live recording in front of another captive audience at San Quentin Prison in 1969. The catchy song "A Boy Named Sue," taken from the San Quentin album, quite unexpectedly became his biggest-selling single, as well as the CMA Single of the Year in 1969, the same year Cash was voted Male Vocalist and Entertainer of the Year.

Cash parlayed that recognition into a prime-time network television variety show, *The Johnny Cash Show,* which captured the nation's attention both for the commanding presence at its core and the eclectic lineup of guests he invited to appear, including Neil Young, Bob Dylan, Louis Armstrong, and Merle Haggard. The show, which ran from 1969 to 1971, was quite the feather in Nashville's cap as well, since it was taped at the Ryman Auditorium, and not Los Angeles or New York, where most national programming originated.

After the show's run ended, Cash continued to tour through the seventies and eighties, and also took parts in several movies. Like many artists of his era, his chart share was shrinking, a disappointment that he answered by saddling up with three of his peers—Kris Kristofferson, Waylon Jennings, and Willie Nelson—and, as the Highwaymen, recorded a series of three albums. A subsequent stint with Mercury Records did not result in commercial success, but an unlikely partnership with rap producer Rick Rubin's American record label did. The deep introspection, raw truth, and stark simplicity captured on the first Rubin-produced Cash album, 1994's *American Recordings,* earned him a Grammy for Best Contemporary Folk Album. The second, *Unchained,* received the 1997 Grammy for Best Country Album. In the late nineties, it seemed as if his creativity and passion for his work soared in adverse proportion to his declining health, which forced him off the road.

Tracks from *American III: Solitary Man* (2000) and *American IV: The Man Comes Around* (2002) earned Grammys for Best Male Country Vocal Performance. His video for "Hurt," a song written and first performed by Nine Inch Nails' Trent Reznor, earned six nominations for the 2003 MTV Video Music Awards.

Cash was the youngest living artist to gain membership to the Country Music Hall of Fame, inducted in 1980 at the age of forty-eight. Fifteen years later, he was possibly one of the oldest living artists to be enshrined in the Rock and Roll Hall of Fame. In 2001, Cash received the National Medal of Arts, the country's highest award for artistic excellence.

No one who knew the couple had any doubt of the deep and abiding love John and June had for each other, nor that they were in every sense of the word soul mates. Johnny Cash was grief-stricken when June died of complications following heart valve replacement surgery on May 15, 2003; she was seventy-three years old. It was her wish that he keep working, so he continued recording, and even returned briefly to the stage, though he was confined to a wheelchair. At a show on May 21, 2003, before singing "Ring of Fire"—the song June Carter co-wrote with Merle Kilgore—he spoke of how her spirit was watching over him. On July 5, 2003, he made his final concert appearance outside Bristol, Tennessee. On September 12, 2003, Johnny Cash died at the age of seventy-one of complications from diabetes. The couple is interred side by side in Hendersonville Memory Gardens, near their cherished lakeside home, which, sadly, burned to the foundation in April 2007.

Johnny Cash could be counted on to whip up a batch of his special Rockabilly Chili for friends, among them Marty Stuart, who had, and then lost, the recipe. When Cash died, Marty felt an urgency to find it, and it turned up in his mother's house just in time for Christmas 2003. "When J.R. was alive, he and I used to go at Christmastime to visit people we knew who were buried at Hendersonville Memory Gardens, and leave them little presents at their grave. Luther Perkins was buried there, and Mother Maybelle. The first Christmas after J.R. died, I made a batch of Rockabilly Chili, and Connie [Smith] and I took a cup out there for him."

Two of the most important women in Cash's life—the others being his four daughters by his first marriage—were his mother, Carrie, and his wife of thirty-five years, June Carter Cash. While the Rockabilly Chili recipe is a family (and close friend) secret, these recipes—from his mother's and wife's cookbooks, respectively—were also favorites of John.

Scripture Cake

Judges 5:25 last clause, ½ cup
I Samuel 14:25, 2 teaspoons
Jeremiah 17:11, 6 separated
I Kings 4:22, 1½ cups
Amos 4:5, 2 teaspoons

II Chronicles 9:9 to taste
Leviticus 2:13, pinch
Nahum 3:12, 2 cups
I Samuel 30:12, 2 cups
Numbers 17:8, 2 cups

Assemble all ingredients; beat together Judges 5:25 and I Samuel 14:25. Add yolks of Jeremiah 17:11. Sift together I Kings 4:22, Amos 4:5, II Chronicles 9.9, and Leviticus 2:13; add alternatively with Judges 5:25, last clause. Add Nahum 3:12, I Samuel 30:12, and Numbers 17:8. Fold in stiffly beaten whites of Jeremiah 17:11 and place in greased 10-inch tube pan, bake 3 hours at 275°. Final product is a light fruit cake of good flavor and keeping quality. Use water under pan while baking to preserve moisture.

June's Special Fruit and Whipped Cream Salad

1 pint fresh strawberries, hulled,
  or 1 package frozen

2 bananas

2 apples

2 bunches grapes, seeded

2 pears

2 oranges, peeled and sectioned

1 can fruit cocktail, drained

Juice of 1 lemon

½ cup sugar

1 package frozen peaches

1 package frozen cherries

2 pints whipping cream

4 tablespoons sugar

Whole cherries or strawberries

Cut fresh fruit into a large serving bowl, add fruit cocktail. Pour the lemon juice over fresh and canned fruit, toss well. Stir in ½ cup sugar. Thaw frozen fruit for 1 hour before serving. Beat whipping cream and 4 tablespoons sugar until soft peaks form. Toss fresh and canned fruit with all the frozen fruit except cherries as frozen fruit starts to thaw and separate. Fold half of whipped cream into the fruit. Add cherries now so as not to mix too much color into the salad. Drop remaining whipped cream by the tablespoon over all the fruit. Put a cherry or strawberry in center of each whipped cream dollop for garnish.

Cool Whip may be used instead of whipping cream and sugar, or half Cool Whip/half fresh whipping cream.

Jimmy C. Newman

Joined the Opry cast in 1956

The French language. Cajun cooking. Music. According to Jimmy C. Newman, born and raised in Big Mamou, Louisiana, those three things compose the trilogy of Cajun culture. And the first Cajun country singer to become a member of the Grand Ole Opry—his golden anniversary was celebrated in August 2006—has all three running through his veins. Having grown up in the southern part of the state, French was a second language (or even the primary tongue) spoken at some of the churches he attended as a youth, where fire and brimstone sermons were delivered *en Francaise.* Music was everywhere, though it wasn't zydeco that inspired him at first, but the cowboy tunes of his boyhood idol Gene Autry. Food of course is akin to religion in Louisiana, capable of provoking worship as devout and discussion as heated.

Jimmy's hometown, founded as Mamou, was named after an American Indian chief. "All of Louisiana was very influenced by Indian tribes, there were so many of them here at one time," Newman explains. "There was an old Cajun song called 'Grand Mamou,' it was sung in French. In the 1950s, a gentleman in Texas did an English version called "Big Mamou," and it became such a big popular hit that everyone started calling the town Big Mamou. It's not very big—only about three thousand people, but I didn't know it was small till I went to Lafayette."

It was in a nearby and slightly larger town that he met his future wife, Mae. Ville Platte—French for "flat town"—is about twenty miles to the east and five thousand people bigger than Big Mamou, large enough to attract touring bands. "Cajun people love to dance," he says. "There was a dance hall there where families would go with their children. There was no alcohol. It had a big post in the middle and benches around the walls where the girls would sit with their mamas, and wait for a boy to ask them to dance. Off they would go, dancing far apart, until they got behind the pole, out of Mama's sight, and the boys would pull the girls close! When

Jimmy C. Newman.

they got older, they graduated to another place, where they went without their mothers. And from there, to a more high-class place, where the big bands would come to play. I went one night with some friends to Ville Platte to dance, and that's where I met Mae."

Courting and eventually marrying Mae also expanded his culinary horizons. "I was raised Protestant and far from town. We ate well but very simply. Mae was Catholic, so they ate a lot of fish and seafood, because back then, Catholics could not eat meat on Fridays. That was when I found out I loved seafood. Mae's brother had a restaurant there, the Pig Stand, a very well-known restaurant. It was already called the Pig Stand when he bought it, it was a barbecue restaurant, but when he ran it, it was Cajun food. Every town in Louisiana, you'll find a family-owned restaurant, with wonderful food. It is still there today, but a different family owns it now." Perhaps because music is so dear to the Cajun culture, Mae's family was not bothered by the idea of their daughter dating a musician; Newman and his band toured the South and Southwest, and he hosted his own radio show in Lake Charles, Louisiana. The exposure from that show led to membership on the famous Louisiana Hayride radio program, then to a television show in Shreveport, and eventually a recording contract with Dot Records. His first country hit was "Cry, Cry Darling" in 1954, a tune he co-wrote. The follow-ups, "Daydreamin'" and "Blue Darlin'," earned him Opry membership in 1956, which necessitated a move to Nashville. Mae stayed behind while he and his fiddle player came first to check the lay of the land and look for places to live. "We stayed with a deejay from WSM, very nice people. His wife was a good cook, but it wasn't what we were used to. We would eat dinner, and still be so hungry we would go to town to eat more! The problem was, there was no rice. Rice is a staple in southern Louisiana. There is a saying, 'How do you tell an intelligent Cajun? He can look at a rice field and tell you how much gravy it will take to cover it!' You eat rice with every meal. Dishes are made with gravy just so you have something to put on the rice. After about two weeks, we were so hungry for Cajun cooking I went back to Louisiana and got Miss Mae!"

Newman wasn't the only one who loved her cooking. Word got out through his band—Cajun Country—and spread through the Opry, and before long, other performers and Opry managers were asking for some of Mae's good cooking. The Newmans would have "big soirees" as Jimmy C. puts it, and the guest list kept getting bigger. So did their houses. "When we first came to town, we lived in a converted garage apartment. We moved around town some, then when we had some success, and I could get a good loan from the bank, we moved to Hendersonville, north of the city. That's where all the country entertainers lived back then. It was far enough away to feel like you were in the country, and quiet, but not too far from the Opry." In 1971, the Newmans bought a 670-acre ranch east of Nashville in Rutherford County and named it Singing Hills Ranch. "Gene Autry was one of my idols, and he had a song called 'Singing Hills.' We thought it fit because the property is surrounded by hills."

Singing Hills is a cattle ranch—beef, not dairy. "Dairy cattle have to be milked twice a day, no matter what. There are no weekends, no holidays. I did that when I was a kid. I didn't want to do that again."

The property is also abundant with wild game, a fact that attracts a number of Opry members and executives who like to hunt. When they come down during wild turkey season, they can count on Mae to cook breakfast, though it won't be bacon and eggs, more likely a gumbo, red beans and rice, or étoufée. Colin Reed, Gaylord chairman and CEO, is especially fond of the hunting, and the food. "When he comes down to the ranch, he says, 'The hunting is great, but Mae's breakfast is the real reason we come!'"

Mae Newman's Cajun Chicken with Sauce Piquante

One 2½-pound fryer chicken, cut up
1 cup flour
1 teaspoon salt
½ teaspoon black pepper
1 cup cooking oil
½ cup chopped onion
¼ cup chopped green onion

¼ cup chopped green bell pepper
¼ cup chopped celery
2 cloves garlic, finely chopped
One 16-ounce can tomato sauce
1 package sliced mushrooms (optional)
Salt, pepper, and red pepper to taste

Dredge chicken in flour mixed with salt and pepper, fry in deep skillet in cooking oil. Cook until brown. Add chopped onion, green onion, green bell pepper, celery, and garlic. Fry until onions are clear and wilted. Add 1 cup water, let simmer with lid on for 15 minutes. Add tomato sauce and mushrooms, if desired; simmer covered for 15 to 20 minutes more. Salt and pepper to taste. Serve over hot rice.

The Cooper Family

Joined the Opry cast in 1957

(Stoney Cooper, 1918–1977; Wilma Lee Cooper, Carol Lee Cooper)

Wilma Lee Leary and Dale Troy "Stoney" Cooper were born and raised on opposite ends of Randolph County, West Virginia. Music brought them together when the Learys—a singing group composed of Wilma, her parents, and her two sisters, Gerry and Peggy—hired the young fiddler to join their act in late 1938. The following year, Wilma and Stoney married, and continued to perform with the Learys until daughter Carol Lee was born. The young parents decided to leave show business and settle down to "normal" lives, she as a housewife and he as a delivery man for the Vaughn Beverage Company in Wheeling, West Virginia. Neither one was happy with the decision, and when a radio station in Nebraska offered Wilma Lee and Stoney Cooper seventy dollars a week to do a regular show, they put baby Carol Lee in the backseat of their car and took off. Their career took off as well, and as their popularity and fame grew, they moved from one city, radio program, and barn dance to another, eventually forming their own touring show under the name the Clinch Mountain Clan and coming home as certified superstars of Wheeling's WWVA Jamboree.

They recorded for a succession of labels, first Rich-R-Tone, then Columbia Records, a partnership that produced some of their signature songs, among them "Sunny Side of the Mountain," "The Legend of the Dogwood Tree," and "West Virginia Polka."

After a decade on the Jamboree, the couple came to the Grand Ole Opry in 1957, filling multiple musical slots thanks to a diverse repertoire that included gospel, bluegrass, honky-tonk, hillbilly, and mountain music; teenage daughter Carol Lee got in on the act as well. They continued recording with Nashville's Hickory Records, appearing on the Opry and touring until Stoney's heart condition forced

Carol Lee, Stoney, and Wilma Lee Cooper.

him to retire from the road in the mid-1970s. He passed away from a heart attack in 1977, ending a thirty-eight-year professional and personal partnership. A few years later, Wilma Lee re-formed the Clinch Mountain Clan and toured on the burgeoning bluegrass and folk music circuit. She remained a regular on the Opry until a stroke she suffered onstage in 2001 prevented her from performing any longer. But it did not keep her out of the spotlight; in 2005, Emmylou Harris brought the matriarch of mountain music onto the Ryman stage during the segment she was hosting, and Wilma Lee was recognized with a rousing standing ovation from a house of appreciative fans.

Though she was not inclined to devote herself exclusively to domestic endeavors, Wilma Lee was known among Opry cast members and staff as a good cook. Grand Ole Opry House manager Jerry Strobel asked for and received her recipe for Meat Loaf–Potato Surprise, a version of shepherd's pie that was originally created as a way to use leftovers from Sunday dinner; in the original dish, leftover roast or lamb was chopped or ground, mixed with gravy and vegetables, and topped with mashed potatoes. This version is made from scratch.

Wilma Lee Cooper's Meat Loaf – Potato Surprise

1½ pounds ground beef
½ cup soft bread crumbs
⅓ cup minced onion
1 egg, beaten
½ cup ketchup

1¼ teaspoons salt
¼ teaspoon pepper
3 cups whipped potatoes
¼ cup minced green onion
1 tablespoon chopped parsley

In large bowl, combine beef, bread crumbs, onion, egg, ketchup, 1 teaspoon salt, and ⅛ teaspoon pepper. Blend well; shape into 4-by-8-inch loaf and place in shallow baking pan. Bake at 350° for 1¼ hours. While meat loaf is cooking, boil potatoes and prepare as desired to make whipped potatoes. Combine potatoes, green onion, parsley, and remaining salt and pepper. Spread over meat loaf surfaces, top and side, like icing a cake. Bake 20 minutes longer. If desired, broil until golden. Garnish with fresh chives. Makes 6 servings.

THE CAROL LEE SINGERS, the quartet of backup singers led by Carol Lee Cooper, appear onstage as often as any Opry member, despite never being official Opry members themselves. The two women and two men occupy four stools behind a Plexiglas tri-fold just a few feet from the band. When cued by Carol Lee, they rise to their feet as one and approach the four microphones; Carol Lee's mike stand is always adorned with a single long-stemmed red rose.

The concept originated in 1973, when Opry general manager Bud Wendell found himself needing subs for then-backup singers the Four Guys. Naturally, he turned to one of country music's most beautiful women, instantly recognized for her hourglass figure, Carol Lee Cooper. "He knew I had a group. We mostly did gospel music, but I felt like we could handle it. The first night we worked, we were so nervous. After the show, Bud came up and asked me, 'How are you doing, Carol?' I said, 'Well, we just tried to fit in as best we could. How did we sound?' He smiled at me, said, 'Terrible,' patted me on the back, and walked away."

Practice makes perfect, and more than three decades later the Carol Lee Singers are as recognized as Porter Wagoner and Little Jimmy Dickens. Svelte Norah Lee Allen, wife of Oak Ridge Boy lead singer Duane Allen, is the longest-tenured; she joined in 1980. Dennis McCall spent years with Barbara Mandrell before retiring from the road and signing on as tenor with the CLS; bass singer Rod Fletcher came to Music City via Walt Disney World in Orlando. Norah Lee "guesti-mates" that they know about three thousand songs. "You have to have a pretty good ear so you can pick it up," she says. Carol Lee agrees. "It's a gift. Once we do a song once, we never forget it."

The Carol Lee Singers join Hairl Hensley at the announcer's podium. L to R: Dennis McCall, Norah Lee Allen, Hairl Hensley, Carol Lee Cooper, and Rod Fletcher.

Porter Wagoner

Joined the Opry cast in 1957

Over the course of a career that spans six decades, Porter Wagoner has made friends in high and low places, and folks from all stations in life have made indelible impressions on him.

The native of West Plains, Missouri, began performing professionally when he was still a teenager. "I was eighteen years old when I started and it was all brand-new to me. I didn't know anything. But I always loved to go out on the road. I just loved to meet new people."

Back in those days, there was very little distance between performer and fan, and friendships were often forged around food and at the table. "For many years, I didn't have a booking agency. I didn't even know what one was. People would just write to me in care of the radio station and say, 'I wonder if you could come to our town to play a show? We've got a schoolhouse and we'll get a good crowd for you, and you can come to our house for dinner.' We played a lot of schoolhouses in those days, and we ate pretty well."

He particularly remembers a letter he received from one family in Missouri. "A woman wrote and told me she had two boys, one eight and one ten, and that their whole family listened to my radio show every morning. She said that when we came to their town, they would have us all out for dinner. She wanted to know what the band and I liked to eat. We were really looking forward to it because we just had a feeling it was going to be a wonderful meal. We got the directions—they lived on a farm—and when we pulled up, the whole family came out to meet us. Those two boys were scrubbed clean, they were wearing their best clothes, and you could tell they had been ordered to be on their best behavior. They were so afraid to make a mistake or do something wrong that they were hardly moving. Well, we all went inside and she had the biggest dinner you could imagine. There were three kinds of meat—beef, pork, and chicken—and every fresh vegetable, corn bread *and* biscuits,

Porter Wagoner.

and of course gravy. In the country, you had gravy with every meal. We were passing the food, making conversation, we were all a little nervous since we didn't know one another. It was real quiet, and suddenly one of those little boys piped up and said, 'Mama, would you pass Mr. Wagoner some of those gravies?' He meant to say biscuits but got confused. It was just so cute, he turned bright red, and everyone laughed; it really broke the ice and we ended up having a wonderful time with those folks. The next morning on the radio show I talked about dinner at their house and how good it was, and how sweet those boys were. They wrote us a letter and said the boys could not have been more excited to hear themselves talked about on the radio."

He got a bit more than biscuits and gravies from another relationship that began in his home state, and has lasted for more than thirty years. He first met John L. Morris when he purchased fishing lures the young man made and sold out of a back room behind his father's Brown Derby Liquor Store in Springfield, Missouri.

Eventually, his business grew too big for his dad's store, so he opened his own place in Springfield in 1972, naming it Bass Pro Shop. "My friendship with John L. developed because of my love of fishing; I was a fan of what he was doing." A few years after starting Bass, Morris sent Wagoner a letter, saying he wanted him to try one of his new boats, the Bass Tracker. The very next morning, the boat—the first "fish ready," professionally rigged boat package—was in Wagoner's driveway, and by that afternoon, he was out on the lake, reeling in his catch. Tracker Marine Group is now the largest manufacturer of fishing boats in the country.

Bass Pro Shops, still headquartered in Springfield, Missouri, has also grown, into the nation's largest outdoor retailer, with thirty-one stores in the United States (two in Canada), including one that serves as an anchor of Opry Mills, the huge mall that is part of the campus that includes the Gaylord Opryland Resort and Convention Center and the Grand Ole Opry House. It was Wagoner who introduced Morris to Bud Wendell—who rose from manager of the Grand Ole Opry to become president and CEO of Gaylord. When Gaylord closed the deal with Bass Pro Shops to bring a store to Nashville, Wendell asked Wagoner to accompany him on the company's private jet to Springfield. During the press conference, John L. Morris presented Wagoner with a plaque acknowledging the role he played in the partnership. Then, paying tribute to their long friendship, he handed Wagoner a ring with two keys: one for a brand-new Tracker boat and another for the truck to haul it.

In 2002, Wagoner was inducted into the Country Music Hall of Fame, and on May 19, 2007, the Grand Ole Opry celebrated Wagoner's fiftieth year as a member. One of the show's most frequent hosts and most recognized stars, he makes his home less than ten minutes from the Opry House. All three of his children live close by—son Richard in a log cabin behind the main house—and gather once weekly for family dinner. Though daughters Debra Jean and Denise are most often the cooks, every once in a while they talk their dad into making his special spaghetti sauce, a recipe he got years ago from his steel player's mother.

Porter's Family Night Dinner Spaghetti Sauce

1½ pounds ground round
1½ pounds Jimmy Dean sausage
2 good-sized onions, chopped
2 good-sized bell peppers, chopped
Salt and pepper to taste

Two 28-ounce cans crushed tomatoes
Two 15-ounce cans tomato sauce
½ teaspoon garlic
1 tablespoon basil
1 tablespoon oregano

Brown meat in large pot, drain grease. Cook onions and peppers with meat until soft. Salt and pepper according to taste. Add tomatoes, tomato sauce, garlic, and herbs and cook on top of stove several hours over very low heat.

Porter Wagoner shows off his rhinestone suit.

Rhinestone Cowboys

I've always said that wardrobe is fifty percent of the act," says Little Jimmy Dickens, standing backstage at the Ryman Auditorium, where the Grand Ole Opry is staged for several months in winter. He is wearing a brilliant blue suit spectacularly adorned with sequins, rhinestones, and intricate embroidery. "You have style in a rhinestone suit; you walk out onstage and people say, 'Wow!'"

Dickens was the first Grand Ole Opry artist to wear a rhinestone suit onstage at the Ryman. He debuted one in 1950, made by famous Hollywood Western-wear designer Nudie, who made all of Dickens' stage wear. When Nudie died in 1984, his primary designer, Manuel, took over and now works out of his shop in Nashville.

Spangled Western/rodeo suits first became popular as the cowboy movie craze hit Hollywood in the twenties; Nudie Cohn, a Ukrainian immigrant, set up shop in North Hollywood, and in the late forties, country stars became drawn to the razzle-dazzle costume's suitability for the stage.

Porter Wagoner can attest to Nudie's brilliant way of building a clientele. He and his band were appearing on the *Ozark Jubilee* in Springfield, Missouri, a national television show that was hosted by Red Foley, when they met. "Mr. Nudie showed up on the set one day," Wagoner recalls. "I was wearing a Western-cut suit, but there was nothing fancy about it. He introduced himself as Nudie from Los Angeles and told me he was a rodeo tailor, and that he also made suits for movie stars. He said his suits were very 'decorative.' He was very nice, and said he was not putting my suit down, but said that I would look so much better in one of his suits. So he offered to make me a suit for free, and said, 'If it does what I think it will do for you, then you'll be buying more.' That sounded okay to me, so he measured me, and then I didn't hear anything from him for about six weeks. One day, I got a box in the mail from California, and when I opened it, there was a peach-colored suit with an embroidered covered wagon on the back. I had never seen anything like it. There was also a shirt and boots, all coordinated to the suit! My sister swears I tried the outfit on about a dozen times the first day I got it. She told me I would wear it out before it ever made it on the show. Mr. Nudie had said that he wanted to make me something so outstanding that when I walked onstage, everyone in the audience would just say, 'Wow!' And it happened exactly like that; I walked out onto the set and the audience went crazy for that suit!" One of Wagoner's most well-known trademarks is the big "Hi!" embroidered inside the left side of his jackets, which he flashes to the audience when he walks out onstage.

Wagoner figures there are about fifty suits in his collection now, jazzing up a long, narrow closet in his home, in every color of the rainbow, and basic black and white. They hang perfectly pressed, shoulder to shoulder, as far back as the rhinestone-blinded eye can see.

"Manuel says I am the only person he has ever dressed for so many years whose size has hardly changed. There is a two-inch difference in my waist from that first suit. Their cost provides some pretty good incentive to watch your weight. When I think about the price I've paid for these suits, I don't eat that much!"

Wagoner admits to a weakness for sweets, particularly the fudge he remembers watching his mother make when he was just a little boy; in fact, he liked it so much, he asked her to show him how to do it. He still loves eating it, but can't indulge often, or his fabulous collection of custommade suits might get uncomfortably snug in the waist!

Porter's Chocolate Fudge

2 cups sugar
2 tablespoons cocoa
½ teaspoon salt
¼ cup Log Cabin syrup
Milk

2 tablespoons butter
1 teaspoon vanilla
2 tablespoons peanut butter
½ cup English walnuts, chopped

Mix sugar, cocoa, salt, and syrup together in a saucepan, then add enough milk to make it soupy, but very thick. Bring to a boil, and boil until sugar is dissolved (4 to 5 minutes). Test by dropping small spoonfuls into water until it forms a ball. Remove from heat and add butter and vanilla. Stir until it begins to cool. Add peanut butter and walnuts. Pour into large platter, and hold a gun on yourself so you'll wait until it cools!

Rudy's Farm and Odom's Tennessee Pride

Opry Sponsors

Good ole country music and big ole country breakfasts found common ground long ago on the Grand Ole Opry when sausage makers recognized that the homespun radio show with hundreds of thousands of listeners would make a fine vehicle for their homemade product. There have been several sausage sponsors in Opry history, and two are thriving still.

Rudy's Farm dates its Tennessee roots back to the late 1800s, when the Rudy family settled on the property that is now in the suburban Nashville community of Donelson, part of which became the home of the Grand Ole Opry complex. Patriarch Daniel Rudy made and sold his own sausage, a trade he passed along to son Jacob, who in turn taught his sons, Frank and Dan. The sausage was packed into large wooden tubs and delivered to merchants in the Nashville area. It was Frank and Dan Rudy who modernized and expanded the operation after their father died in 1936. By the late 1950s, about five thousand pounds of sausage were being produced every month in the twenty-seven-hundred-square-foot sausage plant.

In the early sixties, Frank Rudy saw a marketing opportunity on the Grand Ole Opry and looked no farther than his own three daughters to literally sing the praises of Rudy's Farm Sausage. Outfitted in identical red-checked dresses, Patricia, Caroline, and Mary Francis Rudy sang the company jingle on radio, television, and the stage of the Grand Ole Opry. A bright yellow antique dinner bell hung on a post was rung by the Opry announcer to signal the beginning and the end of the Rudy's Farm segment. Veteran cast and crew remember the night that a practical jokester attached a stink bomb to the bell's clapper, which went off when Grant Turner rang it following the jingle.

Odom's Tennessee Pride Real Country Sausage is another homegrown business, dating back well before the Opry began. At the turn of the twentieth century, Will Seifert Odom started a door-to-door meat wagon in Nashville before opening his own meat market next to a small grocery. His two sons, Doug and Will, went into the family business when they were old enough, and then in 1943, Doug struck out on his own, starting Odom Sausage Company in Madison, about ten miles outside of Nashville. With assistance from his wife, Louise, he experimented with several spice formulas before coming up with the secret recipe for Tennessee Pride. Douglas Odom, Jr., and his brother Richard took over the company from their father, and were in turn succeeded by Douglas Jr.'s son Larry D. Odom.

In the late 1950s, the company hired Opry cast members Lonzo and Oscar to sing and perform on mandolin and guitar the Tennessee Pride jingle for television commercials. They first came on board the Opry as sponsors of the Friday night show in the 1970s, but have been Saturday night staples for some time. The jingle played now for their Opry segment was recorded by bluegrass band Pine Mountain Railroad: "For real country sausage, the best you ever tried, pick up a pound or two of Tennessee Pride!"

Tennessee Pride Country Kitchen Casserole

1½ pounds Tennessee Pride Real Country
   Sausage (hot or mild)
One 5½-ounce package herb-seasoned
   croutons
2 cups shredded sharp cheddar cheese
2 cups shredded pepper jack cheese
¼ cup minced onion

8 eggs
2 cups half-and-half
1½ cups milk
1½ teaspoons dry hot mustard
Salt and pepper to taste
Chopped red and green peppers,
   for garnish

Cook sausage in large skillet until browned. Drain, crumble, and set aside. Spread croutons on bottom of lightly greased 9-by-13-inch baking dish. Cover croutons with cheddar and pepper jack cheeses. Sprinkle cooked sausage and onion over cheeses. In a large bowl, beat together eggs, half-and-half, milk, mustard, salt, and pepper; pour mixture evenly over sausage. Cover and refrigerate casserole for 8 hours. Bake at 350° for 45 to 60 minutes. Let stand 20 minutes before serving. Garnish with chopped peppers.

Hank Locklin

Joined the Opry cast in 1960

Hank Locklin's enduring career began by accident, literally and figuratively, and he knows better than anyone how a twist of fate can lead to destiny. His life-defining moment came when he was just nine years old, on a road near his home in McClellan, Florida, where he was run over by a school bus. "My sister gathered me up in her arms, carried me back to the house, and laid me on the bed. I stayed there for a good long time." To pass the bedridden hours—no television back then—Locklin learned to play the guitar. In a family that produced doctors, the notion of a professional musician was startling to say the least, but having discovered his passion, Locklin could think of nothing else. He began entering amateur talent contests as soon as he was mobile, debuting the voice that would develop into one of the greatest tenors in country music.

While still a teenager, Locklin was a featured performer—just him and his guitar—on WCOA radio in Pensacola. In the forties, he began playing venues in Mississippi, Louisiana, and Texas, and by the end of that decade, he and his Rocky Mountain Playboys—a racy name for a conservative era and genre of music— snagged a morning radio show on KLEE in Houston. He kicked off his recording career on Gold Star, then joined Four Star Records, where he honed his songwriting with such classics as "Send Me the Pillow That You Dream On," "Same Sweet Girl," "The Last Look at Mother," and "Born to Ramble." He also found radio airplay with "Let Me Be the One" and "Knocking at Your Door."

National fame knocked on Locklin's door when he signed with RCA Records in 1955, and a recording session two weeks later produced "Geisha Girl"—which spent thirty-nine weeks on the *Billboard* country chart—and a remake of "Send Me the Pillow That You Dream On."

But it was "Please Help Me I'm Falling" that rocketed Locklin up not just the country charts, but helped insert the term "crossover" into Music City's vernacular.

The crooning ballad held the number 1 spot on *Billboard*'s country chart for a remarkable fourteen consecutive weeks and stayed on the chart a total of thirty-six weeks. The song also went to number 8 on the trade publication's pop chart. "Please Help Me" was also nominated for a Grammy, precipitating Locklin's membership to the Grand Ole Opry.

The singer's smooth, sophisticated style had a tremendous impact on the recordings of his era, helping to popularize the Nashville Sound, as country music's rough edges were polished with full vocal and orchestral backing. The opening notes of "Please Help Me" feature Floyd Cramer's distinct slip-note piano style that would resonate in that era, and launch Cramer's solo career. The song has stood the test of time, with versions recorded through the years by Dean Martin, Roy Rogers, Dolly Parton, and Dwight Yoakam. Thirty-five years after his induction, a Grand Ole Opry audience was delighted when Vince Gill came onstage to harmonize with Locklin on "Send Me the Pillow That You Dream On."

Hank Locklin.

Nearly fifty years after joining the venerable institution, the entertainer—whose voice has only grown richer with time—travels with his wife, Anita, from their home in Brewton, Alabama, a couple times a year to perform his beloved chestnuts on the Opry stage. While in Nashville, the couple spends time with son Hank Adam Locklin, a senior executive with the Country Music Association, who is as well known and well liked behind the scenes in the industry as his father is in the spotlight.

Though singing and songwriting are the talents Hank Locklin is most known for, it is his skills in his wood shop that hold a special place in the hearts—and the homes—of family and friends. His handmade furniture

graces nearly every room of his son and daughter-in-law Jennifer's home. According to Hank Adam, "We have a pie safe made out of mahogany with a copper screen on it. He made that about twenty-five years ago. We get so many compliments on that; it's a beautiful piece. We don't bake many pies in our house, so we keep the good china in it. He made us an oak dining room table, with eight seats. We have a dry bar, and a coffee table made of black walnut. And he made the head- and footboard of our bed. It's something he really enjoys doing, and he has such a natural gift for it."

"It's just something I like to fool with," Locklin says. "Back in the days when I was coming up, we didn't have any money, and I could make things people wanted to buy. Later, I just did it for neighbors and my family. It's just something I enjoy, working with my hands, being off by myself, having time to think. I use all kinds of wood, whatever I have. When I came back from Texas, I bought some land where I had grown up. There was a bunch of trees on the property and I had some cut down and taken to the mill to make lumber, then put that in my shop so I could make furniture.

The first big piece of furniture I made was a pie safe, my mother had one that I loved. She used to keep her tea cakes in the bottom of the pie safe. They weren't fancy—she made them out of whatever was on hand—but I loved them. I remember when I was a little boy watching her make them, rolling out the dough, cutting out the cakes, then patting them with her fingertips. Her fingerprints would be on the tops of the tea cakes. I can still see them today."

Old-Fashioned Tea Cakes

1½ cups sugar
1 cup butter
1 egg, beaten

1 teaspoon vanilla
2½ cups self-rising flour
½ teaspoon nutmeg

Cream together sugar and butter. Add beaten egg and vanilla, stir. Add flour and nutmeg and mix until it forms a soft dough. Roll out on floured board about ½ inch thick and cut into circles. Pat down gently with fingertips. Bake at 325° about 10 minutes until light brown. Cool and store in pie safe. Makes about 3 dozen.

Bill Anderson.

Bill Anderson

Joined the Opry cast in 1961

At the thirty-ninth annual CMA Awards held in November 2005 in New York City's Madison Square Garden, country music veteran Bill Anderson sat beside young country music singer-songwriter Jon Randall, waiting to hear if their co-penned tune, "Whiskey Lullaby," would take home Song of the Year honors. Anderson turned to Randall and whispered, "I hope we win tonight, but if we don't, it's been a hell of a ride." Randall leaned towards the Country Music Hall of Fame member and irreverently replied, "Well, I hope we win for your sake because at your age, you need to win now."

"Whiskey Lullaby," recorded as a duet by Grand Ole Opry members Brad Paisley and Alison Krauss, was indeed named the 2005 Song of the Year, and it's hard to say who was more gratified: Randall, for winning his first, or Anderson, a member of the Nashville Songwriters Hall of Fame since 1975 whose catalogue bulges with hit records dating all the way back to 1958 when Ray Price recorded "City Lights."

"'City Lights' was really my calling card to Nashville," recalls Anderson, who was born in North Carolina but raised largely in Atlanta, Georgia. "I was studying journalism at the University of Georgia; I was going to be the best sportswriter ever. But I was also piddling around in Nashville in the late fifties and began guesting on the Opry. I moved to Nashville in 1960 and became a member of the Grand Ole Opry in the summer of sixty-one. I don't remember much specifically about that night; the induction wasn't such a big deal then."

Neither were the CMA Awards, which in the beginning were simply one part of what was then known as DJ Week, when country music disc jockeys from all over the country gathered in Nashville for a week of camaraderie and carousing. "The awards were given out at a breakfast held at Municipal Auditorium. It was 'Here's your bacon and biscuit, and here's your award.'" In 1960, it was Anderson's pop/country smash "Still" that brought him the bacon, named Song of the Year.

"I feel like I have had two songwriting careers," Anderson explains over lunch at Nick & Rudy's, a restaurant on the outer perimeter of Music Row; the Rudy refers to Rudy Caduff, who for years served as food and beverage director at the Opryland Hotel and came to know all the Opry members. "From the late fifties through early eighties, I wrote by myself, and I had good success. Then there was a period when I didn't write. I was doing a lot of other things. The music had changed and I wasn't sure I knew what it was. Then, in 1997, Steve Wariner recorded "Tips of My Fingers" and it was a hit. I thought to myself, 'Wow, that song is thirty years old. I could write something like that again.' But, I also knew I needed to tap into the new generation of country writers, so I got together with Vince [Gill] and we wrote 'Which Bridge to Cross, Which Bridge to Burn.' At the time, I had no idea how true those words were for him. So, that song gave me a bit of legitimacy with young writers, and I started co-writing. I'm very comfortable with it. I like writing with someone who comes at it from a different place than I do. That's when I feel like we get the best vibe going. I come from here, you come from there, and let's meet in the middle."

One such merger with Dean Dillon in the first part of the new millennium produced a poignant song called "A Lot of Things Different," recorded by Kenny Chesney and voted by members of Nashville Songwriters Association as one of the "Ten Songs I Wish I Had Written" at their 2003 awards dinner. "I am really proud of that song. Of all the songs I have written, I have had more people tell me how much they relate to that one than any other."

"Whiskey Lullaby" was written about the same time, but it sat on a shelf for three and a half years. No one would cut it. "It was too long, too slow, too dark. It was about suicide, not exactly a happy ending. Jon made a beautiful demo of it, and the Dixie Chicks had it on hold, but then they had their own troubles. Somehow, Brad Paisley's secretary heard it, loved it, and played it for Brad. His producer Frank Rogers came up with the idea of making it a duet, and Brad thought Alison would be the perfect choice. If you ask me, the video is what allowed people to understand it, and put it over the top."

While Anderson—known as "Whispering Bill Anderson" back in the day—has found common ground with a new generation of songwriters, he believes there is a vast divide between his era of Opry members and the newer inductees when it comes to the mechanics of the music business, as well as the more human side, the fans. "The difference between the old Ryman and the Opry House is like the difference between touring today on luxury buses and private jets, and traveling like we did in cars. You don't know anyone until you've ridden a thousand miles with them crammed in the backseat of a car! Catering was whatever your fans brought to the show and left for you backstage, or handed you on your way into the theater. We know that in certain cities we will get certain things—the best sugar cookies ever in Maryland, and cheesecakes in Pennsylvania. And lots of cakes! After one show, we had a dozen cakes on the bus!"

One summer tour found Anderson and his Po' Folks band doing back-to-back shows in Cedar Rapids and Des Moines, and one of those nights was his birthday. During the first show, his band suddenly stopped playing on a cue, and a huge birthday cake shaped like one of Anderson's signature white boots was wheeled out onto the stage by a female fan who had baked it herself. Everyone sang to the birthday boy, he blew out the candles, cut the cake, and finished the show. The next night, at the exact same point in the show, the band again stopped, and a boot-shaped birthday cake was wheeled out onto the stage by the same woman. After he thanked her, he asked her privately, "Didn't you already bring me a birthday boot last night?" "That woman looked at me in all seriousness and said, 'That was the *right* boot. This is the *left* boot.' And darned if she wasn't right!"

The Maryland sugar cookie baker is Barb Phillips, a member of the Bill Anderson fan club, who contributes this recipe.

Maryland Sugar Cookies

1 cup margarine or butter

1 cup vegetable oil

2 eggs

1 cup granulated sugar

1 cup 10X sugar (powdered sugar)

4 cups flour

1 teaspoon salt

1 teaspoon cream of tartar

1 teaspoon baking soda

1 teaspoon vanilla

Blend margarine or butter and oil together. Add eggs one at a time, then add sugar and powdered sugar, then add dry ingredients. Add vanilla. Mix well. Chill at least 2 hours. Form into balls about the size of a walnut, dip bottom of glass into sugar, and press ball on cookie sheet. Bake at 375° for about 8 minutes or until light brown. Remove from cookie sheet. Eat and enjoy!

Key Lime Pie
Kenny Chesney/Bill Anderson/Buddy Cannon

Big straw hat, banana drink
I can't remember what it is I think
And my, my, my—my Key lime pie

Ocean breeze, tire swing
Coconut fall if you shake that thing
And my, my, my—my Key lime pie

[Chorus]
Not too tart, not too sweet
My baby loves to watch me eat

Her Key lime pie
Her Key lime pie

Tall green tree, yellow bird
Bikini bottom and a tie-dyed shirt
And my, my, my—my Key lime pie

Big white sail, red sunset
Lobster tail and don't forget
My, my, my—my Key lime pie

A six string, ten shots
Of Cruzan rum, hey, I like it a lot
With my, my, my—my Key lime pie

Tortola, a full moon
Shining down on a blue lagoon
And my, my, my—my Key lime pie

[Repeat chorus]

We got Ginger and Mary Ann
Cookin' up a real good tan
And my, my, my—my Key lime pie

Key lime pie, Key lime pie
Key lime pie, my my my
My, my, my Key lime pie
Key lime pie, Key lime pie
My, my, my Key lime pie

Jim Ed Brown performs on the Grand Ole Opry Cruise.

Jim Ed Brown

Joined the Opry cast in 1963

Jim Ed Brown grew up surrounded by food in Arkansas. His mother served in a series of restaurants the family owned and operated starting when Brown was still not much more than a child. "The first place she had was the Dollarway Drive-In in Pine Bluff, Arkansas," he remembers. "There was a little café on one side and a market on the other. There was an arsenal close by and the soldiers would come in to have a beer and Mother would fix them burgers and sandwiches. I was too young to work in the restaurant side because of the beer, but I could help in the market and I would go into the kitchen, so I was always around the cooking."

Thanks to the success of that venture, the family decided to expand, and in 1955 they built a larger restaurant, which they called the Trio, named in honor of Jim Ed and his singing sisters, Maxine and Bonnie, who performed together as The Browns. Who better to be the house band when the Browns decided to add a small room with a stage to the back of the restaurant? It wasn't long before they expanded that room, naming the place the Trio Restaurant and Supper Club, which hosted many traveling entertainers, one of whom went on to become a country music superstar.

"There was a fellow who used to sell cleaning products to commercial clients; he is actually the person who invented Pine-Sol, mixed it up in his garage and sold it out of the trunk of his car. Anyway, he told us he had a friend named Harold Jenkins who was a really good singer, and wondered if he could play our Supper Club, so we said sure, and so Harold came and played at the Trio Supper Club. My sisters and I were on the road sometime after that, and I can't remember where we were, but while we were backstage we heard a voice that seemed really familiar to us, but we didn't recognize the name on the marquee. It turned out to be Harold Jenkins, but by then, he was calling himself Conway Twitty!"

In 1956, the Trio Restaurant and Supper Club burned to the ground from a

Jim Ed Brown and his sister Maxine Brown, early 1960s.

grease fire. By then, Jim Ed was working in his father's saw mill after a two-year stint in the service, while also performing as The Browns. In 1959, they decided to rebuild the Trio as a Key Club and sell memberships, which in Brown's view was similar enough to a private country club that they could sell liquor by the drink. Unfortunately, the local sheriff didn't quite see it that way, and eventually told Brown that his Key Club was going to lock down.

As The Browns continued to find success on country music charts, Jim Ed and his wife, Becky, moved to Nashville in 1963, settling in what was then a quiet area south of town, Brentwood. As Jim Ed's career as a solo artist took off, Becky opened—and still operates—a dance studio that was built in the rear of the home. For Supper Club impresario Jim Ed Brown, it was déjà vu all over again.

"I thought it would be fun to have people over to eat and visit. Her dance studio was big enough that we could set up some long tables and get a bunch of chairs in there. Becky and I saw it as a way to get the Opry family together, and what better way to do that than over a meal, sitting together at a table? It was Jeanne Pruett who came up with the name Eatin' Meetin'. She is such a good cook and our biggest helper. We ask everyone to bring a dish, and we spread them out on one table, and everyone helps themselves.

"We started them several years ago. Bill Monroe was still alive, so was Grandpa Jones and Roy Acuff, Bill Carlisle. They'd all come out, it's so much fun. No cameras, no tape recorders. After we eat, we all sit around and tell old war stories. The Opry has changed a lot over the years, the members have changed, but the heart and soul of the Opry is still the same. If it weren't for music, if it weren't for the Opry, none of us would know one another, so it's important to come together and celebrate those relationships."

Jim Ed says wife Becky is a wonderful cook, and handles most of their own daily eatin' meetin's, but that when time allows, he likes to stretch himself in the kitchen. He enjoys trying new recipes in his home kitchen, often using the game brought back from the Opry Duck Hunt.

Sautéed Duck in Vinegar Sauce

1 quart orange juice	2 tablespoons chopped onion
2 cups kosher salt	1 teaspoon chopped garlic
2 wild ducks	⅓ cup red wine
1 cup honey	6 tablespoons balsamic vinegar
2 cups soy sauce	1 tablespoon tomato paste
3 cups black coffee, cold	1 tablespoon sugar
2 heads garlic, bruised	2 tablespoons fresh, chopped chives

Mix together 2 gallons of water, orange juice, and kosher salt; soak duck in this brine at least 24 hours. Debone breasts from the body, leaving skin on the meat. Mix honey, soy sauce, coffee, and bruised garlic in a large zip-lock bag. Add duck breasts and marinate 8 to 24 hours.

In a hot skillet, place breasts skin side down and sauté for a few minutes; the purpose is to render the fat from the skin in order to use it for cooking the meat. After there is a good amount of fat in the pan, remove the breasts from the pan, take off the skin, and salt and pepper the meat. Place back in pan and sauté until meat is cooked, about 2 minutes per side. Put meat on a warmed platter and tent with foil to keep warm.

Add onion to pan and sauté. When soft, add chopped garlic, followed by wine and vinegar. Cook until the liquid is reduced to about ¼ cup. Add tomato paste, sugar, and ¼ cup water and bring to a boil. Pour any accumulated juice in the pan with the duck breast into the sauce and simmer. Add salt and pepper to taste, garnish with chives, and serve.

Duck Soup with Wild Mushrooms

2 duck bodies, breasts removed
1 onion, quartered
4 garlic cloves, bruised
2 leek tops, bottom parts reserved
2 celery stalks, with leaves
2 carrots, coarsely chopped
6 sprigs parsley
6 stems fresh thyme
10 peppercorns
1 ounce dried porcini mushrooms,
   soaked in wine

½ pound fresh mushrooms, button and
   cremini
1 cup red wine
2 leek bottoms, sliced
1 onion, diced
1 clove garlic, chopped
2 tablespoons fresh, chopped thyme
3 fresh plums, peeled and chopped

Simmer duck carcasses, quartered onion, bruised garlic cloves, leek tops, celery stalks, carrots, parsley, thyme stems, and peppercorns, covered with cold water in a stockpot for 1½ hours. Remove the duck carcass and let cool. When cool enough to touch, remove any meat attached and set aside. Strain duck stock and refrigerate overnight. When ready to use, skim off the duck fat that will be congealed on the top of the broth, reserve. Drain the soaking porcini mushrooms, reserving the liquid. Coarsely chop the mushrooms. Heat a sauté pan, put in 2 tablespoons of reserved duck fat, and sauté fresh mushrooms until seared. Remove from the pan, add more duck fat, and sauté leeks and onions until soft. Add the porcini mushrooms, garlic, and thyme. Sauté briefly, then add reserved wine/mushroom liquid, the seared mushrooms, and the duck stock. Simmer for 30 minutes until the flavors come together. Add salt and pepper to taste, and add reserved duck meat. Cook until heated through. Place some chopped plums in serving bowls and ladle hot soup over top.

Meat 'n' Threes

If there were a signature cuisine of Nashville, it would be the meat 'n' threes that are as ubiquitous to that city as church steeples, and provoke nearly as much fervent worship. The term describes a style—a meal consists of a meat with three choices of vegetable—rather than a particular food. But the foods cooked, served, and consumed at meat 'n' threes fit into the good ole country cookin' category. Meat 'n' three restaurants, which traditionally serve lunch, though some extend hours through supper, offer three to four different types of meat a day—such as fried chicken, catfish, beef tips, roast beef, pork chops, baked fish, or roast chicken—and a dozen or so vegetable choices, if you count macaroni and cheese as a vegetable, and Southerners sure do. Pick your bread—corn bread, biscuits, or rolls—add a glass of sweet tea and a slice of pie, and you've got yourself a fine meat 'n' three meal. Service comes two ways: at the table or pushing a tray through a cafeteria-type line; either way, you won't get out without someone calling you hon' or sugah or dahlin'.

The simple, substantial food and warm, friendly attention typical of meat 'n' threes make them very popular among country music entertainers, musicians, and industry members. On any given weekday, the dining rooms of the Elliston Place Soda Shop, the Pie Wagon, Monell's, the White Trash Café, Sylvan Park in Nashville, and the famous Loveless Café about twenty miles outside of town are dotted with singers, writers, pickers, and producers. Sylvan Park is one of the most enduring; the original location is in an area of town known as Sylvan Park, and has been there so long that its lack of public restrooms has been grandfathered in as perfectly legal, if a tad disconcerting for first-time visitors. The newer location, on Eighth Avenue South in the Melrose area, is in a squat building that has long operated as a restaurant, though under a series of owners. Opry member Steve Wariner remembers meeting Chet Atkins there for lunch when it was the Melrose Diner, though that's not what Chet called it. "When Chet wanted to meet there for lunch, he'd say, 'Let's go eat at the car wash,' 'cause that's what had been on that spot before it was a restaurant. The old-timers, when they said they were having lunch at the car wash, that's what they meant."

On a clear, cold winter afternoon, Jim Ed Brown settles into a booth at the Melrose Sylvan Park. Eddy Arnold has already come and gone, but Jerry Reed is seated at the next booth and turns around to say hello. A minute later, songwriter Even Stevens and legendary producer Jim Malloy pause to say hello on the way to their seats. "People come here because the food is so good," says Brown. 'It's just good old-fashioned country-style food, and that's what most of us grew up on."

Tex Ritter

Joined the Opry cast in 1965

(1905–1974)

Born and raised on a ranch in Carthage, Texas, Tex Ritter graduated with honors from South Park High School in Beaumont, moving to Austin in the fall of 1922 to enroll at the University of Texas. His interest in music was piqued by three UT professors who collected cowboy folk songs, and he became an avid fan and student of that genre. He joined the glee club (eventually becoming its president) and began acting; for the next several years he vacillated between education—spending a year in UT's School of Law—and entertainment. He moved briefly to New York in 1928, long enough to land a spot in the men's chorus of a Broadway show, *The New Moon,* but then enrolled in Northwest University for a year. In 1929, he turned in his textbooks for good, picked up a guitar, and took the first step on a lifelong career in radio at KRPC in Houston, singing cowboy songs on a thirty-minute radio program. He toured the South and Midwest with a musical troupe before making the leap in 1931 to New York, joining the Theatre Guild when he landed a part as "The Cowboy" in the play *Green Grow the Lilacs* (the basis for the musical *Oklahoma*). That role brought him to the Madison Square Garden Rodeo as their featured singer, firmly establishing the cowboy identity that would make him the natural choice to host New York's first radio Western, *The Lone Rangers,* on WOR, among other roles on radio and TV.

It wasn't long before Hollywood came calling, and in 1936, Ritter moved to Los Angeles, where he appeared in eighty-five movies, seventy-eight of them Westerns. For six years, he was ranked among the top ten money-making stars in Hollywood. Ritter distinguished himself from other movie cowboy singers of the time with his faithfulness to traditional folk songs—thanks to his exposure while in college in Austin—rather than the modern Western ditties that were then the rage. Among

Tex Ritter.

the more respected films in his vast catalogue were *Arizona Frontier, The Utah Trail,* and *Roll, Wagons, Roll.*

One of his most fortuitous contracts was with Monogram Pictures, which cast him with actress Dorothy Fay in 1938's *Song of the Buckaroo.* The two would eventually make three other films together, before making their pairing legal and lasting, marrying on June 14, 1941. The couple had two sons: Thomas Ritter, who was discovered to have cerebral palsy shortly after his birth, an affliction that committed the entire family to passionate awareness efforts and fundraising; and John Ritter, who became a famous and beloved actor in his own right.

Through the forties and fifties, Ritter enjoyed international success on record, stage, radio, television, and film. While still living in Los Angeles, Ritter became one of the founders of the Country Music Association, serving as its president from 1963 to 1965. In 1964, he was elected the fifth member of the Country Music Hall of Fame, and in 1965, he moved to Nashville to join the Grand Ole Opry. Dorothy and the children remained in Los Angeles until John graduated high school, then joined Tex in Music City. Dorothy immediately immersed herself in the local arts scene and volunteer community, and was an engaging and extremely popular presence backstage at the Ryman whenever her husband performed.

Tex Ritter died in Nashville on January 2, 1974, after suffering a heart attack. Funeral services were held in Nashville and in Nederland, Texas, and he was buried in Port Neches, just outside of Nederland.

Though John was by then following his parents' footsteps and pursuing an acting career in Los Angeles, Dorothy stayed in Nashville, where she had developed many friendships, thanks in no small part to her generous spirit and gracious hospitality. Not long after Tex died, then Opry manager Bud Wendell hit upon a brilliant idea that would offer some solace to Mrs. Ritter in her grief while making an invaluable contribution to the institution she and her husband loved. "Mrs. Ritter was such an outgoing woman," he says. "Everyone who ever met her just loved her. After Tex died in 1974, we asked her if she would be our official Opry hostess. When we had special guests, Dorothy would meet them, take them around backstage, introduce them to cast members, tell them stories, get them a little goodie bag with things like GooGoos and Martha White products, then she'd escort them to their seats. It was a perfect position for her personality."

One of the Opry's most famous VIP visits was, in fact, arranged by Mrs. Ritter. Knowing artists Andy Warhol and Jamie Wyeth would be in Nashville for an exhibit and reception at the Cheekwood Botanical Garden and Museum of Art, she invited them to attend a performance of the Opry, which the pair eagerly accepted, and on January 29, 1977, Warhol and Wyeth happily mingled backstage with members of the Grand Ole Opry.

Opry announcer Keith Bilbrey remembers a more personal invitation from Mrs. Ritter that made his first Thanksgiving in Nashville very special. "The year I moved to Nashville, in 1974, Dorothy Ritter invited everyone who worked at WSM—the radio stations and television station—who had no family here, to come to their home on Franklin Road for Thanksgiving dinner. She knew we had to work, and most of us were just kids and had come from somewhere else to work in Nashville. Since we couldn't get home for the holiday, she invited us to hers. Tex had passed away

Andy Warhol and Dorothy Ritter backstage at the Opry.

that January, but the boys were there for the holiday. I think she ended up with more people than she expected, though. There was quite a crowd. I overheard her telling her boys, 'Jonathan and Tom, run over to the neighbor's house and see if they can give us some of their food so we can feed these folks.' That's exactly what they did, and they came back with enough food to feed everyone there. She was such a gracious, generous woman, you just wanted to be gracious and generous back!"

Charlie Walker

Joined the Opry cast in 1967

Before Charlie Walker recorded hit records, the long, tall Texan became famous spinning them. Though he had a promising start onstage when the Texas-based Cowboy Ramblers hired him as a singer-guitarist after he graduated high school, his singing career got sidetracked by Uncle Sam not long after that. During World War II (Walker is the only WWII vet in the Opry cast) he was stationed with Eighth Army Signal Corps occupation forces in Tokyo; it was there he honed his skills in the booth when he became the first American to broadcast country music from Japan. When he returned to the States, he got a job at San Antonio's KMAC, and was immediately embraced by his local audience, ultimately becoming one of the country's top disc jockeys. "I was the first person to be on the air five hours a day," he says proudly. "I had a split shift, from six to eight a.m. and then came back and was on from three to six p.m., both drive times, so we had lots of listeners."

Though he kept his day job, on the side Walker recorded a couple of songs that achieved regional success. Through his friend Ray Price, he received a copy of a song written by a new and relatively unknown songwriter then living in California, Harlan Howard. In 1958, Walker's recording of "Pick Me Up on Your Way Down" became a million-seller for Columbia Records, and one of the first stepping stones in Howard's path to musical immortality and enshrinement in the Country Music Hall of Fame in 1997. What it did not do was pluck Walker from the deejay booth or out of the Lone Star State, where President Lyndon B. Johnson regularly tuned in when he took a break from the Beltway to spend time on his ranch. Walker remained in radio in San Antonio until 1967, when he moved to Nashville and joined the cast of the Grand Ole Opry.

Charlene Walker, the oldest of Charlie and Virginia Walker's five children born in Nashville (he has five children by two previous marriages in Texas), says her first memory is of the Grand Ole Opry. "Daddy used to take me with him, and one

Charlie Walker.

Saturday night I just ran out onto the stage and stood out there singing along with him," she recalls. "I remember the lights and looking at all the people in the audience and being a little bit confused. But it was exciting, too. The Opry was still at the Ryman then, so I can always say that I have sung onstage at the Ryman."

With the move to the Grand Ole Opry House in 1976, there was a lot more room backstage for Walker's growing brood. "He and my mother brought us all out there with them when he played; he was there every weekend that he wasn't on the road. Everyone was so nice to us, like a family, we just looked forward to going. Miss Rosa always gave us lemonade; we loved her, like everybody did. Another woman that worked there, Debbie [Logue], used to keep track of everyone who performed, what they sang, maybe it was for the union. She sat on a bench on the side of the stage and used to let me sit there with her. That was back when Roy and Minnie were there, and Dolly was still singing there. You can only imagine as a young girl what it was like to see Dolly Parton."

Charlene Walker was named for her father, and like her younger siblings, Catherine, Christine, Caroline, and Charlton, shares his initials. Though her singing career began and ended on the Ryman stage more than thirty years ago, she did go into the entertainment business. Before she could legally drink, she began bartending at the upscale Morton's steak house in downtown Nashville, and entered their management program a few years later. Her warmth and professionalism earned her a devoted following among the movers and shakers who regularly wined and dined at Morton's, so much so that when New York's famous Palm restaurant opened just a half block off Lower Broad in 2000, they went right to the woman who knows everyone who is anyone, and treats everyone like they are someone. The Palm is a popular between-show dining spot for Opry cast members and guests when the show returns to the Ryman for a few months every winter, and Walker a familiar face at the door.

The original Palm was opened on Second Avenue in New York City in 1926 by immigrants Pio Bozzi and John Ganzi. Though it was their plan to open an Italian restaurant, they were located in the heart of New York's thriving newspaper district, and reporters and editors were quite inclined to bourbon and beef. When a request came in for a steak, one of the men would run to a nearby butcher shop, then run it back to cook to order, and the restaurant's reputation as a steak house took hold.

By the time of its eightieth anniversary in 2006, there were thirty Palms in the country, but thanks to a decor element that is unique to this restaurant since its inception, each has a personal connection to its individual city. When Pio Bozzi and John Ganzi opened the first restaurant, they had no budget for decorating. Fortuitously, many of their customers—writers and cartoonists—had no budget for dining. In exchange for a plate of spaghetti, the cartoonists drew their signature characters on the wall; the originals—including Popeye, Beetle Bailey, and characters from the Family Circus—are still there, signed by their creators. It was King Features artist Jolly Bill Steinke who began the caricature tradition when he was asked by regulars to draw their likenesses—or his amusing view of their likeness—on the walls above the booths where they dined. The drawings in the original Palm were painstakingly hand-restored in 1995, and the walls in each of the two dining rooms are insured for half a million dollars each. As each new Palm opened, well-known citizens in each city were asked to supply a photograph of themselves, which in turn is given to a Palm artist and made into a drawing for the walls of their own Palm. A place on the Palm wall is coveted by customers, considered a status symbol and measure of celebrity.

Among the Opry members whose faces can be found on the walls of the Nashville location of the Palm—just two blocks from the original front door of the Ryman—are Johnny Cash, George Jones, Porter Wagoner, Little Jimmy Dickens, Reba McEntire, Trisha Yearwood, Dolly Parton, Alan Jackson, Martina McBride, Bill Anderson, Lorrie Morgan,

Vince Gill, Ricky Skaggs, Marty Stuart, Pam Tillis, Brad Paisley, and of course, Charlie Walker.

According to Charlene, her mother "couldn't boil water when they married." With five children to feed, Virginia got plenty of on-the-job training, but when it was chili time in the Walker house, Charlie manned the stove. "He makes the best chili," Charlene says. "He's a Texan through and through, and likes to use ingredients that are made there, so maybe that's his secret." His recommendations for products are personal and so noted.

Charlie Walker's Texas Hold 'Em Chili

- 1 pound lean ground beef; or, if available, ½ pound ground beef, ½ pound ground venison, antelope, or bison
- 1 pound hot sausage, preferably Jimmy Dean's ("I bought him his first cowboy hat.")
- 1 large onion, chopped small
- 1 clove garlic, minced
- 1 tablespoon (at least) chili powder ("I think Texas-made Gebhardt chili powder is the best. I stock up when I'm down there.")
- 1 teaspoon salt
- ½ tablespoon cumin
- Two 14.5-ounce cans diced tomatoes with green chilis, do not drain
- One 14.5-ounce can ranch-style beans or kidney beans
- ½ cup picante sauce, mild, medium, or hot ("I use Pace's, because the company is in San Antonio and I used to golf with the owner.")

Brown meats with onions and garlic and cook until onions are softened. Add chili powder, salt, and cumin; mix well. Add tomatoes, beans, and enough water to make it soupy. Add picante sauce (mild, medium, or hot depending on your taste). Cook on low for about 1 hour; serve with oyster crackers or corn bread.

Jeannie Seely

Joined the Opry cast in 1967

Since she was a child growing up in Townville, Pennsylvania, Jeannie Seely has marched to her own drum—challenging rules, breaking stereotypes, and blazing trails. Within the industry, she is renowned as much for her keen insight, wry wit, and unique social commentary referred to in the Opry as "Seely-isms," as she is for the records that brought her fame. Unfailingly generous to family, friends, fans, and colleagues, she is an independent spirit who is proud of her many "firsts": first—and still only—Pennsylvania native to become an Opry member, first woman to wear a miniskirt on the Grand Ole Opry stage, and first female artist to regularly host half-hour segments of the Grand Ole Opry. That career and gender achievement happened in 1981, and took an act of God to achieve. A totally unexpected snowstorm had blanketed the city and made roads nearly impassable; she was the only Opry member in the building when it came time for the show to start, so producers had no choice but to let her take the wheel and drive.

But, to hear Jeannie tell it, there was never a grand life plan, only a lifelong passion for performing, and a career fueled by equal parts talent, drive, and an insatiable curiosity to find out what was around the next bend in the road.

Like so many of the artists of my era, I grew up listening to the Opry on the car radio. We'd put on our pajamas and get our blankets, then lay in the backyard, eat popcorn, and listen to the Opry. Mother says when I was little, I would fuss when I couldn't find it on the radio whenever I wanted; I was too little to understand that it only came on at a certain time. My father built a chicken coop that my mother didn't want. While they argued about it, I moved in and made it a playhouse. It wasn't too long before we made a little stage in there. I would put a Mason jar on a floor-lamp pole and that was my microphone. The first time I performed in public was at a variety show; I was eight years old and I sang "One

Jeannie Seely.

Has My Name, the Other Has My Heart." That's appropriate for a little girl, now, isn't it?

Not long after high school graduation, the majorette/cheerleader/honor student, who thought she "owned the world," shipped her things to "General Delivery, Los Angeles," hopped into her MG Roadster and didn't stop until she hit Hollywood. She first worked for a bank, but intent on learning the music industry she took a secretarial job at Liberty and Imperial Records. She began writing songs—which were cut—and released some records of her own on a small label. At the urging of Dottie West, who had recorded one of her tunes, and songwriter Hank Cochran—whom she met in L.A. and eventually married and divorced in Nashville—Jeannie Seely landed in Music City in 1965, with only fifty dollars and a Ford Falcon to her name.

Not long after, however, Porter Wagoner hired her to fill in for Norma Jean as the "girl singer" on his road and television show. When Norma Jean came back, Seely stayed on.

Everyone told Porter he was crazy to have two women on his bus, but it was great. We had someone to talk to, go to museums with, go shopping, to help each other out.

It was tough back in those days. The role you played with a man depended on the man. You were one way with one and another way with another, and you were a different way still as a songwriter. That was a tough nut to crack, the songwriting world; Dottie West and I were the ones who were always trying to push our way into that boys' club.

Jack Greene

When Jack Greene's first single, "There Goes My Everything," hit number 1 on the *Billboard* country chart in 1966, he was sitting on top of the world. He was also still sitting on a stool behind a drum kit looking at Ernest Tubb's back night after night.

The East Tennessee native was a Peachtree Cowboy before he became a Texas Troubador; he joined Ernest Tubb's band as a drummer in 1962 and stayed with the trailblazing honky-tonker for five years. It was Tubb who introduced Greene to legendary Nashville producer Owen Bradley, a meeting that led to the recording of the classic that resulted in an astounding year in 1967.

His solo career might never have gotten off the ground had Greene not gotten kicked off Tubb's bus one night in Virginia. "Back when Ernest was drinking, he seldom got drunk, but when he did, it was all over," Greene recalls one morning over breakfast at the Opryland Hotel. "We had three dates booked up in Virginia, and the first night we were there, Ernest got drunk. The band did the first set, and he didn't show; the second set, and he didn't show; and the last set, and he didn't show. I went back to the bus to take my costume off, and Ernest was in there, drunk and fussin'. He says, 'Move over, Big Ears'—that was his nickname for me—'I want to talk to you.' He was slapping my leg to make his point; he always wore a lot of rings, so it was painful. He says, 'When we get back to Nashville, you no longer work for Ernest Tubb.' I said, 'Why wait till Nashville? I'll get off right now!' And so I did. I was still in my costume and I got my bag and I'm walking down the side of this old road. The bus was creeping along beside me, but I just told 'em to go on. I was mad and I was through. About three miles down the road, I come to a little diner, and I asked them if a bus might come through there and they said yeah, at 5:30 A.M. So I sat down and had some coffee. When I got on the bus, I pulled out all the money I had and asked the driver how far it would take me. He told me I

Jack Greene.

could get as far as Knoxville on it. Then I hear this voice from the back of the bus; 'I'll lend you five dollars, Big Ears, so you can get all the way to Nashville.' It was [fellow bandmember] Cal Smith. He had gotten kicked off the bus, too."

Once Tubb sobered up, Greene got his job back, as well as an introduction to Owen Bradley. "I think Ernest felt a little guilty. He quit drinking, and introduced me to Owen, and that was how I came to record 'There Goes My Everything.'"

On the strength of that hit, Greene and the song swept the 1967 CMA Awards show, taking home the trophy for Single of the Year, Album of the Year, Male Vocalist of the Year, and Song of the Year. "Ernest encouraged me to go out on my own, and told me that if things didn't work out, I could always come back."

Needless to say, Greene didn't have to go back, but went on instead to a career that earned him Opry membership on December 23, 1967, and endures nearly forty years later. He has toured all over the country, but one of his favorite cities has always been New Orleans, and one of his favorite places to eat is Deanie's Seafood, a family-owned and family-friendly seafood restaurant that has been in Metairie, Louisiana, for forty-five years. It was purchased in 1982 by the Chifici family, who opened a French Quarter location in 2001. "They have great seafood, any way you want it, but what we love are the hot potatoes. Whenever we go to New Orleans, we look forward to going to Deanie's for their hot potatoes. We take the ones we don't finish with us, and walk around the French Quarter eatin' them like they were apples."

Rather than a bread basket, diners at Deanie's seafood restaurants in Metairie and New Orleans get a bowl of "spicy potatoes" to stave off hunger pangs while perusing the menu. "My father, Frank, did that from day one," says his daughter Shandra, who has worked at Deanie's almost since birth. "He just wanted something different. People love them. Before Katrina, we went through fifty or sixty twenty-pound bags of potatoes a week. That's one of the things we've always been known for."

Deanie's Seafood Hot Potatoes

Small red potatoes, scrubbed, unpeeled
1 package crab or seafood boil

Bring a pot of water to a boil. Add potatoes and seasoning bag, bring back up to boil, and cook until a fork can be inserted easily into the potato, about 10 minutes. Place in bowl, and serve with plenty of butter on the side.

Dolly Parton.

Dolly Parton

The first song Dolly Parton recorded that made the country charts was "Dumb Blonde" in 1967. The spectacular career she has built in the forty years since refutes the very notion, something she has pointed out more than once in her trademark self-deprecating style: "I'm not offended by dumb blonde jokes because I know that I'm not dumb. I also know I'm not blonde."

Photographs taken during her hardscrabble childhood in East Tennessee show a fair-haired girl, though since she became an entertainer, she has relied on wigs—an entire closet full—to help maintain her over-the-top image, one she says she cultivated by observing the town tramps and emulating their big hair, long fingernails, and tight-fitting clothes.

Dolly Rebecca Parton was the fourth of twelve children born to Avie Lee Owens and Robert Lee Parton; she was raised in a one-room mountain cabin in Sevier County with no electricity, running water, or indoor plumbing. Though there was little in the way of material goods, music flowed from every branch of the large extended family; all of the children participated in sing-alongs, and five of the surviving eleven eventually became professional musicians. But more than any of her siblings, Dolly was intent on discovering the world outside of the Smoky Mountains.

She began by learning to play the guitar her uncle Bill Owens bought her, and by the time she was ten years old, she had landed a spot on a television variety show in Knoxville, enlisting an aunt to drive her the forty miles there on weekends. She gained some regional attention and made her first Grand Ole Opry appearance in 1959 when she was thirteen years old. The taste of fame fueled her desire to get to Nashville. The morning after she became the first member of her family to graduate high school, she was on a bus bound for Music City with a suitcase and her guitar.

She first gained attention not for her looks or her voice, but her songwriting—a natural-born gift she cultivated before she was even old enough to know how to read. Though she took clerical and waitress jobs to pay the rent, she was soon signed to a songwriting contract by Columbine Music, and a cut she co-wrote with her uncle Bill Owens became a hit in 1966 for Bill Phillips. That earned her a shot with Monument Records, and "Dumb Blonde"—which actually attacked female stereotyping—made the Top 25 in early 1967. It also brought her to the attention of Porter Wagoner, then one of country music's biggest stars. He was looking for a "girl singer" to replace his duet partner Norma Jean on his popular syndicated television series, *The Porter Wagoner Show,* and once he met Dolly, he looked no further. Though Norma Jean fans were initially cold to her replacement, Dolly's vivacious personality, angelic voice, and breathtaking beauty won them over, and the duo took off. Wagoner helped grease the wheels for a deal that took Dolly from the small Monument Records to the powerhouse RCA label. Her first record under that contract was a duet with Wagoner, "The Last Thing on My Mind." The next release—the title track of her debut album, *Just Because I'm a Woman*—was pure Dolly, somewhat controversial in 1968 for its frank lyrics and condemnation of the double standard applied to male and female sexuality.

In 1969, she fulfilled a childhood dream when she joined the cast of the Grand Ole Opry, and her first number 1 came in 1971 with her own composition, "Joshua." Three more hit the top in 1974, "Jolene," "Love Is Like a Butterfly," and the poignant and bittersweet "I Will Always Love You." The last was acknowledged to be a personal yet very public farewell to Wagoner, whose fame she was clearly eclipsing, a fact that was creating an uncomfortable work environment. She left the show that year, emerging like a butterfly from its cocoon.

Over the three decades that she has flown solo, Dolly has become an international superstar, one of the most well-known and recognized women in the world. In 1986, she was inducted into the Nashville Songwriters Hall of Fame, and in 1999 saw her bronze plaque installed as she took her place in the Country Music Hall of Fame. She received the Living Legend medal by the U.S. Library of Congress in 2004, and is also a recipient of the National Medal of the Arts. She has starred in films, landed atop the pop charts, written songs for movies, lent her distinctive voice to animation, and paid homage to the music of her childhood by recording acoustic, bluegrass, and spiritual albums.

She and fellow Opry star Vince Gill had a huge hit in 1996 when they recorded "I Will Always Love You" as a duet, and in 2006, she changed partners and danced again, taking "When I Get Where I'm Going" to number 1 with one of the Opry's newest members, Brad Paisley.

As high as Dolly has soared in the world, she has never risen above her raisin'. Dollywood, the theme park she built in Sevierville, Tennessee in 1985, changed the economic landscape of her birthplace, and she funds scholarships to high school students in Sevier County.

Though her Barbie-doll figure implies that hardly more than a pea ever passes between her voluptuous lips, and less than that ever sticks to her tiny hips, Dolly remains a fan of the kind of simple country cooking she grew up on, and even published a cookbook, *Dolly's Dixie Fixin's Cookbook.* But Dolly isn't the only Parton with a flare for cooking. Willadeene Parton, the oldest of the Parton children, compiled the recipes she and Avie Lee devised from what was on hand to feed the large family, with an occasional treat like chocolate syrup, in her 1997 book *All-Day Singing and Dinner on the Grounds,* which included the following three recipes.

Eggplant Pancakes

1 medium-size eggplant	5 tablespoons flour
¼ cup water	1 teaspoon salt
2 eggs	

Bake eggplant with water, covered, at 350° until tender. Peel and remove seeds. Mash, add well-beaten eggs, flour, and salt. Mix all ingredients. Drop by spoonfuls on a hot buttered pan. Turn and brown on both sides.

Syrup made from Violets

1 quart spring or distilled water
¼ cup fresh violet petals, collected and gently washed
1 pound sugar

Bring water to a boil, pour over violet petals, mash to a paste. Keep adding water, add sugar. Boil until clear. Strain through cheesecloth folded four times. Pour into hot sterilized jars, seal, and place in hot bath.

Wild Rose Jelly

1 quart spring or distilled water
¼ cup rose petals, collected and gently washed
1 pound sugar

Bring water to a boil, pour over rose petals. Add sugar, boil until clear. Pour through fine cloth or cheesecloth. Reheat. Pour into hot, sterilized jars, seal, and place in hot bath.

GOLL-Y, DOLL-YS

Grand Ole Opry member Jeanne Pruett has a special recipe for potatoes that's very popular. "My friend Dolly Parton and I can eat our weight in these. After I fixed them for her the first time, she brought me the biggest iron skillet I've ever seen. The note she left with the skillet said, 'Anytime you can cook 'em, I can eat 'em.' So, since 1974 I've called them Goll-y, Doll-ys."

This recipe appeared in her appropriately named *Feedin' Friends Cookbook*.

Dolly Parton and Porter Wagoner welcome Jeanne Pruett as an Opry member, 1973.

"GOLL-Y, DOLL-YS" (FRIED POTATOES AND ONIONS)

> Wesson oil
> 6 medium Irish potatoes, peeled and shoe-stringed into medium-sized pieces
> 1 medium to medium-large onion, diced
> Salt and pepper to taste

Heat Wesson oil in skillet. Cover and fry potatoes until they are tender to the touch, just before they start to brown. Add the diced onion and cover and leave covered for about 5 minutes. Uncover and turn heat up to lightly brown potatoes and onions. Salt and pepper to taste.

The Opry Duck Hunt, 1974. L to R: Grandpa Jones, Charlie Walker, Stu Phillips, Neil Craig, Jimmy C. Newman, and E. W. "Bud" Wendell.

The Opry Duck Hunt, 2006. Front, L to R: Ricky Skaggs, Jimmy Dickens, Colin Reed, Craig Morgan, and Marty Roe. Back, L to R: Jim Ed Brown, Brian Abrahamson, Steve Buchanan, Jimmy C. Newman, Blake Shelton, and Pete Fisher.

The Opry Duck Hunt

The Opry Duck Hunt, an annual celebration of camaraderie and gamesmanship that began in 1970, had its genesis in a casual conversation in 1969 between Bud Wendell—then just one year into a six-year tenure as the Opry general manager—and one of its most beloved stars, Tex Ritter. "I've always liked to bird hunt," says Wendell, who retired in 1997 as president and CEO of Gaylord Entertainment, and one year later was elected to the Country Music Hall of Fame. "I was talking to Tex Ritter one night at the Opry about it, and he said he liked to hunt, too. I started nosing around, and it turned out Grandpa Jones was also a duck hunter. So I said, okay, I'll set us up on a hunt. It was me, Tex, Grandpa, Charlie Walker, and a photographer from WSM television that first time. He ended up liking to hunt more than taking pictures, so the next year we took [Opry staff photographer] Les Leverett, and he went on every one."

Soon, more Opry members wanted to be included, which eventually necessitated getting a bus for the trip to Reelfoot Lake, in the northwest corner of Tennessee. "It was Opry members, and sometimes executives with National Life and WSM. Not everyone wants to get up before dawn to sit in the cold and in the water, hoping some ducks will come along." But over the years, Tom T. Hall, Bob Luman, Stu Phillips, Jimmy C. Newman, Porter Wagoner, Little Jimmy Dickens, and Jim Ed Brown were among those who took the bus to the tiny town of Samburg, where they checked into the South Shore Motel. "We'd leave Sunday morning, after the Saturday night show, so we could get settled in. We would get a couple blinds and hire a guide and hunt Monday and Tuesday mornings. Samburg was just a duck hunting, fish camp little town. Our guide, Son Cochran, was a second-generation guide. Nothing much went on there except during duck season, and then the whole place came alive at four A.M. Hunters milling around, dogs barking, kids running, the whole place is jumpin'! Of course, by eight at night, everybody's in bed because you have to get up so early."

Before getting some shut-eye, the group would have dinner at Boyette's, which aside from being "a wonderful restaurant" enjoyed a distinction that appealed to the group. "It was the only place in the state where it was legal to serve crappie. People that lived around there and hunted there knew it was where we ate, so business would really pick up for them when we were in town. One year, we went hunting right before Christmas, and Boyette's was all decorated for the holiday. They had a piano there, and after we ate, Roy Clark sat down at the piano, and Tex and Grandpa got up there with him and started singing Christmas carols. They got everyone in the restaurant to sing along, it was really a special night."

For a few years, Wendell recalls, the group went to Stuttgart, Arkansas, site of the World Champion Duck Calling Contest, when the chamber of commerce asked for an Opry star to serve as emcee for the event. Stuttgart went one better on Samburg when it came to feeding the hunters. "The first night, they had the Critter Dinner for invited guests. It was a buffet, with every kind of game you could imagine, from beaver to deer. There was one platter with something on it that none of us were quite sure what it was. Jim Ed Brown knew; they were squirrel heads. The rest of us wouldn't go near them, which was fine with Jim Ed, because he loved them. I think they must have been fried. There wasn't much meat on them; you would suck the brains out."

Much more to the group's liking was a cheese dip made by Julio Pierpaoli, who came to Nashville in the early seventies to work for Opryland, first as food and beverage director at the hotel, then, when the Opryland amusement park opened, as the park manager. Because he brought the treat on the trips to the Duck Calling Contest, it was dubbed Stuttgart Delight no matter where it was served. "Julio just loved the Opry Duck Hunt. Every year, I would have something made to give out to everyone with the logo on it, a T-shirt or bag or a hat. When Julio passed away in 2005, his family placed two hats in his casket, a UT cap and an Opry Duck Hunt cap. That really meant a lot to me."

According to son Kenny Pierpaoli, his father was passionate about two things: University of Tennessee Football and duck hunting. "I'm not sure which one he loved more, probably duck hunting. He started taking me when I was just a boy, and it's something we loved to do together. He was from Arkansas, so we often went to Stuttgart to hunt. He had lots of friends there, and we were always going to a party or a dinner at someone's house. One time, we had a cheese dip at someone's house that was so good, my dad asked for the recipe and started making it at home. He changed it up a little like food people do to other people's recipes. At Christmas, the Opryland chef would make it up in a big batch, and then he'd put it in smaller tins for gifts."

Wendell was named president and CEO of WSM in 1978, and in time he handed over the reins of the Duck Hunt to Opry general manager Bob Whitaker. "We had fun hunting," Wendell remembers, "but most of all, it was about being together, telling stories. Tex Ritter was the master storyteller; everyone would gather round him. Those were wonderful times."

Like the Grand Ole Opry, the location and members of the cast of the Duck Hunt have changed over the years, but Pete Fisher, who became the Opry's general manager in 1999, says the spirit remains the same.

"It's most importantly a chance to spend time together," he says. "The younger artists are so impressed with the older members, to hear their stories; it's such a gift, a great experience, a way for them to connect with the Opry's past and move it forward."

"Another thing that hasn't changed is Little Jimmy's appetite for crappie," adds Colin Reed, Gaylord chairman and CEO, and Duck Hunt host since 2002. "We no longer have to look for a restaurant in town that serves crappie. We just send Little Jimmy out with a cane pole in the afternoon and fry up the filets in the lodge that evening!"

In 2004, the Opry Duck Hunt moved to Greenwood, Mississippi, an outdoorsman's paradise where Reed has a hunting farm. "I think some Opry members were a bit surprised to learn that I'm an avid duck hunter and outdoorsman," Reed acknowledges. "In fact, I was delighted to discover that it would be my responsibility to carry on the tradition and host the annual Opry Duck Hunt. It's one of the best parts of my job description!"

The group that flew down in 2006 reflected the Opry's diversity of experience and genre: Reed; Gaylord executive vice president and CFO David Kloeppel; executive director of communications, Brian Abrahamson; Gaylord's senior vice president of media and entertainment, Steve Buchanan; and Fisher from the management side. Artists included the Opry's longest-tenured member, Little Jimmy Dickens, along with Jimmy

C. Newman, Jim Ed Brown, Ricky Skaggs, Diamond Rio's Marty Roe, and two of the Opry's most frequent guests, Craig Morgan and Blake Shelton.

"The Opry Duck Hunt—which since we came to Greenwood now includes other wild game—is a really important opportunity for Opry artists to spend time with Opry management in a nonmanagerial way," says Fisher. "It's a unique way to get to know one another; you have a big breakfast together, then stand in flooded timber in the cold, pitch dark. After dinner, we pass the guitar and sing, tell stories, then get up and hunt again the next day. It's a wonderful experience that is a remarkably enduring and rich chapter of Opry history."

Reed feels much the same way. "My memories of the Duck Hunt are less about the hunting and more about the camaraderie and storytelling that goes on around the fire. The singing is another highlight, though my participation in that is limited to being an appreciative listener, passing the guitar from the person on my left to the person on my right," Reed admits with a laugh. "Fresh crappie, country music, and ducks in the decoy—that's my favorite recipe."

Opry Duck Hunt's Stuttgart Delight

Julio Pierpaoli's brother Gene is the keeper of this recipe, a classic in Arkansas duck clubs. He recommends making it a couple days in advance to let the flavors settle in.

1 pound bacon	1 bunch green onions
1 pound sharp cheddar cheese, grated	1 small package sliced almonds
One 8-ounce jar mayonnaise	Dash of garlic powder

Cook bacon until very crisp, drain, and pat as much fat off as possible. Crumble into bowl and mix with all other ingredients. Place in a cheese jar or bowl and refrigerate for at least 2 hours, preferably 2 days. Remove from refrigerator 1 hour before serving and return to room temperature. Serve with crackers.

Tom T. Hall

Joined the Opry cast in 1971

In a time-honored plot line, Tom T. Hall's life story has come full circle: His first appearances as a professional musician were with the bluegrass band he formed as a teen, the Kentucky Travelers. Since he officially retired from public performance in 1997, he and his wife Miss Dixie have become, in his words, "patrons of bluegrass music," providing living quarters for bluegrass musicians while they avail themselves of the studio at Fox Hollow Farm, the Hall's rural estate about twenty miles south of Nashville. In the years between, the quiet and thoughtful man built a distinguished career in country music based on his incredible gift for writing, earning him the title the Storyteller, as well as hit singles and countless songwriter and performance awards.

The native of Olive Hill, Kentucky, got his first guitar when he was just eight years old from his father, a bricklayer and Baptist preacher. A natural-born poet, with an instrument at his fingertips, Hall began putting his words to music. The Kentucky Travelers played at high schools and for a local radio station before disbanding, leaving Hall as a deejay at the station. A four-year stint in the army put Hall in Germany, where he worked on his craft and took advantage of a captive audience for his original material that he performed at local noncomissioned officers clubs and on the Armed Forces Radio Network. When he returned to the States, he used the G.I. Bill to enroll at Roanoke College as a journalism major, earning living expenses spinning records at a radio station in Salem.

A Nashville songwriter visiting the station was so impressed with Hall's own material that he sent along some of his songs to Music Row publisher Jimmy Key at New Key Publishing, who signed Hall and began sending the tunes out to producers. Grand Ole Opry member Jimmy C. Newman was the first to record one of Tom's songs; "DJ for a Day" hit the Top 10 in 1963, a chart accomplishment repeated by Dave Dudley the next year with Hall's song "Mad." The back-to-back

Tom T. Hall.

success convinced Hall to move to Music City to become a full-time songwriter. Not long after Hall's arrival, Opry member Johnnie Wright took his song "Hello Vietnam" all the way to number 1, a first for both men. Though Hall was content writing for others, Nashville producer Jerry Kennedy thought he should step out of the shadows and into a studio to make some records, telling the reluctant performer that if he didn't, some of his songs would never be heard. That wasn't exactly true, as Jeannie C. Riley proved in 1968 when her recording of Hall's song "Harper Valley PTA" became not only a major hit, but a political and cultural phenomenon, named Single of the Year by the Country Music Association.

With his reputation firmly established in the Nashville writer community, Tom T.'s own recording career finally took off when "Ballad of Forty Dollars" hit number 4 on the country charts. "The Year That Clayton Delaney Died," based on remembrances of neighbor and childhood musical mentor Lonnie Easterly, was released in 1971, and became his biggest hit, earning him induction into the Grand Ole Opry. Through the seventies and into the eighties, Hall was a consistent presence on the radio; he also toured, appeared on television, and continued writing, of course, not only songs, but also a couple of books.

Though Hall had a reputation as somewhat of a loner, he and his English-born wife—who wrote several cookbooks herself—often entertained Opry members and staff at their home, as Opry announcer Keith Bilbrey recalls. "Dixie and Tom T. used to put on a big feed. Miss Dixie was a wonderful cook. It was a real family-style gathering. It was fun to get together and be together away from the Opry. Music was the last thing we would talk about, but by the end of the night, somebody would pull out a guitar, and before you knew it, it was being passed around."

In the eighties, Hall's narrative style–songs–stories that ran through without a chorus—were no longer connecting with three-minutes-and-out country radio, and in 1986, he decided to retire from recording. His songs still resonated with a new generation of artists, and in 1996, super-star Alan Jackson took "Little Bitty"—which Hall began writing in Australia and finished in Florida—to number 1, where it stayed for three consecutive weeks. That same year, the Storyteller announced his retire-ment from touring and live performances, though he hardly settled into a rocking chair on the front porch. He just retreated from what he calls "the big-time music business" and spends his time painting, gardening, wood-working, golfing, and writing songs with Miss Dixie for the young blue-grass artists and bands that gravitate to Fox Hollow.

For years, Hall turned down offers to "come out of retirement" to perform, until the Country Music Hall of Fame extended an invitation that intrigued him. Miss Dixie also had a hand in convincing her husband to serve as the institution's 2005 artist in residence. For three consecutive Wednesday nights in August, Hall appeared in the Hall's Ford Theater. The first evening, "Tom T's Bio in Song," told Hall's life story through his autobiographical compositions; the second, "Songs I Wish I'd Written and Some I'm Glad I Did," focused on his favorite songwriters; and the third, "Tom T's Return to Roots," was devoted to his first and lasting love, blue-grass music.

While Hall's catalogue is filled with thoughtful ruminations on life's darkest and most hopeful moments, he's not adverse to fun, as one of his more lighthearted hits—an ode to hops with a rousing chorus—attests.

I Like Beer
Tom T. Hall

In some of my songs I have casually mentioned
The fact that I like to drink beer
This little song is more to the point
Roll out the barrel and lend me your ears

[Chorus]
I like beer
It makes me a jolly good fellow
I like beer
It helps me unwind and sometimes it makes me feel mellow
*   (makes him feel mellow)*
Whiskey's too rough, champagne costs too much, vodka puts
*   my mouth in gear*
This little refrain should help me explain as a matter of fact
*   I like beer*
(He likes beer)

My wife often frowns when we're out on the town
And I'm wearing a suit and a tie
She's sipping vermouth and she thinks I'm uncouth
When I yell as the waiter goes by

[Repeat chorus]

Last night I dreamed that I passed from the scene
And I went to a place so sublime
Aw, the water was clear and tasted like beer
Then they turned it all into wine (awww)

I like beer
It makes me a jolly good fellow
I like beer
It helps me unwind and sometimes it makes me feel mellow
*   (makes him feel mellow)*
Whiskey's too rough, champagne costs too much, and vodka
*   puts my mouth in gear*
Aw, this little refrain should help me explain as a matter of
*   fact I love beer*
(Yes, he likes beer)

Tootsies Orchid Lounge

Opry Sponsor

Before Tootsies Orchid Lounge became an official sponsor of the Grand Ole Opry, it provided support of a different nature to the show. The back door of World Famous Tootsies, as it truthfully touts itself, is directly across the alley from the stage door at the Ryman. When the Opry was still broadcast from the auditorium, cast members were known to slip out between performances for a "holler and a swaller." Bud Wendell, general manager of the Opry from 1968 to 1974, remembers having to sprint between stage and bar to round up missing singers and musicians in time to hit their cue.

Of all the honky-tonks on Lower Broadway—the blocks between Fifth Avenue and the Cumberland River—Tootsies was distinguished by its orchid-painted exterior and the generous woman inside who gave the place her name and her heart. The bar was originally known as Mom's; when Hattie Louise "Tootsie" Bess bought it in 1960, she changed the name to Tootsies. A singer-comedienne herself with husband Jeff Bess's outfit, Big Jeff and the Radio Playboys, Tootsie provided countless singer-songwriters a place to play and nurse a beer—or ten—while working on their craft, among them Willie Nelson, Kris Kristofferson, Faron Young, Hank Cochran, Waylon Jennings, Roger Miller, and Tom T. Hall. The photos and memorabilia that cover the smoke-stained walls chronicle the famous, the infamous, and the legion whose fame never spread beyond a song or two on the tiny corner stage. Tootsie took care of them all, slipping five- and ten-dollar bills into empty pockets and keeping a cigar box of IOUs behind the bar. At the end of the year, Opry members would take up a collection among themselves to pay them off. When Bess died on February 18, 1978—just sixty-three years old—she was buried in an orchid gown in an orchid casket with an orchid in her hand. Her funeral was attended by Opry members Tom T. Hall, Roy Acuff, Faron Young, and others, and Connie Smith sang some of her favorite hymns.

Like many downtowns across the country, downtown Nashville suffered an exodus of business and retail tenants through the seventies and eighties. Lower Broadway became tawdry and seedy, and at one point in the early 1990s, Tootsies would have been torn down if not for the efforts of Steve Smith and John Taylor, who bought it in 1992. They devoted themselves to honoring the memory of Tootsie Bess by preserving her namesake. The resurrection of the bar as a vital and exuberant Nashville hotspot coincided with the reopening of the gorgeously renovated Ryman as an acclaimed performance venue. In 1999, the Opry returned to the Ryman for one weekend, and it was so successful that it often returns to the Mother Church of Country Music for a month or more in the winter. In 2000, Tootsies Orchid Lounge officially came on board as an Opry sponsor, an unbroken circle indeed.

Jan Howard

G rowing up poor as dirt on a farm in West Plains, Missouri, third from the bottom of eleven children, Lula Grace Johnson seemed destined to repeat her mother's life. Married at fifteen after dropping out of school, she bore three boys before she turned twenty-one. Her first husband was an abuser, her second a bigamist.

When Lula boarded a Greyhound bus headed to Los Angeles, she left everything behind but her children, looking for a fresh start; she never could have imagined that she would emerge a few years later with a new name—Jan Howard—on her first single, "Yankee Go Home," a duet with Wynn Stewart.

She acquired the last name when she married Stewart's friend, aspiring songwriter Harlan Howard, whose day job was in a printing factory. "We were married a year before he ever heard me sing, and that was by accident," she recalls. "He came in one evening while I was washing dishes and overheard me. He asked if I would record a song he and Buck Owens had written called 'Daddy for a Day.' Since I was singing it, they changed it to 'Mommy for a Day' and sent it to Kitty Wells. She recorded it, and it became their first BMI award. After that, I was the official demo singer. It was fun, but I didn't give up my day job. Harlan was making fifty-five dollars a week in the factory, but I was making eighty-five dollars a week as a secretary."

The couple made some visits to Nashville to test the waters. Harlan Howard was finding that his songs were striking a chord on Music Row, and Jan Howard made her Opry debut on the Prince Albert–sponsored segment of the show, one of the first times she had ever performed live. In 1960, the couple and her children moved to Nashville; that same year, her first solo single, "The One You Slip Around With," became a Top 10 hit. More hits followed, often written by her husband. In 1965, she began a professional partnership with Bill Anderson that earned them acclaim and success as a duo. Unfortunately, her partnership with Harlan ended in divorce in 1967. Unimaginable tragedy was right around the corner. In 1968, her oldest son, Jimmy, was killed in Vietnam, just weeks after a song she penned for him, "My Son," was released. Four years later, her youngest boy committed suicide. She wrote movingly of the grief, pain, and healing process in her autobiography, *Sunshine and Shadow.*

Because of her personal loss, Jan Howard is passionately devoted to supporting the armed forces and frequently entertains servicemen and -women. In 1992, her efforts on behalf of the armed forces, the Veterans Administration, Vietnam veterans, and the Vietnam Veterans Memorial earned her the Tennessee Adjutant General's Distinguished Patriot Medal, its highest civilian honor. In 2005, the commander in chief of Veterans of Foreign Wars presented her with the Medal of Merit, awarded for "exceptional service rendered to country, community, and mankind."

Jan Howard.

She is a regular performer on the Opry, and spends as much time as possible on the golf course, frequently as the only female member of foursomes in fund-raising tournaments. Just as she did back in the days when female entertainers were often dismissed as "girl singers," she holds her own with the good ole boys and then some.

Her tall, slim figure is the envy of her peers. "I hate going to lunch with Jan Howard," says Jeannie Seely. "She can eat whatever she wants and never gains a pound."

Not exactly true, Howard says. "I eat what I want, and I don't mess with any of that low-fat stuff. I eat butter, not margarine. But I watch portion size."

Except when it comes to coconut meringue pie. "I like to bake, but when I do, I need to have someone to give it to or I'll eat the whole thing. One night, I don't know what got into me, I made a coconut cream pie, and once it cooled, I sat down on the floor of my house and I ate that whole pie. I was sick for four days. Now, I let myself have one piece of something, and then take the rest and put it in the band room at the Opry."

Jan Howard says no one taught her to cook; she learned by trial and error. The first pie she made was a big error. "I was just a kid, and had never made anything. I thought I'd make a cream pie, so I poured cream in a pie shell and put it in the oven. What a mess. My pies have gotten a lot better, but I think Pillsbury has the crust down pat, so I use theirs instead of making my own."

Jan Howard's Coconut Meringue Pie

Crust
1 Pillsbury ready-made pie crust

My instructions: Take it out of the box and place in a 9- or 10-inch pie pan. Bake as directed on box.

Filling
¾ cup sugar

¼ cup cornstarch or ½ cup all-purpose flour

3 cups whole milk

4 eggs separated, set whites aside for meringue

1 tablespoon butter or margarine ("I prefer butter.")

1½ teaspoons vanilla

1⅓ cups flaked coconut

Combine sugar and cornstarch (or flour) in a saucepan and stir in milk. Cook over medium heat until thickened and bubbly. Cook a couple minutes more, stirring constantly. Remove from heat. Slightly beat egg yolks, then stir a cup of hot filling into egg yolks. Pour egg yolk mixture into hot filling in pan. Bring to a gentle boil and cook approximately 2 minutes. Remove from heat. Stir in butter, vanilla, and 1 cup coconut. Pour into prepared pie crust.

Meringue

4 egg whites	½ teaspoon cream of tartar
1 teaspoon vanilla	½ cup sugar

In a large mixing bowl, combine egg whites with vanilla and cream of tartar. Beat with electric mixer on medium speed until soft peaks form. Gradually add ½ cup sugar (one tablespoonful at a time), beating on high until stiff peaks form and sugar dissolves. Immediately spread over warm filling, being careful to seal edges with meringue. Sprinkle top with remaining ⅓ cup of coconut. Bake in 350° oven until meringue is a nice, golden brown, about 10 to 15 minutes. Do not overbake. Cool on wire rack for at least 1 hour, then chill a couple hours before serving. Enjoy, but don't eat the whole pie by yourself!

VIP DINING

Jan Howard counts many current and retired members of the military as her friends, and they in turn are big fans of hers and the Grand Ole Opry. Among them is Joe McClure, who lives in Dover, Tennessee, with his wife, Bernice. During a visit to their home for "some good food, good fellowship, and a lot of pickin' and grinnin'," Howard was looking at photos and mementos from McClure's service days, and found out he had been flight steward on Air Force One and other VIP planes during the Nixon/Ford administration. Over dinner, she asked him what was the dish most requested by the passengers on those planes, and he replied, "You're eating it right now!"

Jan Howard at a fan club brunch.

JOE MCCLURE'S **AIR FORCE ONE WALDORF SALAD**

½ cup mayonnaise

½ cup marshmallow cream

1 tablespoon lemon juice

Sugar (or sweetener) to taste

3 medium, unpeeled, chopped McIntosh apples

3 stalks celery, chopped

½ cup raisins, soaked in warm water

½ cup chopped pecans or walnuts

½ cup small or sliced grapes

3 chopped red maraschino cherries for color

Mix mayonnaise, marshmallow cream, lemon juice, and sugar (or sweetener) in large bowl. Add remaining ingredients. Mix together until thoroughly coated. Chill at least 1 hour before serving.

George Jones.

George Jones

Joined the Opry cast in 1973

There is probably no singer in country music history whose life mirrored myths or begged to be told more than George Jones. He says he wrote his autobiography, *I Lived to Tell It All,* to set the record straight. "I got tired of hearing things I'd done blown out of proportion," he explains.

In the sixty-five years from his birth in the East Texas community of Saratoga until the book was published in 1996, Jones logged more charted singles than any other artist in any other genre of music; received a string of trade, industry, fan-voted, and achievement awards; and had four wives and three divorces. He battled alcoholism, drug addiction, poor health, legal problems, and financial woes. He became a member of the Grand Ole Opry on two different occasions seventeen years apart, and was inducted into the Country Music Hall of Fame in 1992. In spite of, or perhaps because of, the tumult that has marked his life and career, Jones is revered by subsequent generations of singers who hope to at least honor the path, if not fill the shoes, of the man many consider the greatest country singer of all time.

Jones was born in a log cabin and raised poor, the eighth child of a truck driver father who played guitar and a mother who was a church pianist. Living within such a musical environment, he began singing and playing guitar as a child, and before he turned thirteen, was a pint-sized performer on the streets of nearby Beaumont, collecting spare change from passersby. Ironically, music first provided an escape for Jones from his alcoholic father, and by the time he was fifteen, he was on his own, having secured a regular spot on a Jasper radio station, followed by a stint at KRIC in Beaumont. At nineteen, he married Dorothy Bonvillion, a union that lasted about one year. The first Mrs. Jones cited her husband's drinking and temper as unacceptable to the covenant of marriage, setting in place a pattern that would affect his relationships for nearly fifty years.

Post-divorce, Jones joined the marines and served in North Korea. When he returned to the States, he again gravitated to music, cutting his first record, "No Money in This Deal" for Starday Records in 1954, and committed himself again to holy matrimony, making Shirley Ann Corley the second Mrs. Jones.

"Why Baby Why," which Jones co-wrote, was his first entry on the country charts, reaching number 4 in *Billboard* in 1955. The following year, he went one notch higher on the charts with "Just One More" and the trade publication prophetically named him their Most Promising Country Vocalist.

Clearly, it was time to move to Nashville and a larger label, and he did both, leaving Starday for Mercury Records, which was responsible for his hits for the next several years, including his first number 1 in 1959, "White Lightning." Other classic Jones songs that came from that relationship were "The Window Up Above," "She Thinks I Still Care," "A Good Year for the Roses," "Love Bug," and "The Race Is On."

George Jones joined the Grand Ole Opry in 1956, but left the cast the following year. His second marriage ended in 1968, and one year later, in a seemingly fated pairing that was the hillbilly equivalent of Elizabeth Taylor and Richard Burton, he married the First Lady of Country Music, Tammy Wynette. Not only did that marriage produce remarkable drama, it also resulted in some of country music's most classic duets, beginning with "Take Me" and continuing—even after their divorce—through "The Ceremony," "We're Gonna Hold On," "Golden Ring," "Near You," and "Two Story House." George rejoined the cast of the Opry in 1973 at the same time as his wife, Tammy, and has been a member ever since.

Jones had begun another challenging but very productive relationship in 1971, with legendary Nashville producer Billy Sherrill on Epic Records. The string of hit records that followed was in contrast to the perilous free fall Jones was taking in his personal life, thanks to increasing alcohol and drug abuse. Wynette first filed for divorce in 1973; the couple reconciled briefly, but ultimately made the break in 1975. They had one child, Tamela Georgette Jones, in 1970.

Jones' downward spiral continued through the next decade, during which he was arrested and hospitalized on numerous occasions. The Possum would disappear for days at a time on binges, earning another nickname, No Show Jones, for the many concert appearances he missed. Yet it was also during this dark period that Jones recorded in 1980 what has been cited on too many lists to mention as the greatest country song of all time, "He Stopped Loving Her Today." The sorrow-soaked ballad became his first million-seller, won a Grammy for Best Male Country Vocal Performance, and contributed toward his winning of the CMA's Male Vocalist of the Year awards in 1980 and 1981.

In 1983, Jones married Nancy Sepulveda and began to shake his addictions. Though he continued to have hit records, country radio was increasingly turning to younger artists. In 1988, he recorded his final album with Billy Sherrill, *One Woman Man.* He next was signed to MCA Records, where he recorded the feisty tune "I Don't Need Your Rocking Chair," which also became a hit video.

Tammy Wynette and George Jones perform a duet on the Opry stage, 1973.

In 1999, Jones was seriously injured in a one-car auto accident near his home. An open bottle of vodka was found in the car, indicating Jones had resumed old habits. He was ordered to undergo treatment, which he did, and has been clean since.

Though his one-of-a-kind voice is rarely heard on contemporary country radio, Jones is still a significant presence and force in the industry. In 1992, he was inducted into the Country Music Hall of Fame, and has continued to win awards from the National Academy of Recording Arts and Sciences (which distributes the Grammy Awards), the Academy of Country Music, and the CMA. In 2002, he received the National Medal of Arts Honor from President George W. Bush, the nation's highest honor for artistic excellence.

The prestigious ceremony in the nation's capital was a walk in high cotton for a country boy, but central to Jones' impassioned popularity and the love he inspires in his fans is his unabashed pride in his rural roots.

One of his more recent collaborations is with the Williams Sausage Company, a West Tennessee–based company that has been making breakfast sausage for nearly a half century. With Jones' involvement, the family-owned company customized a special blend of sausage, available mild, hot, or premade as sausage and biscuits. Every box is printed with "Fables and Truths," amusing and embellished facts about Jones' life that somehow connect to sausage.

Like many country artists who were actually raised in the country—a dwindling number these days—Jones likes good old country cooking. His favorite home-cooked meal, he once replied to the question from a fan, is "fried potatoes with onions, fried okra, baby lima beans, and fried corn bread. I'm not a big meat eater, but if I had to include meat, it would be smoked ham. I'm not against eating meat and I do eat it, but I prefer homegrown vegetables."

He did develop a fondness for one classic beef dish, after he sampled it during the recording of *The Bradley Barn Sessions,* which took place in 1993 at the late Owen Bradley's studio in rural Mount Juliet. Nashville caterer Monica Holmes, whose Clean Plate Club has fed country music singers since 1980, was in charge of the grub that week.

"I had roast beef as the entrée one day. I had prepared it sort of like the classic French bourguignonne, where the beef is braised in red wine, and all the musicians were loving it," Holmes remembers. "George wasn't going to eat, but they kept telling him it was so good he just had to try it. So finally he told me to cut him off a piece and put it on a roll. Well, even though he said he wasn't a big beef fan, he loved it, and ended up having lots more. About ten years later, my business had grown and I had moved my catering kitchen to a new building. One of the first calls I got was from this woman. She said, 'You don't know me, but my name is Nancy Jones and I'm married to George Jones.' She told me that she had asked George what he wanted for Christmas dinner and he told her he'd like the roast beef that girl made that year at Bradley's Barn. So she asked me if I could make it again and I said sure. They sent one of their people over to pick it up, the roast beef and the same side dishes I made that day. I couldn't believe that of all the catered meals he has had in his career, he remembered that one. But since he liked it so much, I have called it Beef Bourgon-Jones ever since."

* * *

Beef bourguignonne is a classic French dish, meaning "as prepared in Burgundy" one of France's most famous gastronomic regions. The beef is braised in red wine, garnished with mushrooms and white pearl onions, and is similar to a stew. Most Americans probably first became familiar with the term watching Julia Child's televised cooking show, or reading one of her cookbooks. There have been countless adaptations since, including this one by Monica Holmes, owner of Nashville's Clean Plate Club catering.

Beef Bourgon-Jones

1 whole rib eye (usually they are around 13 to 15 pounds)

Marinade

2 packages McCormick meat marinade	2 tablespoons fresh, chopped thyme
1 cup olive oil	Black pepper
1 cup red wine	4 tablespoons coarse-grain mustard
3 cloves fresh garlic, chopped	

Rub

Cracked black pepper	Dried thyme
Salt	Granulated garlic

Mix marinade ingredients together. Place beef in zip-lock bag, pour marinade in bag, refrigerate for 2 to 3 days, turning to cover a couple times a day.

Preheat oven to 375°. Remove beef from bag. Mix together ingredients for rub. Coat beef in mixture. Cook 2 to 2½ hours for medium rare; using meat thermometer, temperature should read about 125°. Serves 10 to 12 hungry musicians.

Jeanne Pruett.

Jeanne Pruett

Joined the Opry cast in 1973

Jeanne Pruett came to Nashville from Pell City, Alabama, in 1956 as a young bride. While raising her children and managing a home, she began writing songs in her so-called spare time, and was understandably thrilled when Marty Robbins signed her as a writer to his publishing company, and recorded several of her compositions. "I had been a fan of his music forever. When we met, I gave him a notebook I had been writing in. There were eleven songs in there. Over the next three or four years, he ended up recording seven of those first eleven songs. I was pretty proud of that. I have always enjoyed writing more than anything else."

In 1963, she began singing herself, and released several singles on RCA, then Decca; in 1973, she signed with MCA. As the label was preparing to release Jeanne's new single, "Satin Sheets," that March, the savvy artist took matters into her own hands, literally. "I went to the fabric store and bought twenty-five yards of pink satin, then I got out my pinking shears and began cutting them into squares. We would wrap them around the record and send out two hundred at a time. Every disc jockey in the country that hadn't yet gotten one was calling, wanting to know where theirs was. We sent out sixteen hundred by the time it was done. It was a great promotion, but it was a better song."

In less than two months, "Satin Sheets" went straight to the top of the country charts, and went on to become Jeanne's signature song, one of the most enduring country music classics of all time. That summer, Jeanne Pruett was inducted into the Grand Ole Opry, the last singing member to join the world's longest-running radio show while it was still at the Ryman Auditorium.

Cutting sixteen hundred squares of satin herself was not at all out of character for Jeanne, who was drawn early on to the tasks of domestic life. While she was beloved around the world for her writing and entertaining, among friends, family, and colleagues, she is known as an immaculate housekeeper, a spectacular cook, a skillful gardener, and a generous hostess.

The youngest girl of ten children—"five of each" she says—Jeanne was raised on a working farm in Pell City, where there was always a lot to be done.

Everyone had jobs to do. My earliest job was every spring I washed out all the fruit jars. My daddy had built shelves down in the cellar and I would wash all the fruit jars, then set them upside down on the shelves to dry. Everything we grew on that farm was eventually put up in a jar, even pork meat. We called it "jar meat." You'd cook it down, and then put it up in its own grease. It made sausage balls. When you wanted to cook them, you'd put the jar in a pot of hot water and the meat would come back to life. We put up all our own vegetables and fruits. We raised chickens and pigs, and we had fish out of the pond. We never had beef because we didn't have cattle. It was a lot of hard work and effort, but it was wonderful food and the best way to grow up.

When my mother was expecting her youngest child, my two oldest sisters were pregnant with their first babies. The way we grew up, the oldest kids helped raise the youngest kids, and then the youngest kids helped raise the oldest kids' children. If there was a baby in the room that needed pickin' up, or their nose wiped, or their diaper changed, whoever was closest did it.

Jeanne's career as an entertainer began as a little girl when she and her father would go into the town to sell extra goods from the farm. "I would get up in the back of the wagon and sing songs to get the attention of the ladies shopping. That's when I started to learn to write, sitting up in the apple tree at home, making up these little songs to sell our stuff."

It was in the kitchen of the family farmhouse that she learned to cook. "My mother and four older sisters were excellent cooks. They could all take nothing and make it into something so special. Everyone cooked. I learned by watching. When I was about five years old, my daddy built me a little stool and attached a rope to it. I would drag that stool around the kitchen and pull it up beside my mother, or whoever was cooking, stand on my stool by their elbows and watch. They never had a recipe written down; it was in their heads and the tips of their fingers. I remember when my mama would open the jar of Watkins Vanilla Flavoring and in that hot Alabama kitchen, the smell would fill the entire room. She kept it up on the very top shelf, in a safe place, because it smelled so good, all the boys would want to get at it. To this day, I still use Watkins Vanilla Flavoring, and I keep it on the top shelf!"

Just as she wrote down the words to the songs she heard in her head, Jeanne eventually began writing down recipes, which was not easy. "When I started writing down recipes, the hardest part was figuring out the measurements." Since 1986, Jeanne has published four cookbooks, *Feedin' Friends,* volumes one, two, and three, and *Satin Sweets,* the fourth in the series. It was the cookbooks that led to her cooking show with country music radio and television personality Ralph Emery. "We had so much fun together. He just couldn't believe I didn't measure. He would say, 'Jeanne, how do you know that's a quarter cup?' And I'd tell him to go ahead and test it. He would, and it would always be right. I can tell you what a quarter cup of sugar is within a grain or two!"

Jeanne's success with the cookbooks and cooking shows, as well as her status as the Grand Ole Opry's best cook, came to the attention of Gaylord Broadcasting Company, which had purchased all the Opryland properties in 1983, including the theme park that had opened in 1972. Executives with the company contacted Jeanne and asked if she would be interested in turning an existing building into a restaurant. She was, and Feedin' Friends restaurant became as popular in the park as the Wabash Cannon-ball and Grizzly River Rampage.

It wasn't uncommon to see two hundred people lined up, waiting to get in. Our most popular item was white beans and fried corn bread. I would go in there and fry the corn bread myself. At the time, I had my own line of cornmeal, too. I loved it there. We had a lot of senior citizens that lived nearby and had season passes; they would come to the park several times a week to walk, it was so pretty there with all the flowers. And they loved the shows and the music. Then they'd come in to Feedin' Friends to eat. We became friends that way, I came to know them by name. I would get worried if a week or so went by and I didn't see them. I miss the folks I met out there more than anything.

Jeanne says she is retired from the Opry. "I felt like it was time to give someone else my place," but not from the music business, and never from the kitchen. "I still put up my own tomatoes, because I have never tasted one from a can that is better than one of mine from a jar." She also cans her own pickles, but everything else from her garden she freezes. And she loves to get together with friends over food. "People ask me all the time what is my favorite recipe or favorite thing to cook. I can't say. Whatever I am cooking at the moment is my favorite thing! I love preparing it, I love presenting it. If you spend hours making something, why not make it look the best it can, and put it on the best thing you own? People are always saving their 'good dishes' for a special occasion. That's silly. It's just stuff. Every day that I am able to make a great dish and cook for family and friends is a special occasion."

The following recipes appeared in Jeanne's first cookbook, *Feedin' Friends,* volume one.

Fried Corn Bread

My mother taught me to make this when I was about eight years old, so I've made it quite a while.

1 cup Martha White® self-rising cornmeal
3 tablespoons cooking oil

In a bowl, add hot water, a little bit at a time, to cornmeal until it becomes a medium-thin mixture. In a heavy-bottom skillet (I used black iron), heat oil for a few seconds. With a large spoon, drop the cornmeal mixture into the frying pan in two to three places, being careful to keep the corn cakes apart from each other, like pancakes. Fry until golden brown, then turn to other side and do the same. Serve with a pat of butter on each.

Hot Chicken Legs

½ cup rock salt crystals
6 tablespoons red pepper flakes
6 tablespoons dry hot mustard
1 package crab boil
3 dozen chicken legs

In large, deep pot, bring approximately 1 gallon of water to boil. Stir in salt, red pepper, mustard, and crab boil. Add chicken and bring back to boil. Turn down heat and continue to cook 1 hour on medium heat.

Russian Fruit Tea Tennessee-Style

1 family-sized tea bag
4 sticks cinnamon
1 quart canned grapefruit juice
1 quart canned pineapple juice
One 12-ounce can frozen orange juice, thawed

In 1 cup of boiling water, place tea bag and cinnamon sticks. Remove from heat and cover to steep for 15 minutes. In large container, mix juices, adding 1 cup of water for orange juice. Mix in tea and cinnamon mixture. Store in refrigerator. Serve hot with gingersnaps.

The Grand Ole Opry House.

Backstage at the
Grand Ole Opry House

A covered, landscaped cobblestone walkway runs from the parking lot to the double glass doors that mark the backstage entrance to the Grand Ole Opry House, home to the Opry since March 16, 1974. The enclosed desk just inside the second set of glass doors is where musicians and cast members get their dressing room assignments, and where guests have their names checked on the pages-long clearance list maintained by Jo Walker and Becky Sanders. Their post is also the receiving department for the gifts that fans bring to Opry members. More often than not, that is something edible, and over the years, those fans have become known by the product they bring, and their deliveries highly anticipated by appreciative recipients. There are the Apple People from North Carolina, and the Country Ham Man from the same state; the Strawberry People from Plant City, Florida, who get up before dawn to pick the luscious red berries, then drive straight through to Tennessee to deliver flats of their goodies that very night. There was the Shrimp Woman from Mississippi, who filled coolers with fresh-caught crustaceans.

Bluegrass artist Bobby Osborne remembers Jim Chestnut, who had a grapefruit farm in Florida. "His son would haul those grapefruits up north, but he would always stop at the Opry on the way up. He'd pull that big truck into the parking lot and we'd go out there while they unloaded some boxes. We'd peel them open right there as soon as they came off the truck so we could tell them how good they were." The Pickle Boys make the trip over from Warsaw, North Carolina, two or three times a year, and if it's May, the Onion People are on their way from Sylvania, Georgia.

There are more than twice as many dressing rooms backstage at the Opry House than there are at the Ryman—seventeen as opposed to eight; Porter Wagoner is in number 14, Little Jimmy Dickens in number 3, and bluegrass bands get number 2. The rest of the entertainers are assigned a place to use for the night; many of the dressing rooms are fairly small, with just enough room for the artist and their band to get dressed. The overflow fills the wide hallways and snakes around to the central greenroom, located just off the stage between one wall of dressing rooms and another. Like many other waiting rooms backstage of performance venues and television studios, the Opry House greenroom is not actually green but just uses the name traditionally assigned to such spaces. The Opry's greenroom is furnished with comfortable upholstered chairs and a television set mounted high on the wall that allows occupants to watch the show in progress. In one corner is a counter set with a bottomless pot of fresh-brewed coffee and a cooler full of bright pink punch. Overseeing hospitality is either Sally Smith or Tommy Huff. Sally Smith was employed by National Life (now American General) and began working at the Opry on weekends, selling tickets, then conducting backstage tours for visitors. Tommy Huff's tenure at the Opry began when he was just fifteen, working as an usher in the house.

When the Grand Ole Opry House opened, Rosa Hodge was in charge of the hospitality counter backstage; Huff started helping her when the man who preceded him collapsed in the Opry House lobby one Saturday night. "When James couldn't come in the next weekend, Miss Rosa asked me to help her until he came back, and I said of course, but he never did come back. I helped her set up, and then would help her clean up, but she stayed behind the desk, because people loved visiting with Miss Rosa. When she retired in 2003, management decided Sally and I could split the job, but nobody could ever replace Miss Rosa."

Occasionally, a fan will drop off a cake or cookies at the backstage desk, one of the Opry members will bring in some goodies, or Huff will bring in a box of cookies to go with the punch and coffee. One weekend, Jean Shepard made him a wager. "One Friday night, I had brought a box of cookies from the store, opened them up, and put the box on the counter. She told me my presentation was lacking. She said to bring cookies Saturday night, and she would buy a package to bring, and hers would be more popular. So, the next night I set out the package of cookies. She had hers in a tin lined with waxed paper; she bought them, but it looked like they were homemade. And she was right; people couldn't get enough of Jean Shepard's homemade store-bought cookies! Hers were gone before the first one of mine was taken out of the bag."

Cracker Barrel Old Country Store®

Opry Sponsor

Whether you're driving around the corner or around the country, chances are you'll find Cracker Barrel Old Country Store® along the way. In fact, Opry members, staff, and guests have for years enjoyed the Cracker Barrel located a half mile away from Opry's backstage entrance on Music Valley Drive. On Saturday nights, many members head to Cracker Barrel in between shows to enjoy some good country cookin' and the "home-away-from-home" atmosphere.

Over the years, the Grand Ole Opry and Cracker Barrel have consistently delivered a quality experience based on friendliness and hospitality. Similar to the Opry's humble beginnings in a tiny studio in the home office headquarters of National Life and Accident Insurance Company, Cracker Barrel's inauspicious start gave little indication of the success that lay ahead.

In the late 1960s, Dan Evins worked as a Shell Oil "jobber" in rural Tennessee. Driving from town to town, he would spend hours thinking of new ways to sell gasoline to folks traveling on the highways and interstates. All that time driving helped him understand people needed a place they could trust when they travel, so in 1969, Evins and a local contractor scratched their building plans in the dirt on Highway 109 in Lebanon, Tennessee. This dusty blueprint marked the spot of the original Cracker Barrel Old Country Store location.

Evins believed a business for travelers should be convenient and trustworthy. He thought travelers would appreciate making one stop to get gasoline, a good meal, candy for the kids, and some rest from the road. To persuade folks to stop, he blended his service station business with the atmosphere of the old country stores he remembered as a child. Those stores were a community's unofficial meeting place where folks gathered around a barrel full of saltine crackers to visit with friends and trade some common-sense wisdom.

News of this "new" old country store spread throughout Tennessee. The word-

Old Country Store ®

of-mouth advertising also made its way to the Grand Ole Opry, and it wasn't long before Opry members like Johnny Cash, Loretta Lynn, Bill Anderson, Stonewall Jackson, Little Jimmy Dickens, and Dolly Parton stopped in for a bite to eat. People driving along Interstate 40 looked forward to pulling off the road to a Cracker Barrel because the experience reminded them so much of a weekend visit to Grandma's house. Families liked sitting down for a home-style meal and visiting with the friendly staff. The kids enjoyed exploring for toys and treats in the old country store, especially when they found a new trinket that would help the miles pass by a little faster.

As the Cracker Barrel concept spread across Tennessee, Georgia, and Kentucky, Evins noticed that many of his guests were traveling to and from Nashville to visit the Grand Ole Opry. In 1977, Cracker Barrel became the sponsor of the 7:30 portion of the Friday night show. The partnership proved so harmonious that in 2004, Cracker Barrel Old Country Store became the first presenting sponsor in the history of the Grand Ole Opry.

As the relationship between the corporate parents of the two entities has expanded, the loyalty Opry members and fans have for the friendly restaurant has never wavered. Roy Acuff, who spent the last years of his life in a home on the grounds of the Grand Ole Opry House, frequently ate at the Cracker Barrel on Music Valley Drive, and was a favorite of the employees there, most of whom he knew by name.

"When we're on the road, we look for a Cracker Barrel because it's the food we grew up with," says Jack Greene. "I like the coleslaw, pinto beans, corn bread, turnip greens, and macaroni and cheese. I could be a vegetarian real quick."

When Alan Jackson had an all-day shoot at the Opry House, he bypassed the elaborate catered buffet for an order of Cracker Barrel's white beans and corn bread to go. "Cracker Barrel has saved us many a time," says John Conlee, speaking for all working men and women.

Vintage Cracker Barrel menu.

And not naming names, but more than one Opry member has decided that one good legend deserves another, and has passed off a tray of Cracker Barrel's legendary corn bread dressing as their own. Secrets of the stars.

Corn Bread Dressing

⅔ cup chopped onion

2 cups chopped celery

2 quarts day-old, grated corn bread

1 quart day-old, grated biscuits

¼ cup dried parsley flakes

2 teaspoons poultry seasoning

2 teaspoons ground sage

1 teaspoon coarse-ground pepper

4 ounces margarine

1 quart plus one 14-ounce can
  chicken broth

Preheat oven to 400°. Mix onion, celery, grated corn bread and biscuits, parsley, poultry seasoning, sage, and pepper in a large mixing bowl. Add melted margarine to mixture. Stir until well blended. Add chicken broth to dry ingredients and mix well. The dressing should have a wet but not soupy consistency like a quick bread batter (banana bread/corn bread). Divide mixture evenly into two (8-by-8-inch) pans sprayed with nonstick spray. Bake uncovered for 1 hour at 400° or until lightly brown on the top. Remove from oven and enjoy! Makes sixteen 6-ounce servings.

Cracker Barrel's tips for great dressing

1. Grate biscuits and corn muffins in a food processor until coarsely ground or using the largest holes on your hand grater.
2. Substitute your own homemade chicken or turkey stock for canned if you prefer.

John Conlee.

John Conlee

Joined the Opry cast in 1981

John Conlee says he doesn't cook; his wife, Gale, is in charge of the kitchen. But when it comes to feeding people, he's been stepping up to the table for more than twenty years.

Raised on the farm that his mother's father bought in 1945—a two-hundred-acre spread in Versailles, Kentucky, not far from Lexington—he learned hard work at a young age, and still finds pleasure and satisfaction in getting his hands dirty. When he comes off the road, he heads to his seventy-five-acre farm north of Nashville, and climbs up on his tractor, works on his bus, cleans his guns, putters in the woodshop, and tends to their fifty chickens and two mules, Kate and Beck. "Farming is just in our blood."

It was the farm crisis of the mideighties, or more specifically, mainstream media's response to it, that set his blood to boiling. "The stories of these farms failing, and farmers going bankrupt, were all buried in the back of newspapers, except maybe in the Midwest, where it was happening. But otherwise, it was completely under the rest of America's radar. I wanted do something. So I called the National Farm Association and asked what we could do to call attention to the situation. It seemed like music was the best way."

He began doing some farm benefit shows, but it was his show in Omaha, Nebraska, in June of 1985 that established the Family Farm Defense, for which he serves as honorary chairman. In September, Willie Nelson announced the first Farm Aid, and Conlee has been involved in every one since. It is a cause he is deeply committed to, but one that frustrates him at the same time.

"The only way to keep the family farm system alive is for prices at the farm level to go up, but as farming becomes more corporate, as the livestock industry becomes more dependent on big confinement operations, the likelihood of that happening is less and less, because they can do it for cheaper the corporate way. Not better, but cheaper. Farm Aid can't bail out the family farm system, but we can help them. We can raise awareness nationally. Some battles we have won, but the war is still being lost, the train is still going down the wrong track. I was back in my hometown recently and every farm I knew growing up is now either a horse farm or a subdivision. That's hard to stomach."

Conlee is equally impassioned by another cause: feeding America's hungry. "I saw something on television about Larry Jones' program called Feed the Children. I was attracted by his mission of feeding hungry people here in America, as opposed to somewhere halfway around the world. I admire the work anyone does to help hungry people everywhere, but it is a disgrace that people are going hungry here in this country. Not long after I saw that on television, we were doing a show somewhere and I was singing "Busted." Somebody brought a dollar bill up and left it on the stage, and then someone else did, too. By the end of the show, we had about sixty dollars. I hung on to it for a while trying to figure out what to do with it, then I remembered Feed the Children, looked them up, and sent it to them. That's how it all started. We got a five-gallon bucket and put it on the stage. Every time we do "Busted," it's the cue for people to start coming up with their money. Some nights we might get fifty dollars, and some nights we might get five hundred dollars."

Over the years, one dollar at a time, Conlee has raised more than two hundred thousand dollars for Feed the Children. The Kentucky farmer may not know how to cook, but he sure can put out a spread.

Ricky Skaggs

Joined the Opry cast in 1982

Border to border, Kentucky and Oregon are about two thousand miles apart, but faith, hope, music, and a pear pie brought two families together in a relationship that has spanned distance and time.

Kent and Susan Adams, who loved country music for its purity, rhythm, and honesty, became Ricky Skaggs' followers the first time they heard him on the Silver Eagle radio show. Kent liked him so much he joined the fan club, keeping an eye on the itinerary to see if it might include a stop in their home state of Oregon. That summer Ricky headlined the Oregon State Fair, and after seeing him live, Kent and Susan became even bigger fans. Their two-year-old son, Ben, heard them play his records so often he even learned the words to his favorite songs: "Heart Ropes" (aka "Heartbroke") and "Don't Give a Bug Your Raisin" (aka "Don't Get Above Your Raisin'").

A few summers later, when Susan saw Ricky was coming to play five miles from their hometown, she thought it might be nice to bring him a present. "I thought that with his schedule he must eat in restaurants a lot. That's when I got the idea to bake him something. Kent really loved my pear pie, so I thought Ricky might, too."

According to Ricky, Susan was right about that. "I was signing autographs after a show, and I could see one couple waiting, hoping they could have a few minutes alone. We talked, and it was clear they were fans of my music, but there was something more there. I noticed they had brought me something. Susan opened the box and pulled out the most beautiful pie I had ever seen. I asked her what kind it was and she said it was pear pie. Well, we had an old pear tree in our front yard when I was a kid growing up in Kentucky, but the only thing those pears were good for was to throw them at mean dogs when they would come around our house, so I never had a pear pie before. We said good-bye, I took the pie on my bus, and left it on the table. A few hours later I went up front to try that pie and I sure am glad I went

Ricky Skaggs.

when I did, since there was just one puny piece of pie left on that whole plate. But that small piece of pie started a relationship with a family that has lasted till this day, and will through eternity. We have shared joy, tears, triumph, disappointments, heartbreak, and about every other emotion you can imagine."

From then on, every time Kent and Susan went to see Ricky play, she brought a pear pie or two for him and his band. They had two more children in the meanwhile, Chris and their youngest, Joel, who had some medical problems when he was born. The Skaggs family joined their prayers with all the others coming his way, and through God's mercy and the staff at the Dornbecker Children's Hospital in Oregon, Joel pulled through. Susan and Kent were so grateful that they became involved as volunteers with the hospital, wanting to help other families who were suffering the same ordeal. Through their friendship with Ricky, they asked if he would be interested in helping with a benefit, and he and his wife, Sharon White (of family band the Whites), agreed, and went together to visit the hospital with the Adamses, spending time with the patients.

A few years later, Kent Adams was diagnosed with brain cancer. "It was such a blow," Ricky remembers. "It was so hard to see this wonderful couple and their kids go through that, but God has a plan for everything."

Kent, Susan, and their boys came to Nashville to attend the Grand Ole Opry, and to meet Ricky and Sharon's children. "It was a wonderful time together, for us and for all the kids. Seeing them go back home was hard because we knew if God didn't heal Kent on this earth, we wouldn't see him again until we got to Heaven."

Kent did pass away. "He had just turned forty years young when he went home to be with Jesus," Susan says. "Brain cancer took a lot of his abilities away, but two things it could not take were his faith in God and his love for a good ole Ricky Skaggs song. For his funeral, Kent requested two songs: 'Amazing Grace' and Ricky's 'A Brand New Me.'"

A few years passed, and Ricky got a call from Susan, asking him if she could come by his upcoming show in Washington, and that she had someone she would like him to meet. Ricky said sure, but only if she brought a pear pie.

"I was really looking forward to seeing her and the boys. It had been too long since I had last seen them and I knew the boys would have grown so much. When I saw them coming towards me, there was Ben and Chris, and a man walking between Susan and Joel, with a hand in each of theirs. It was her new fiancé, Rob, and after meeting him and talking to him, I certainly did approve. Susan had that same pie box with her as she did the first day I met her and Kent. It was a little bittersweet to see them without Kent, but I could not help but shed a tear seeing that family walking together, loving God, getting better, not bitter. It's so amazing how God took a little piece of pear pie, and from it, made such a message of His love."

Susan Adams-Messmer's Pear Pie

Pastry for a 9-inch, two-crust pie
6 Anjou, Bosc, or Comice pears, ripened
¾ cup sugar
3 tablespoons flour
1 teaspoon cinnamon

¼ teaspoon ginger
¼ teaspoon salt
1 tablespoon grated orange rind
2 tablespoons orange juice
2 tablespoons butter

Spray pie pan with nonstick spray. Line pan with pastry for bottom crust. Pare, core, and slice pears; arrange half of pears in bottom of pastry-lined pie pan. Combine sugar, flour, spices, and salt. Sprinkle part of mixture over pears. Add remaining pears and spice mixture. Sprinkle orange rind and orange juice over top of pears and dot with butter. Cover with top crust, flute edges. Bake at 450° for 10 minutes, reduce to 350° and bake 50 minutes longer. Serve warm and top with French vanilla ice cream. Go to local gym for 3 hours, or run 10 miles to prevent having this pie with you forever!

Riders in the Sky. L to R: Joey the CowPolka King, Woody Paul, Ranger Doug, and Too Slim.

Riders in the Sky

Joined the Opry cast in 1982

(Ranger Doug, Woody Paul, Too Slim, Joey the CowPolka King)

Riders in the Sky is inarguably the Grand Ole Opry's most unique act, so it's not surprising that the route they took to be inducted veered quite a bit off the beaten path. As Ranger Doug remembers it, the comedic cowboys made their debut as a threesome at a Nashville nightclub called Phranks and Steins, which, as the name implies, served up hot dogs and beers along with a repertoire of live folk music. When the scheduled act canceled at the last minute, Ranger Doug, Woody, and Too Slim rode to the rescue.

Oddly enough, that first show was the essence of who we are today. Dressing up in outlandish costumes, bantering with the audience, making jokes. The eight drunks that were there that night loved us. We woke up the next morning laughing, it was so much fun. We played again the next night and ended up making twenty-five dollars for both nights. Musically, we weren't very good then, but we thought that otherwise it worked. We were on our way.

Before they hit the road, they improved their musicality, so much so that their first album, *Three on the Trail,* hit a chord with an audience that included everyone from tiny tykes to rocking-chair seniors, who shared an affection for old-fashioned cowboy music. And just two years later, they became the first exclusively Western music artists to join the Grand Ole Opry. "It was Hal Durham, bless his heart, who was managing the Opry at the time," explains Ranger Doug. "He was interested in an act that honored tradition. God knows we didn't have a hit record; we still haven't, we wouldn't want to hurt our career. We were not only the first Western music artists, but the first sort of counterculture act. We were big fans of the Smothers Brothers, their comedy and their musicianship. Hal saw that we had that. There had always been a great tradition of humor on the Opry that adds texture to the show, and we think that's what we do. Hal really took a chance on us. But we were reliable, we'd show up sober and on time, we still do."

The Riders boast two royal members: Woody Paul, King of the Cowboy Fiddlers, and since 1988, accordionist Joey the CowPolka King; as well as the Idol of American Youth, Ranger Doug, and Too Slim, the Quickest Wit in the West. Galloping onto the stage in their colorful Western wear, they elicit a wave of laughs before the first word comes out of their mouths. Perfectly rendered Western classics like "Tumbling Tumbleweeds," "Happy Trails," "Red River Valley," and "Navajo Trail" strung together with wacky humor and witty banter make the Riders one of the most crowd-pleasing acts on the Opry. Their harmonious onstage partnership segues into strong friendships away from the spotlight as well, though their backgrounds are quite different.

Ranger Doug's mother was born in the jack pine forest of northern Michigan, the Upper Peninsula, an area where many Finns have settled; her father was among them when he first came to America. One of the most traditional of Finnish foods is the pasty, a mixture of meat and vegetables wrapped in dough that was particularly popular sustenance for miners. The origin of the dish is Cornwall, England, though many countries claim its adoption and development, among them Finland, Ireland, Sweden, Poland, Italy, and France. Everyone agrees that pasties must contain two things: potatoes and onions. Their popularity was due in part to their hearty nature, as well as portability, and the fact that they can be eaten without utensils.

"My aunt Margaret makes the best pasties of any I have ever had," Ranger Doug testifies. "She made the gold standard of pasties, even though she married outside of the Finnish clan. I've never made them myself, but when I get a craving, I have had pasties overnighted from Joe's Pasty Shop. They're pretty good, but they're not Aunt Margaret's."

Joe's Pasty Shop, in Ironwood, Michigan, since 1946 (they boast of being the first pasty shop in the Upper Peninsula), still uses their old-world family recipe that started their business; Joe calls himself the Pasty King.

Equally enamored of his culinary heritage is Joey the CowPolka King, the master musician who apprenticed with the late polka master Frank

Yankovich. Joey is first-generation American, his parents immigrated to America from Slovenia (then part of the Austro-Hungarian Empire) in 1910. He was raised in Chicago, where he says "there were so many pockets of ethnicity, Jewish, Italian, German. On Sundays, we would go to Maxwell Street, which was a Jewish neighborhood. Their Sabbath is Saturday, so every Sunday they had a big sidewalk sale, and there was always wonderful food, knishes, beef hot dogs, egg creams. It was the same thing in the Italian neighborhoods, and German neighborhoods; the smells of the foods cooking there, in the kitchens and in restaurants, was just amazing. At home, we had Slovenian cooking, which resembles German food, but has some differences. Slovenian sausage is more like Polish sausage; we had stuffed peppers, stuffed cabbage, kidney stew. Our desserts were very typically Slovenian: *flancitas,* a pastry shaped like a bow tie, with powdered sugar; *krofe,* which is like a doughnut without the hole; strudels; and the best thing, *potica* [po-teet-sah]. I remember my grandmother rolling it out on her kitchen table. You had to have potica for holidays and special occasions, it's a Slovenian tradition!"

Though Woody Paul's background is pure country—he grew up on a farm—some of his favorite foods might be considered exotic by city folk. "I'm not real particular," admits the laconic fiddle player. "I'll pretty much eat whatever's put in front of me. We raised and killed hogs, and I love everything from the hog: souse, pig's feet, cracklin's. I really love menudo; there's lots of different ways to make it, but I don't like to fancy it up. I like the kind that just has the tripe in it. I like organ meats a lot, and I love brains and eggs. There's a place on Lower Broad in Nashville, Layla's Bluegrass Inn, that has the best hot dogs, that's some high-quality organ meat there. They taste like the ones I remember as a kid; you just can't get those anymore, like you can't get a good piece of bologna.

"There wasn't much game where I grew up, just squirrel and rabbit and maybe some birds. I like squirrel better than rabbit. Every once in a while I'll get a craving for squirrel so I'll go shoot me a couple, and then my momma will cook 'em. If it's a big ol' squirrel, you have to pressure cook 'em. My momma knows how to do it right."

When it comes to cooking, Too Slim defers to the singing cowboy's camp cook, Side Meat. Rider legend has it that way back during the Gold Rush in the Yukon, Meat had an unfortunate accident, slipping into an icy crevice where he was frozen solid for eighty years, until the Riders stumbled upon him on a Western trail ride and thawed him out. Meat's campfire skills earned him a bunk on the Rider's bus—it's the cowboy way, after all—and he's been repaying the favor with Momma Meat's recipes ever since. Bean soup and Bachelor Biscuits are a particular favorite.

Side Meat's Momma's Bean Soup

- 1 pound navy beans
- 1 meaty ham bone
- Two 15-ounce cans diced tomatoes
- 1 medium onion, diced
- 1 cup diced celery
- 2 bay leaves
- Salt and pepper to taste

Soak beans overnight; drain. Return to pot and add 6 cups of water. Add meaty ham bone, tomatoes, onion, celery, bay leaves, salt, and pepper; don't be stingy with the salt because that can cover up lots of bad things. Simmer on medium heat, covered, for 2 to 3 hours. Remove meat from bone, remove bone, give to good dog. Here's the secret to Momma Meat's Bean Soup: take 1 cup of soup and put in blender, blend it all up, then return to pot and stir it in for good body.

Bachelor Biscuits

- ¼ cup shortening
- 2 cups sifted all-purpose flour
- 1 cup milk

Cut shortening into flour, add milk, mix it together, but not too much. Be gentle on your biscuits. Drop by spoonfuls onto baking sheet, cook at 450° until golden brown. Serve Bachelor Biscuits with bean soup; use biscuits to sop the bottom of the bowl.

Joey The Cow Polka King's Slovenian Walnut Potica

Dough

1 tablespoon dry active yeast

¼ cup warm milk

1 teaspoon sugar

¼ cup butter

¼ cup sugar

¼ cup sour cream

3 egg yolks

4 cups all-purpose flour

8 ounces evaporated milk

Filling

¼ cup honey

¼ cup (4 tablespoons) butter

½ cup milk

2 cups granulated sugar

1 pound ground walnuts

½ lemon rind, grated

3 egg whites, whipped

1 tablespoon vanilla

Mix yeast, ¼ cup warm milk, and 1 teaspoon sugar and set aside until foamy.

Mix ¼ cup butter, ¼ cup sugar, sour cream, egg yolks, flour, and evaporated milk to make dough, then add yeast mixture. Set aside.

To make filling, mix honey, ¼ cup butter, ½ cup milk, and 2 cups granulated sugar in saucepan, heat gently until everything is melted, keep warm. Add ground walnuts, lemon rind, whipped egg whites, and vanilla, mix well. Add cinnamon and nutmeg to taste.

On a floured surface with a floured rolling pin, roll dough out very, very thin into a rectangle. Tradition calls for potica dough to be rolled so thin and wide a newspaper can be read through it. Gently spread filling onto dough. Roll up as for a jelly roll. Place in a greased loaf pan. Cover with towel and set aside in a warm place until it rises twice in size. Bake in 340° oven for 1 hour. Brush with salad oil. Let cool to room temperature, slice, and serve.

Aunt Margaret La Forest's Pasties

Filling

2 large potatoes, peeled and cut up into ½-inch cubes

½ small rutabaga, cut up into ½-inch cubes

I large onion, chopped

½ pound steak (sirloin or flank), cut in ½-inch cubes

I tablespoon ground beef suet in each pasty

Crust

2 cups flour

I teaspoon salt

½ cup (I stick) plus 2 tablespoons butter or margarine, chilled and cut into bits

Mix all filling ingredients together in a bowl. Set aside.

For crust, mix together flour and salt, cut in butter. Add ⅓ cup of very cold water a spoonful at a time to form a dough. Knead the dough lightly, then form a ball, dust with flour, wrap in waxed paper, and chill for about 30 minutes. Divide dough in half, then with floured rolling pin on floured surface, roll each half out to a circle about ¼ inch thick. Place half of filling in each circle of dough; fold dough over to close, sides touching. With moistened fingers, pinch to close, using fork to crimp along edge. With a knife make a slash on top so steam can escape while cooking. Place on a greased cookie sheet and bake in a 400° oven for 1 hour.

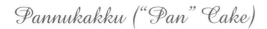

Pannukakku ("Pan" Cake)

3 eggs

3 cups milk

1¼ cups all-purpose flour

1 teaspoon salt

½ cup (1 stick) unsalted butter

¼ cup sugar

Sliced fresh fruit (optional)

Beat eggs on high speed with electric hand mixer until volume is nearly doubled; add ½ cup milk and continue beating on high 1 minute. Gradually add the remaining milk, flour, and salt and mix well until smooth and slightly thickened. Put 1 stick butter in 10- to 12-inch cast-iron skillet or other ovenproof pan. Place skillet in 450° oven until butter is melted and sizzling slightly. Remove carefully from oven and pour batter into pan. Return to oven for approximately 30 minutes. Remove from oven and allow top to settle. Sprinkle generously with sugar. If desired, add sliced fruit such as peaches or pears.

This dish can be served as a breakfast bread or dessert.

The Whites

(Buck, Cheryl, and Sharon White)

The Whites might never have come to be one of bluegrass music's favorite acts had it not been for a neighbor who—banjo in hand—knocked on their door shortly after they moved to Arkansas and asked Buck if it was true he played music. "Daddy said, 'Come on in,' and that was that," says Sharon.

Back in his hometown of Wichita Falls, Texas, Buck White—the son and grandson of plumbers—was a plumber by trade as well, but at night, he put his wrenches away and took out his mandolin, playing with a succession of bands. When he met his wife, Pat, he was a member of a three-piece, the Blue Sage Boys, who would play just about anywhere within a 120-mile radius.

Concerned about the impact such a schedule was having on his young family, Buck White moved them all to western Arkansas, where the intention was to give up performing and lead a quiet life in the country. But then opportunity knocked, and soon enough, Pat and Buck White had informally teamed up with Arnold and Peggy Johnston. The Down Home Folks—as they called themselves—jammed in the Whites' living room, recording tapes that they would take to nearby radio stations. As their music hit the air, requests for public appearances began coming in. "Mama didn't want to at first," Sharon tells. "She said singing in the living room was one thing, but singing onstage another. Daddy talked her into it, and once she did it, she loved it." The White girls weren't shy either; along with the Johnston children, they made up the Down Home Kids, and would sing a song or two during shows. Eventually, the four Whites, with a banjo player, began performing together, apart from the other family. Their first professional gig was in Walker, Louisiana, in 1967. "We knew it was professional 'cause we crossed a state line and they paid us!"

For some time, Buck and Pat pondered moving to Nashville, but Sharon and

Cheryl wanted to finish high school in Arkansas. In the summer of 1971, just before Sharon's senior year, the family was invited to Bill Monroe's Bean Blossom festival. "It was such an unforgettable experience, being around all of those performers. When we were asked to get up onstage, we were really well received, and for Cheryl and I, that was it. In the car on the way home to Arkansas, we told Mama and Daddy that if they were ready to go to Nashville, we were, too. Daddy didn't say anything, but when we pulled into the driveway at home, Daddy got out of the car, went into the garage, and came out a minute later with a For Sale sign that he tacked up in the front yard. Then we unloaded the car. That was in June of 1971, and by September, we were in Nashville."

Their reputation within the music industry grew, even as they continued touring the country, sometimes on the road for as long as a month at a time. In 1973, with two younger daughters—Rosie and Melissa—at home, Pat retired from the band to be with them. "She said to us, 'You go on, be blessed.' She was always so supportive and encouraging. It has always been a family effort, no matter who was on the road and who was at home." The Whites continued on, appearing on other artists' albums, making independent records, and touring with Emmylou Harris, which is where the courtship between Sharon and Harris's Hot Band member, Ricky Skaggs, took place. The two were married in 1981.

Though Sharon's vocal and musical gifts were unquestioned, her skills in the kitchen were lacking a bit, but then, so were Pat's when she and Buck first married. "Mama came from a big family. They were sharecroppers, they pulled cotton and worked very hard, but were really poor. They ate whatever they had on hand. Daddy's father and his grandfather were plumbers, but his great-grandfather was a cook and a pastry chef. He taught Great-Grandmother to cook, who taught Buck's mother. When Daddy and Mama got married, she was just seventeen, and she didn't know how to cook, so Daddy's mother taught her. All of the recipes we have are from Daddy's side of the family, and were passed down to my mother. When we were growing up, Mama gave us jobs to do in the kitchen. At first, it was just cleaning up and doing dishes, but as we got older, we did more. Cheryl made tea and set the table, and I peeled and mashed potatoes. Mama always made the meat. We had meat every night and it was always fried, so she made the gravy, too.

"When I got married, I made great mashed potatoes, but I couldn't make tea or meat or almost anything else. The first time I made gravy, I was scared to death. I called Mama and between her talking me through it, and me praying through it, I did it. But I never did learn to make biscuits!"

All the girls did learn to make a pot of pinto beans, a staple in the White household. "Mama made the best pinto beans. She cooked a pot about once a week and we'd have them with corn bread. When Ricky and I were dating and he was coming over for dinner, I told him we were having beans and corn bread and he said, 'No meat?' In his house, beans were a side dish; in our house, they were the main course!

"Mama always made her corn bread with a little bit of sugar, and it rose real high, almost like a cake. So that's how I made it, and Ricky used to wear me out about it. He said the only real corn bread was buttermilk corn bread. He had a whole routine he used to do onstage about teaching me to cook corn bread. I got the recipe off the Martha White sack and it made him happy."

Shortly after Pat White suddenly passed away on June 16, 2002—which even more sadly was Father's Day that year—daughter Cheryl remembers that she had to teach her father how to make a pot of pinto beans. "He called me on the phone and said, 'I'm sitting here looking at a sack of beans and as many times as I saw your mother make them, I have no idea how she did it.' Mama never wrote any of the recipes down, she just made what she knew. I told him how to do it, and he still makes a pot of beans every week. We think it's one of his ways of keeping her close. We did figure out how to make her corn bread dressing, and we still make that every holiday. She made the best, but we get pretty close. Ricky's favorite part was the part that cooked inside the turkey. We always had cranberry sauce, potato salad, Waldorf salad, giblet gravy, and sometimes fresh fruit salad with whipped cream and pecans. Passing down family recipes is the best way to keep memories alive."

Pat White's Pinto Beans

Pinto beans
Salt
Oil or bacon grease
Ham or ham bone (optional)

Pick through the sack of dry beans for gravel and bad beans. Put the sorted beans in a colander and rinse very well. Put in a large pot and add enough cold water to cover well. Bring to a good, strong boil. Lower heat, and continue to boil over medium heat. Cover pan, but with lid slightly ajar. Keep adding warm water as needed, cook for several hours, 4 or more, until beans are soft and broth is thick. Add salt to taste and a bit of oil or bacon grease. If you have a ham bone, or leftover ham, cut that up and add. Serve over corn bread.

Martha White®'s Southern Corn Bread

1 egg
1⅓ cups milk or 1¾ cups buttermilk
¼ cup vegetable oil or melted shortening
2 cups Martha White® Self-Rising Corn Meal Mix

Preheat oven to 450°. Grease a 9-inch cast-iron skillet or baking pan and place in oven to heat. Beat egg in mixing bowl. Add remaining ingredients; stir until smooth. (Batter should be creamy and pourable. If batter seems too thick, add a little more liquid.) Pour batter into prepared skillet or pan. Bake for 20 to 25 minutes or until golden brown. Makes 6 to 8 servings.

Patty White's Corn Bread Dressing

1 whole Turkey
1 loaf white bread
4 large onions
2 stalks celery
1 tablespoon Wesson oil

2 pans baked corn bread
6 hard-boiled eggs
Salt and pepper to taste
Ground sage
¼ cup white vinegar

Parboil turkey the night before in a large pot of water. Save water. Toast loaf of bread in oven. Dice onions and celery; sauté in large skillet in oil. Crumble corn bread and tear the toast into small, bite-sized pieces and mix together in large bowl. When onions and celery are translucent, add to bread mixture. Chop eggs finely and add. Add enough of reserved broth to make bread moist. Season to your taste with salt, pepper, and lots of ground sage. Grandma White taught Patty White to make the dressing, and she always put in some vinegar. No one knows what the vinegar does, but everyone is afraid to leave it out!

After all ingredients are mixed and you are happy with flavor, put the parboiled turkey and dressing in a large pan. Bake uncovered in a 350° oven until the turkey is brown and the dressing is done.

Lorrie Morgan

Joined the Opry cast in 1984

As one of the "Opry brats"—which is how Opry members and staff affectionately referred to the children of Opry stars who congregated on the sides of the Ryman stage while their parents performed—Lorrie Morgan lost count of the number of times she heard her father, Country Music Hall of Fame member George Morgan, croon his 1949 signature song, "Candy Kisses."

Lorrie, born Loretta Lynn Morgan, literally grew up backstage at the Opry, going with her dad on weekends back when it was at the Ryman. "It was so much fun. Not only getting to see all the big stars sing, but getting to hang out with the other kids and teenagers. Marty Stuart was so cute! I had lots of crushes back then. But as a child, the Opry was my family, and coming down to the Opry was just like going to see your family. That's what made me love it so."

Morgan made her Opry debut when she was just thirteen years old; she sang "Paper Roses," got a standing ovation from the audience, and a bucket of tears from her proud dad. "I knew then that was what I always wanted to do. I love the Opry. To me, it represents my dad and my childhood. And I'm so glad I got to be a part of it while it was still at the Ryman."

Otherwise, she and her father may never have stumbled upon another passion they shared: hot chicken. A dish with roots in the African American community, hot chicken is a product peculiar to Nashville. Though each establishment that specializes in hot chicken—some cooking it commercially for more than half a century—zealously guards their recipe, the common elements are lard and cayenne pepper. At Prince's Hot Chicken Shack, one of Nashville's longest-operating purveyors, breast quarters or leg quarters of chicken are dredged through a top-secret mix, then fried in large, ancient, black cast-iron skillets. The chicken comes in four degrees: mild is just a tad spicy, medium will raise your internal temperature a bit, hot will make you break out in a sweat, and extra-hot will set your tongue on fire

Lorrie Morgan.

and make smoke come out of your ears. "People say they like hot food, but they don't usually know what hot chicken is," says Lorrie.

After frying, the chicken is laid atop two slices of white bread to soak up the grease, which is an alarming russet shade thanks to the cayenne, and stabbed with a toothpick skewer of pickle chips to help soothe the burn.

George Morgan first discovered hot chicken simply by following his nose. "When he drove to the Opry on Saturday nights, he said he could smell something really wonderful but couldn't figure out where it was coming from. One night he was determined to find it and drove around until he stumbled upon it." He went in to Thornton's—which later became Prince's—at Seventeenth and Charlotte, and met Bolton Polk, who was manning the skillets, and later went on to open his own place, Colombo's Hot Chicken. George Morgan was hooked from his first bite of the fiery treat, and Lorrie remembers that every time they went to the Ryman, they would stop for some hot chicken. "How I feel about the Opry is sort of how I feel about hot chicken; it was something I did with my dad. The restaurant was segregated, but with a twist: the black customers ate in the front, and the white customers had to come in through the rear and eat in the back. I remember Mr. Bolton would always come out to say hello and give my dad a little something extra. It made you feel special."

One thing he did not give Lorrie Morgan, despite rumors to the contrary, is his recipe for hot chicken. Before his death in the early 2000s, Polk denied reports that he gave his recipe to George Morgan either, who died in 1975 when Lorrie was just sixteen. "George Morgan used to come by often to get hot chicken to take home, and he was a very nice man," Polk said. "I first met Lorrie when she was about eleven years old, and she's a very nice girl. But I didn't give my recipe to her daddy or to her and I won't sell it either."

Morgan says her father came up with his own recipe, which is the one she used when she and husband Sammy Kershaw had their own place, HOTChickens.com, about ten miles outside of Nashville. They offered six levels: plain, mild, medium, hot, extra hot, and Atomic Bomb. Her preferred level is hot, and she advises folks to stay away from carbonated beverages when eating hot chicken. "The bubbles kick up the heat level and you don't want that. When I'm having hot chicken, I always drink 2 percent milk with ice."

Several years ago, when fellow Opry member George Jones had a terrible car accident, she was among the friends who—in typical Southern tradition—brought home-cooked food to his house during his recuperation. Arriving at his front gate, she ran into Kershaw, whom she had known for years, but was not even dating at the time. "It was such a funny

Lorrie Morgan's first Opry appearance in 1973.

coincidence. He had a big bowl of crawfish, and I had brought chicken and dumplin's."

The recipe for this classic comfort food came from her father's mother, Ethel, who taught her mother, Anna, to cook, and is a staple in her repertoire of family recipes. "Every once in a while I get the urge to make it on the bus. Sometimes when you're out on the road, you just want a taste of home. It's easy to make, but hard to find the room on the bus to roll out the dough. But I'll tell you this, you definitely don't want to be eatin' hot chicken before you get on the bus!"

Ethel Morgan's Chicken and Dumplin's

2 to 3 pounds chicken thighs, bone-in, skin-on	3 cups all-purpose flour
6 chicken bouillon cubes	3 rounded tablespoons shortening
Salt	3 teaspoons salt (optional if on a
Pepper	low-sodium diet)
Crushed red pepper flakes	2 cups water

Put pot of water (about 6 cups) on the stove, add chicken thighs, and bring to boil. Add bouillon cubes, salt and pepper to taste, and a pinch of crushed red pepper flakes. Boil until bouillon cubes are dissolved, turn down heat, and simmer two hours.

Meanwhile, mix together flour and shortening with fingers to get a mealy texture. Add salt, if using, and mix thoroughly. Begin adding 2 cups of water a little at a time, mixing in until a dough is formed. Continue adding water until the dough is of a rubbery consistency and smacks back at you as you turn it. Flour your surface and rolling pin; roll out fairly thin. Cut into strips about 1 inch wide, then cut into 2-inch lengths.

Remove thighs from pot; keeping heat low, drop strips of dough into broth one at a time. Cook for approximately 15 to 20 minutes. When they drop to the bottom, they are done. Pour into bowl. Some people pull the meat off the thigh bones and put back into the broth, but I just like to serve the dumplin's with fried chicken.

Patty Loveless

Joined the Opry cast in 1988

Growing up in Pikeville, Kentucky, the daughter of a coal miner and a homemaker, the soundtrack to Patty Loveless' youth was the Appalachian music of the region, particularly the mountain bluegrass music of the Stanley Brothers, Lester Flatt and Earl Scruggs, and Bill Monroe, artists her father loved. She began listening to the Friday and Saturday night Opry when she was still a toddler, but her musical frame of reference also included the rock and roll records her older brother played.

Patty took her first stab at Nashville when she was just fourteen, and two years later, the Wilburn Brothers hired her to replace their "girl singer," Loretta Lynn. Her path to popular and critical acclaim was temporarily sidetracked when she married the Wilburn's drummer, moved to North Carolina, and with her husband, performed in several rock and roll bands. Neither the marriage nor that style of singing took, and Patty followed her heart back to Nashville, where she signed to MCA Records and made her mark on the country music scene at the time as a new traditionalist. It was that devotion to the true core of country that paved the way to Patty's induction as a member of the Opry in 1988. In 1989, she married renowned producer and musician Emory Gordy, Jr., and the two have collaborated on every musical project since. In 2001, she went back to her roots, paying homage to her Kentucky home and her father, with *Mountain Soul.* Her recordings since—*On Your Way Home* and *Dreamin' My Dreams*—have brilliantly blended her eclectic musical influences: bluegrass, honky-tonk, country, gospel, folk, and rock.

She and Gordy split their time between their country home outside of Atlanta—"It used to be in the boonies, but there is so much building going on that it's not anymore"—and a condo in Nashville, but when she wants to reconnect to her childhood, she doesn't have to go any farther than whatever kitchen she is in.

Mama had a lot of mouths to feed when we were kids. There were seven children, though my brother Roger says eight because of cousin Dixie. She came to live with Mama and Daddy when they were first married, and my oldest sister, Ruth, is so close to her. That's the way it was back then. You had a cousin show up, and next thing you know you were sharing a bed, making another place at the table, doing chores together. Back then, people didn't pick up a telephone. You went to visit, and then you stayed a while.

Patty remembers a hot breakfast of some kind every morning before school, oatmeal or "sweet rice," which was rice with sugar, cream, and a little bit of vanilla. But it was on weekends that her mother put out the breakfast spread, and Patty's favorite thing was tomato gravy. "Those breakfasts when we were all home together, the kitchen smelled so good. Those mornings are some of my most wonderful memories of family and food."

Patty Loveless.

When Patty makes a big breakfast, it includes tomato gravy, which is spooned over biscuits, hash browns, or her personal favorite, home fries. "People sort of raise their eyebrows when you offer them tomato gravy, but I've won over a lot of stomachs with it. Back when I was playing in rock and roll clubs, the whole band would come back to our place after the clubs closed, and the girls would make breakfast at three o'clock in the morning. My rock and roll friends called it pink gravy."

When she and Emory really want a country dinner, they make fried pork chops, black-eyed peas, and greens. "I mix up my greens; I use collard, mustard, and turnip. When I make beans, I try to make them healthy. Instead of fatback I use canola oil and bouillon cubes. I made some thataway for my mother without telling her, and she said they were the best beans she ever had. She didn't believe me when I told her how they were made!" The tomato gravy makes an appearance at their dinner table, too. "After I fry up the pork chops, I let them sit in a pan of tomato gravy. It makes the meat tender and adds a lot of flavor."

Patty Loveless' Tomato Gravy

¼ cup flour
¼ cup bacon or pork chop drippings
1½ cups tomato juice

½ cup milk
Salt
Pepper

In a cast-iron skillet over low heat, stir flour into bacon or pork drippings to make a paste. Mix tomato juice and milk together, then pour all at once into skillet. Add salt to taste and plenty of fresh-cracked pepper. Cook and stir over medium heat until the gravy thickens and starts to bubble up. Turn down heat and keep warm until ready to serve.

Alan Jackson plays to the balcony at Carnegie Hall during the Opry's special 80th Anniversary concert.

Alan Jackson

Joined the Opry cast in 1991

From 1989's tribute to his parents, "Home"—which Alan says is his favorite of the songs he has written—to the heartbreaking memorial to the events of September 11, 2001, "Where Were You (When the World Stopped Turning)," to "Remember When," a deeply personal and poignant look back at love and marriage, Alan Jackson consistently reveals himself as a man from a humble background who finds great relevance and importance in the simple things life brings.

Even his lighthearted tunes celebrate his affinity for the basics. Two from his album *When Somebody Loves You* make his culinary tastes clear: "Meat and Potato Man," written by Harley Lee Allen and John Pennell, and his own song, "Where I Come From."

> *Where I come from, it's corn bread and chicken*
> *Where I come from, a lotta front-porch sittin'*
> *Where I come from, tryin' to make a livin'*
> *And workin' hard to get to Heaven*
> *Where I come from*

Where Alan comes from—Newnan, Georgia—it is most definitely corn bread and chicken, meat and potatoes, and all of it preferably fried. He was raised on Mama Ruth's good, old-fashioned country cooking, and with four older sisters, there was little reason for Alan to ever go in the kitchen unless it was to dig around in the refrigerator for a jug of milk.

Even so, those close to him say that when he has a hankering for country food, and is far from home, he can cook up some mean fried corn bread and black-eyed peas on the bus.

One of his two favorite things to eat—the other being Brunswick stew—is pineapple and mayonnaise sandwiches: pineapple rings on white bread with mayonnaise. But it can't be just any mayonnaise. It has to be Blue Plate, which in some parts is considered the *only* mayonnaise worth having.

It wasn't until the mid-1920s that commercially made mayonnaise began to appear on market shelves; prior to that, it was made in home kitchens. In the late twenties, according to the New Orleans paper *Gambit Weekly,* a chemical engineer named J. B. Geiger, who was working for a subsidiary company of Wesson-Snowdrift Oil, was assigned to head the research team to begin producing mayonnaise. Within three years, a separate plant was up and running, with its own label, Blue Plate. In 1941, operations were moved to a newly constructed, art deco–designed facility in Mid-City, with a huge neon sign that quickly became a city landmark as Blue Plate mayo was establishing itself as a local treasure. In 1974, Blue Plate Foods—which also produced peanut butter, jams, and jellies—was purchased by Reilly Foods, another New Orleans tradition, the parent company for CDM coffee and Luzianne tea. Though Blue Plate has been made in Knoxville, Tennessee, since 2000, the sign survived Hurricane Katrina and remains a landmark in New Orleans, just as the product maintains its stature among fans as the South's best mayonnaise. Alan Jackson will accept no other, stocking it in his homes as well as on the bus.

When it comes to dining out, he is a man of predictable tastes, with little interest in experimentation. He likes his iceberg lettuce salad plain, with Catalina dressing, or sometimes O'Charley's honey mustard, though he is also fond of Olive Garden's bottomless salad bowls and breadsticks. When it comes to fast food, he likes an Arby's roast beef sandwich with Arby sauce and a chocolate shake; at Taco Bell, it's one bean burrito, one beef burrito, no onions.

When he finds himself in Los Angeles for television appearances, he is exclusively committed to Jerry's Deli and their Napoli pizza—extra sauce with sun-dried tomatoes is a bit of a stretch. But it was back to the basics when he was in Manhattan in November 2005 for the CMA Awards. Forsaking the veritable global market of culinary options available in what many consider the best food city in the world, Alan refused to take a bite of the Big Apple. Instead, bus driver Billy Jones was dispatched to find a jar of pimientos. When he finally hunted one down, and brought it back to the bus, Alan whipped up a batch of pimiento cheese, with Blue Plate mayo, of course.

Alan's Pimiento Cheese Salad

One 2-ounce jar diced pimientos
3 cups grated extra sharp cheddar cheese
¼ to ½ cup Blue Plate mayonnaise
Black pepper to taste (optional)

Smash pimientos and juice with a fork until blended. Add grated cheese. Add the Blue Plate mayo and mix well. (Use less or more for the consistency you prefer.) Add pepper to taste. Spread on crackers or white bread.

Catering Country Style

Monica Holmes, who started her Clean Plate Club catering company as a single mother on a song and a prayer in 1980, has a clientele that includes the upper echelon of Nashville society, top business groups, national and local politicians, community institutions, and some of country music's most recognized superstars. But way back when, much of her business came from providing meals at studios during recording sessions. Though she was eager to experiment and try new things, what she discovered was that country entertainers' tastes generally reflected their backgrounds. "They like good country cooking, like their mamas made. Maybe it's because they are on the road so much, but when they can get it, they like basic comfort food. Keep it simple. Because the same studio musicians tended to be hired over and over, I learned their tastes pretty well; the artists sometimes had special requests."

She remembers putting out a buffet for an Alan Jackson session at the Castle recording studio that was quite substantial, both in choice and type of food. "He came looking for me and asked me if I had any ketchup. I like ketchup as much as the next person, but I couldn't think of a single thing on the buffet that needed ketchup, so I hadn't brought any. I asked him what he needed ketchup for and he looked at me like I was a complete idiot. He said, 'The lima beans.' I said, 'No, I'm sorry. I have no ketchup.' He looked very disappointed. From that time on, I brought ketchup to every session that I catered. I figured you just could never tell what some people might put ketchup on."

Another early misjudgment she made was on a session for George Strait. "I made these beautiful big jumbo pasta shells stuffed with ricotta cheese and spinach. I saw him standing at the buffet and he looked disgusted. The woman in charge of hiring and booking the session, Jesse Noble, came over to me and whispered, 'He's a meat-and-potato kind of guy.' I've learned they pretty much all are."

There are exceptions to the meat-and-potatoes rule. When Reba McEntire started watching her weight, she specifically requested oven-fried catfish. Conway Twitty always asked for her chicken pot pie. And Vince Gill loves her chicken noodle soup.

Angie Reynolds, Grand Ole Opry interactive marketing manager, used to work for the Country Music Association, and was responsible for coordinating the photo shoot promoting Gill as the host of the annual awards telecast. As she remembers, "One day, the photo shoot took place during Fan Fair. I called Monica at Clean Plate Club to set up the catering for the day. When she faxed me over her menu suggestions, it included chicken noodle soup. I thought that was pretty strange for a hot, steamy day in June and asked if we could substitute it for something else. She insisted this was one of Vince's favorite dishes, so we left it in the menu. Sure enough, it was one of the first things Vince gravitated to. I had my doubts, not being a huge fan of chicken noodle soup, but I discovered just what Vince loved about it. Simple comfort food. It was definitely one of the favorite items of the day."

Clean Plate Club's Chicken Noodle Soup for the Country Soul

2 whole chickens

1 large sweet onion, preferably Vidalia, chopped

Half bunch of celery, chopped

3 or 4 medium carrots, chopped

White pepper

Thyme

Chicken base (sold in grocery stores in plastic jars, or in bouillons)

One 16-ounce package egg noodles, cooked and drained

1 bunch fresh parsley, chopped

Place 2 whole chickens in large pot, cover with water, simmer until done. After chickens cool down somewhat, take out of broth and refrigerate overnight. Cover pot of broth and refrigerate as well. The following day, carefully skim fat from top of broth and discard. Pull meat from bones and save. Discard bones. Put broth on stove to simmer; most likely you will need to add more water or canned chicken broth. Add chopped onion, celery, and carrots, simmer until they are no longer crunchy. Season with white pepper and chopped fresh thyme; add some chicken base. Stir; taste before salting because chicken base has lots of sodium.

After flavors are right, add chopped or torn chicken meat, and egg noodles. Before serving, chop one bunch of fresh parsley and add.

Vince Gill.

Vince Gill

Joined the Opry cast in 1991

More than any other contemporary member of the Grand Ole Opry, Vince Gill honors the heritage and history of the institution while encouraging its evolution as a vital and viable component of country music's modern era. Long before he was inducted in 1991, Vince was an avid fan and dedicated disciple of some of the Opry's most revered members, among them Chet Atkins, Roy Acuff, and Bill Monroe. His frequent appearances on the Opry are a labor of love, playing alongside some of his closest friends and fellow members, like Ricky Skaggs, Steve Wariner, Patty Loveless, Alison Krauss, Marty Stuart, and Del McCoury; trying out new material as he did when recording his most critically acclaimed album, 1998's *The Key;* performing more than forty times in a nine-month period in 1997 and 1998; or introducing stellar artists from other genres to Opry audiences. In February 2006, it was jazz singer-pianist Diana Krall, who had come to Nashville to record a duet with Vince for the new album he was recording. A fan of her music and playing, Vince met Krall backstage at a Grammy awards show some years before, and had always hoped they might one day record together. She was equally enthused by the proposition, and after Vince wrote "The Faint of Heart" with her in mind, she came to town with her husband, rock musician Elvis Costello. A lifelong fan of the Grand Ole Opry, Costello saw a dream come true when he was invited to appear in the seven to eight P.M. time slot with Emmylou Harris, Gillian Welch, and David Rawlings. On the last segment of the first show—Vince on guitar and Krall on piano—they debuted the new song, and were rewarded with a standing ovation from the packed house of the Ryman Auditorium.

By the time Vince moved to Nashville in 1983, he had already been on the road for nearly ten years. The constant touring not only honed his skills as a musician, the lifestyle helped develop another gift that has come in handy over the years: an intuitive knack for dining out. "I can pretty much go anywhere and pick out what will be the best thing on the menu," he says with his familiar self-deprecating laugh. "I don't think it's any secret that I am a serious student of eating. Some people eat to live and some people live to eat; I'm sorta right there in the middle."

Opry announcer Eddie Stubbs can attest to the fact that gasoline isn't the only fuel the entourage relies on. Stubbs, who emceed his first Opry show on June 23, 1995, and handles the last shift—10:30 P.M. until midnight—on Saturday nights, was the announcer on the Grand Ole Opry American Road Show tour. The package featured Gill, Patty Loveless, Del McCoury, and Rebecca Lynn Howard. For fifteen dates, Stubbs rode with Gill and his band, which is when the quick-witted singer nicknamed him Chubby; Stubbs, at six feet three inches and 140 pounds, almost disappears when he turns sideways. "The pantry of their bus was very well stocked," he says with gentlemanly understatement. "It was a little like a mobile convenience store. And after every show, hot food would be delivered to the bus—burgers, tacos, wings, pizza. I can't eat like that late at night. I took a lot of kidding because of my eating habits. I brought my own cereal on the bus, and whenever Vince caught me eating it, he'd tell the band they needed to get me some cheese and mayonnaise. It was on that trip that he started calling me Chubby; he does it onstage if I announce his portion of the show. For the obvious reasons, it gets a lot of laughs." Off the bus, from coast to coast, Vince finds what he likes, wherever he is, and then sticks to it. "In Oklahoma City, I go to Ted's Escondito, and get the shredded beef and cheese rellenos. They also make the best homemade flour tortillas. In New York, I only eat pizza, and I actually found a place called Vinny's that I really like. I also eat pizza in Chicago, at a place called Gino's. In L.A., it's gotta be Pink's, and I get their chili dog."

Closer to home, Vince tags some favorite Nashville places and the dishes that call his name. "We like Sportsman's Grille and their chicken tortilla soup. At Brown's diner it's the cheeseburger. The Palm downtown is great because it's right across the street from the Arena, so we go there before hockey games, or between shows when the Opry is at the Ryman. It's all about the steak and potatoes at the Palm, no need to mess with anything else. When I'm trying to watch my weight, I'll eat breakfast at Noshville and get some scrambled egg whites or an egg white omelet.

Otherwise, I'll do breakfast at the Pancake Pantry. I miss Joyce though [the retired thirty-plus-year veteran server of the legendary diner and favorite prenoon gathering spot for Music Row's power brokers]; she used to make toast especially for me, it was a sourdough toast that we called She-nay-nay toast, after Shania Twain: very desirable toast!"

Even more irresistible to Vince as a boy and young man were his grandmother's yeast rolls, a treat he feasted upon every time they went to visit her in Saint John, Kansas, about a four-hour drive from their home in Norman, Oklahoma. "Believe it or not, when I was a kid, I was so skinny my family either called me Bean Pole or Skelly, short for skeleton. I was a very picky eater. When we would go visit, she would cook everything, fried chicken, mashed potatoes, every kind of vegetable you can imagine. But I went straight to the yeast rolls. I could put some away. When my grandmother passed, the only thing I wanted of hers was the old green bowl that she always made those yeast rolls in."

Vince has the bowl, but his grandmother's recipe did not come with it. Shannon Lumpkin, who has been baking breads and desserts for various Nashville caterers for more than twenty years, always uses this recipe when she knows that Gill will be on site.

Vince's Favorite Yeast Rolls

2 packages active dry yeast
1½ cups, plus 2 tablesoons sugar
6 to 7 cups bread flour
1½ tablespoons salt
3 eggs

2 cups mashed potatoes
1½ cups butter or margarine
  (room temperature)
1½ cups potato water
½ cup milk

Preheat oven to 350° and butter a cookie sheet. Mix yeast, 2 tablespoons sugar, and ¾ cup warm water (between 105° and 115°) and let sit for 5 to 10 minutes.

In a mixing bowl combine 4 cups flour, 1½ cups sugar, and salt. In a heavy saucepan bring 1 quart of water to boil, add 4 medium potatoes (Yukon Gold) cut in a small dice; once the potatoes are very soft, drain off the remaining water but reserve it for use later. Mash the potatoes until there are no lumps, measure out 2 cups of mashed potatoes and add to the flour mixture. Take 1½ cups of the potato water you reserved and also add to the flour mixture. Add butter and begin mixing. Once the flour mixture starts to get moist, add the eggs, milk, and yeast mixture. This mixture will be very moist; slowly start to add the remaining flour until it starts getting a doughy consistency. Place dough in a buttered bowl and cover with a towel, allow dough to sit in a warm place. When dough doubles in size, pour dough out onto a floured board and roll out dough to about ¼ to ½ inch thick. Cut your rolls any size or shape you wish and place on buttered cookie sheet. Allow dough to rise again until the rolls have doubled in size, and bake in the oven for approximately 20 minutes or until rolls get brown on top. Brush with melted butter and serve.

Dough can be refrigerated overnight and used the next day.

Depending on size of rolls, makes approximately sixty 2-inch dinner rolls.

Marty Stuart and Connie Smith

Joined the Opry cast in 1992 and 1965 respectively

It was Opry star Goldie Hill, a Texas singer known in the 1950s as the Golden Hillbilly, who pinned a nickname on Marty Stuart that stuck. She called him Dandelion, "because he pops up everywhere." There are few other contemporary artists who have dug deeper into the roots of country music, studied its history more devotedly, paid homage to its legends more reverently, or painted his own career with a broader brush.

Stuart first popped up as something of an instrumental prodigy, renowned in his hometown of Philadelphia, Mississippi, for mature-beyond-his-years skill on stringed instruments. By the time he was twelve, he was playing mandolin on the road with the Sullivan Family Singers, a gig that led to a meeting with Roland White at a bluegrass festival in Indiana. White was the mandolin player with Lester Flatt's Nashville Grass; hearing the thirteen-year-old play, Flatt offered him a job as a rhythm guitarist. When White left the band, Stuart took his place on mandolin. After Flatt passed away, Stuart went on to play electric guitar with Vassar Clements in the group Hillbilly Jazz, acoustic guitar with Doc and Merle Watson, and played sessions on albums by Willie Nelson, Emmylou Harris, and Neil Young. In 1980, the versatile musician—he plays guitar, bass, mandolin, and fiddle—joined Johnny Cash's band, where he remained for six years, accepted as a member of the family even before marrying daughter Cindy Cash in 1983. Though they divorced in 1988, Stuart remained extremely close to Johnny and June until their deaths in 2003.

Connie Smith, a member of the Opry since 1965, had never aggressively sought the spotlight; after being talked into entering, and then winning, a talent contest at a music park in Columbus, Ohio, she met Bill Anderson, who subsequently invited her to Nashville to record some demos. Producer Chet Atkins, who had developed the Nashville Sound in the fifties, signed her to RCA Records in 1964. Her first single, "Once a Day," was penned by Anderson, and after climbing to the number 1

Connie Smith and husband Marty Stuart.

position on the country charts, it remained there for eight weeks. But even as she was being touted as "the next big thing," her heart was at home with the first of what would eventually be five children; Darren was just two when her record hit. Though she enjoyed a successful recording career, earned the respect and admiration of her peers and critics, and toured for another fifteen years, she never was comfortable being away from her children. She left the life in 1979, though she returned to performing on the Opry in 1985, when her youngest started kindergarten. When the last of her children left home more than a decade later, she decided to go back in the studio again and make a record, which was when she turned to her friend Marty Stuart.

Marty and Connie had met in 1970 when Stuart attended one of her shows. He was twelve and instantly infatuated, and vowed he would marry her one day. When their paths crossed again years later, they became friends, and he seemed the logical choice to produce her comeback album for Warner Bros. They wrote nearly forty songs together, and somewhere in the process the professional partnership turned personal. On July 7, 1997, they wed, and have been inseparable since.

Along with producing his wife's album, in the past two decades Dandelion has popped up just about everywhere: on mainstream country radio as a solo artist and with his friend Travis Tritt; at the podium as a four-time Grammy winner; exploring the sources of country music through the acclaimed concept album *The Pilgrim;* in the studio as a producer; at the helm of the Country Music Hall of Fame and Museum's board of directors; as an author for *Oxford American* magazine; looking through the viewfinder at friends Bill Monroe, Johnny Cash, Merle Haggard, and others, whom he

Alison Krauss

Joined the Opry cast in 1993

What's the difference between a fiddle and a violin? Alison Krauss, who began studying classical violin when she was just five years old, answered that question when she first heard and fell in love with bluegrass music. From that moment on, her violin became a fiddle, and a pickin' prodigy was born. She began entering talent contests when she was eight, had her own band at ten, and at twelve won her first state fiddle championship, leading the Society for the Preservation of Bluegrass Music in America to name her the Most Promising Fiddler in the Midwest. By fourteen, she had a contract with Rounder Records, launching her recording career three years later with her well-received 1987 solo album *Too Late to Cry,* backed up by her band Union Station. The follow-up album, *Two Highways,* was a group effort, and was nominated for a Grammy in 1989 for Best Bluegrass Recording. The next album, *I've Got That Old Feeling,* received the first of a record-setting twenty Grammys she earned over the next fifteen years as a solo artist, a group member, and a producer.

She and Union Station made their Opry debut that same year; her poised and guileless performance won the seventeen-year-old Krauss the respect of Opry veterans and the adoration of the audience. Union Station's spectacular musicianship hearkened back to the days of the Opry's most legendary bluegrass performers. In 1993, when Alison joined the cast, she was the first bluegrass artist inducted in twenty-nine years, and the youngest cast member at the time. On the night of her induction on July 3, 1993, just twenty days shy of her twenty-second birthday, her parents, Fred and Louise Krauss, and grandmother Ruth Rigotti were in the wings. They and everyone in the Grand Ole Opry House that night were thrilled when country superstar and 1990 Opry inductee Garth Brooks came onto the stage to welcome the newest member to the family. Just as meaningful to Krauss were these words written on that night's printed program: "Alison Krauss is a fine singer and she really knows how to play bluegrass music like it should be played. Alison will be a wonderful addition to the Grand Ole Opry." The testimony came from the Father of Bluegrass, Bill Monroe.

Though she first gained acclaim as an instrumentalist, it is her delicate yet emotionally rich soprano that sang its way into the hearts of more mainstream music fans. *Now That I've Found You: A Collection* made bluegrass sales history when it was certified double platinum for more than two million sales. Her work on the soundtrack for the 2000 film *O Brother,*

Alison Krauss. *Where Art Thou?* brought her, and Union Station member Dan Tyminski,

even greater exposure, and she has been in demand for movie soundtracks since. Her collaboration with rock musician Sting on "You Will Be My Ain True Love," one of two tracks she recorded for the 2003 film *Cold Mountain,* earned her first Oscar nomination for Best Song.

Though Krauss has lived in the South for more than half her life, she was born and raised a Yankee in Champaign, Illinois. Her recipe for Pretty Good for a Yankee Chicken Pot Pie is typically modest in its description, and she notes, "This is what I would make if Larry Sparks came to dinner." Sparks, a fiercely independent bluegrass singer and guitar stylist, calls himself "the youngest of the old-timers." A fellow Yankee, he and Krauss have performed on the Grand Ole Opry together, and he was her musical guest at the National Academy of Recording Arts and Sciences honors dinner in 2005 when she received a Musical Achievement Award. Introduced by Dobro master and Union Station Band member Jerry Douglas as "one of Alison's favorite singers," the two-time winner of the International Bluegrass Music Association's Male Vocalist of the Year prize sang the bluegrass standard "Doin' My Time," which Krauss had requested. "I never thought I'd ever do anything like this," said Krauss as she accepted her award. "I never thought I'd do this for a living."

Pretty Good for a Yankee Chicken Pot Pie

1½ boneless, skinless chicken breasts, boiled and cut into bite-sized pieces
1 can cream of chicken soup (undiluted)
1 can (use soup can) buttermilk
1½ teaspoons Better Than Bouillon chicken base
1¼ teaspoons black pepper
4 tablespoons (½ stick) unsalted butter, melted
One-half 15-ounce can young peas, drained
1 cup carrots, cut into bite-sized pieces (not diced) and boiled until tender
3 Idaho baking potatoes, cut into bite-sized pieces and boiled until tender
1 cup broccoli, steamed
1 Pillsbury refrigerated pie crust

Preheat oven to 350°. Mix all the ingredients (except the pie crust) in a large bowl. Pour mixed ingredients into a 9-by-13-inch casserole. Unfold the pie crust and cut the ends off to make it a rectangle. Place pie crust over the casserole, using pieces that were cut to cover the ends of the casserole. Bake for about an hour (might need more time, depending on your oven) until the crust is golden brown.

Martina McBride at legendary Carnegie Hall.

Martina McBride

Joined the Opry cast in 1995

Martina McBride is an award-winning certified superstar, but few accolades have meant more to her than her induction into the Grand Ole Opry on November 30, 1995, particularly when the honor was bestowed by none other than Loretta Lynn, who had preceded her into the august body thirty-three years before. "I have always admired her straightforwardness and courage. She agreed to induct me at a time that was personally very hard for her. Doo was very sick, so I was surprised and touched that she would come into Nashville and be a part of my special night." Though McBride was inducted by Lynn, that night she performed a signature song by one of Loretta's most beloved friends, Patsy Cline. "I sang 'Crazy,' which seemed fitting because Patsy and Loretta had been such close friends. In a way, it was paying tribute to someone who meant a lot to both of us, but couldn't be there."

McBride has always been an involved hands-on mom to her three daughters. A busy family life with husband John and the demands of a successful career keep her from the Opry all but a few times a year, but every time is special. "It is a privilege and an honor to play the Opry. It's an institution that has stood the test of time because of the music, and because of the heart and soul of the people there. Whenever I perform there, it always feels like the first time. I still get nervous."

Since the girls started school, Martina limits much of her touring to summer months, when the entire family can hit the road, bunking up in the bus, which provides most of the comforts of a home, though in a much smaller space. One thing everyone—family and extended family—misses after a while is a good, home-cooked meal.

Sometimes when you are out playing the fair circuit, catering leaves a bit to be desired! We had a particularly bad string of catering a couple of years ago; four shows in a row with basically horrible food! Now, I don't know about anyone else, but I feel that catering and the quality of the food is important on the road. Sometimes there are days when there is really nothing to do and you are kind of out in the middle of nowhere, and sitting down to a good, hot, healthy meal with your family, band, and crew is something you really look forward to. So after the fourth bad meal in a row, I decided to take matters into my own hands and cook for my band and crew. I guess it's the mother in me, but I feel like they work so hard all day and it's important that they have a good meal. Anyway, I have a cooktop on the bus so I made chili for everyone. It was quite a sight to see, all the guys lined up inside and outside the bus, bowls in hand, ready for their ladle full of chili! We had our own little soup kitchen going! They were all very grateful for the hot chow and I felt like I had really done something to take care of them. We have done this more than once over the years. I always make sure I have a cooktop on my bus for just such an occasion.

Martina's Bus Stop White Chili

3 to 4 boneless, skinless chicken breasts
Two 14½-ounce cans chicken broth
1½ teaspoons white pepper
1 teaspoon garlic powder
3 tablespoons vegetable oil
Two 15-ounce cans great northern beans
Two 4½-ounce cans chopped green chilies
One 10½-ounce can cream of chicken soup
3 tablespoons (or less, to taste) jalapeño pepper juice
2 tablespoons minced fresh cilantro
1 teaspoon salt

Garnish
6 to 8 flour tortillas (6 inch)
1 cup sour cream
1½ cups (6 ounces) grated mozzarella cheese

To cook chicken breasts, I put them in a glass baking dish, pour in 1 can of Campbell's chicken broth, cover the dish with tinfoil, and bake them at 350° for about an hour. Remove chicken from baking dish, reserve broth. Cut chicken into small pieces and season with white pepper and garlic powder. Sauté chicken in oil in stockpot for 2 to 3 minutes. Add great northern beans, reserved chicken broth plus second can, green chilies, cream of chicken soup, jalapeño pepper juice, fresh cilantro, and salt, and bring to a boil. Reduce heat and simmer for 30 minutes.

To serve, cut tortillas into ¼-inch strips. Place tortilla strips in individual serving bowls with strips extended beyond edges. Ladle chili into bowls. Garnish with sour cream and cheese if desired.

Steve Wariner

Joined the Opry cast in 1996

Well before he ever moved to Nashville, Steve Wariner was a member of the Nashville Country Club, which was not exactly a country club, and definitely not in Nashville. In reality, it was a country music club on the west side of Indianapolis where Wariner—who was still in high school in his hometown of Noblesville, Indiana—was playing on weekends. A tour stop for nationally known acts, the NCC was presenting Dottie West one such weekend that Wariner was playing, and after catching his performance, the star country vocalist invited him to sit in with her band. Little did he know it was an audition, and right afterwards, she offered him a job as her bass player. "I was a senior in high school, and was on winter break at the time, so I went back and worked it out with my teachers so I could do it. Looking back, I can't believe my parents let me go!"

Off he went, doing homework and keeping up with assignments backstage and on the bus; he got his diploma, but rather than walking across his high school stage to "Pomp and Circumstance," he graduated on the road, playing West's huge hit "Country Sunshine" on stages all over the country.

It was with West that he first appeared on the Grand Ole Opry, which was nearing the end of its thirty-one-year tenure at the Ryman. Due to West's issues with punctuality, he nearly missed his own debut. "Because it was going to be my first time, Dottie told me to come to her house and we'd ride down together. It was a Saturday night show, and I was so nervous and excited I could hardly stand it. We jumped in her white Cadillac and were flying down Belmont Boulevard; she was always running late. She had WSM on the radio and just as we pulled into the alley behind the Ryman, the announcer was saying, 'And now, here's a lady from McMinnville, Tennessee, Dottie West!' Somebody was standing at the back door waiting on her and pulled her inside, but I was left standing there with my bass, no idea where to go or where to plug in. I remember running past Marty Robbins and Minnie Pearl. I was so scared that first time."

The Opry stage came to be a second home of sorts for the talented young musician, who began playing bass for Opry member Bob Luman when he was just twenty-two; it was Luman who not only encouraged Wariner in his dream to be a solo artist, but nudged his song-writing efforts along.

In 1977, Luman had plans to record an album for Epic Records that would be produced by his good friend and neighbor Johnny Cash. "We were playing Faron Young's club on Lower Broad in Nashville one night and Johnny and June came in and sat in with us. The place went crazy. I'll never forget it. A few weeks later, we went in the studio and I was so nervous because I had some songs that Bob wanted to cut, but I was sure that Cash would throw them out. So we played the first one for him, "Labor of Love," and after he listened, he says in that deep voice, 'I like this real well. We'll cut it.' He liked every one of the songs; they were the first songs I had written that I ever had cut; I started my publishing company, Steve Wariner Music, with those four cuts. I remember Waylon ended up coming in on those sessions. What a time that was."

Steve Wariner.

Session player Paul Yandell passed some of Wariner's music on to guitar maestro, producer, and label head Chet Atkins, who signed him to an artist contract at RCA. "I played the Opry with Chet quite a bit, and once I started to have some success with some singles, I played on my own, but I wasn't asked to join until 1996. I was out there one night playing, and Bob Whitaker, who was the manager at the time, pulled me into dressing room number 1 and asked if I'd like to become a member. It meant a lot to me, partly because of what the Opry meant to my mom and dad. You don't hear it so much anymore from new artists, but it was true in my case;

we used to listen to it together on the radio on Saturday nights. I was so excited I couldn't hold it in, so I found Skaggs and told him. I was playing with him that night, and while we were singing, Sharon [White] leaned over and whispered, 'Welcome home.' It felt so good. The night I was inducted, I had Chet playing with me, and I was sorta goin' on and on, I said, 'I'll always make you proud of me.' And about then Chet leans over and says, 'I think it's time to sing now.' When I walked offstage I saw my dad standing in the wings talking with George Jones and Chet; it was so cool. They had a little celebration for me backstage. Little Jimmy Dickens was the first to congratulate me, and Jean Shepard. It means so much to have worked with all those people. What I love these days is the mix of the old and the young, the legends and the new artists."

Just as Dottie West, Bob Luman, and Chet Atkins did for him, Wariner is mentoring a new generation of musicians; sons Ryan and Ross have both been bitten by the music bug, and avail themselves of the studio Wariner built a few years ago on his property. In 2005, songwriter Rick Carnes invited Wariner to check out a young trio at a writers' night in town. "They blew me away, their songwriting is so good, and their harmonies are great, I knew I wanted to work with them. So we went into my home studio and cut some acoustic stuff. Tim DuBois [then president of Universal South Records] called me and said that he had heard we had some stuff he needed to hear. We played it for him, and he flipped. He gave us a budget and we went back in the studio." Shortly after, DuBois and Tony Brown signed Alvarado Road Show to the label, with Wariner at the helm of the project. "This is my first foray into producing. Being around Chet like I was made such an impression on me, seeing how he was in the studio. I've always seen him as a role model, both as a guitarist and a producer, he produced so many great records. I've always loved the studio; even as a young kid I was a studio rat. I'm just where I want to be right now, doing things that make me smile."

Wariner doesn't often find himself in the kitchen, noting that wife Caryn is a great cook, but when he does, it's usually to make this cherry pie, a recipe he got from his aunt Doris.

Steve Wariner's Luscious Cherry Pie

Two 1-pound cans pitted, tart red cherries, drained
(in season, use 1 quart fresh pitted red cherries)
1¼ cups sugar
2½ tablespoons flour
¼ teaspoon salt
Pastry for 2-crust 9-inch pie

Mix together cherries, sugar, flour, and salt. Spoon into pastry-lined pie plate. Roll out remaining pastry, cut into ½-inch-wide strips. Interlace strips in crisscross fashion over filling to make lattice top. Trim strips even with pie edge. Turn bottom crust up over ends of strips. Press firmly to seal edge. Flute edge.

Bake in 450° oven 10 minutes. Reduce heat to 350° and bake 30 minutes or until golden brown and filling is bubbly. Cool on rack. Makes 6 to 8 servings.

Tips from Steve Wariner on the perfect lattice top:
- I roll the dough into an oval, a little larger than the bottom
- Dust with flour so it isn't sticky
- Using a pastry jagger, cut 10 strips (I like to cut about ¾" each)
- Some use a ruler to score, but I eyeball it
- Start laying strips according to diagrams, then continue back and forth
- When finished, I use water on my fingers to smooth down strips or repair any rip

Pam Tillis with her father, Mel.

Pam Tillis

Joined the Opry cast in 2000

Pam Tillis' Grand Ole Opry debut took place on the historic Ryman Auditorium stage, singing "Tom Dooley" with her father, Mel Tillis. She was just eight years old, but already studying classical piano, and resolutely determined to follow the path her father had forged. Mel, an aspiring songwriter, moved his young family from Pahokee, Florida, to Nashville in the late fifties; he brought his baby girl along with him on writing sessions, using an empty guitar case as a "hillbilly crib" according to family lore. As Mel's career as a writer and entertainer took off, other songwriters and singers were frequent guests in the Tillis home, and Pam gravitated to music like a moth to the flame, grabbing a chance to perform wherever she could: school contests, summer camp musicals, and self-produced and -directed home garage shows, which always starred Pam.

But music was not the only family passion. "Food has always played a very prominent role in my family," she says. "The kitchen is the center of everything. That's part of the culture of the South, where food isn't seen as a necessity but a lifestyle. We're either planning and cooking the meal, eating the meal, or talking about what the next meal will be. That makes us happy. In my family, it's not unusual to call each other up to chat and the first question is, 'What did you fix for dinner tonight?' A perfectly acceptable gift is a bag of okra frozen out of the garden. I'll go visit my aunt and on the way out, she's handing me bags of vegetables, saying, 'You'll want to take this with you.' Well, of course I do!"

The love of food and cooking is in the Tillis family blood. "My grandfather was a baker. When he was asked one time what his idea of happiness was, he answered, 'Five good laying hens and my own bakery.' Eventually, he did get his own bakery. After my father got out of high school, he wanted to be a pilot, so he enlisted in the service. He was turned down for flight school, and when he took an aptitude test, it showed he was best suited to be a baker!"

It was after getting out of the service that Mel came to Nashville, and when he snagged a fifty-dollar-a-week writing job, his baking skills were put on a back burner professionally, but frequently called upon in the family home.

"My dad is a really excellent cook, but he's a better baker. My mom has always been the day-to-day cook; there were five children in the family and my father was on the road quite a bit. My mom was just seventeen when they married, and my dad's mother taught her to cook. You know, both my parents are painters, and their styles are reflected in their cooking. Dad is very much the realist, he is very precise, it's all about the measuring, the temperature, the time, that's what baking is all about. My mother is an impressionist, she loves to experiment, she doesn't color in the lines! I know lots of chefs like to claim this, but it was actually my mother who invented nouvelle Southern cuisine, at least in our house."

The name of Pam's publishing company, Mystic Biscuit, was in fact inspired by Doris Tillis. "Whenever my mother would make biscuits, they would start out as regular biscuits, then she would cut up some fresh rosemary from her garden and put that in the dough. Or she might brush the tops with melted butter and dill. There was always something unique and creative about everything she cooked."

Pam's touring schedule keeps her out of the kitchen, but when she is off the road, that is frequently where she'll be found, with friends and family. "When I'm at home, I like to cook every meal, not just dinner, but breakfast and lunch, too. A bowl of cereal is *not* breakfast. And I like to cook with people; it's not a chore, it's a social occasion. Some of my closest friends are people I cook with. My friend Callie Khouri [screenwriter of the 1991 movie *Thelma & Louise*] and I would come home from a late night out and decide to bake cookies. I love to get in the kitchen with friends."

She knew early on that her son Ben has the gift. "When he was just six years old, he had some friends over to spend the night. They got up early the next morning, before I did, and Ben decided to make breakfast. He made scrambled eggs, which I thought was pretty good for a six-year-old. But when I was cleaning up the kitchen, on the counter I found the evidence of fresh-chopped herbs that he had used for the eggs. Now that's a chef! One of the first times he came home from college to visit, I asked him what he wanted to do, and he said, 'I want to cook you dinner.' I'm just so glad to know that it's something he enjoys."

Though her children and grandchildren are scattered about, Doris Tillis still cooks the family holiday dinners, and Georgia ham is a favorite. True to her impressionist style, Doris took a recipe and made it her own. "For several years, my father performed at campaign fund-raisers for a Georgia congressman. My mother would go down with him, and got to know the congressman's wife. She told my mother how to make this Boston butt ham. Then my mother came up with the idea of adding the pastry and making a ham Wellington. When she gave me the recipe, the dough was pretty free-form, a little of this, a pinch of that. I called my friend Lona Hines, who went to Culinary Institute of America, to help me figure out the pastry. What she and I came up with is a little bit more rustic type of bread. I called my mother up to tell her we had succeeded in making it, but that we had used a bread-making machine to do it. Technology is a great thing, but cooking together, sharing food, that is our heart. Recipes are more than directions for cooking something; passed from one person to another, they are part of our history, our family lore. There are dishes that provoke thoughts of particular occasions or honor a person's memory. They are love."

Doris Tillis' Georgia Ham

This is a Boston butt wrapped "en croute" or in crust. I added the au jus as my own touch—you could thicken this for more gravy. Feel free to vary it as everyone before you has done! It's also fantastic with mint jelly on the side or a mango chutney.

   Note: *Read recipe through before cooking as it is multiple steps.*

Roast

5½ pound Boston butt ham (if smaller, adjust proportions accordingly)

2 teaspoons whole cloves

1 teaspoon black peppercorns

2 bay leaves

Put ham in stockpot and cover with water seasoned with cloves, peppercorns, and bay leaves. Boil for 30 minutes, then reduce heat and simmer low. Check at 2 hours; temperature should reach 175°. Remove from heat. Reserve liquid for au jus.

Dough

1 package yeast (fast acting)	¼ cup flour, plus 1 tablespoon more
¼ teaspoon salt	2¼ cups flour

Prepare an hour or so before the roast is done. Mix yeast, salt, ¼ cup water, and ¼ cup flour thoroughly in mixing bowl till spongy. Then sprinkle 1 tablespoon flour on top. Set in a warm, draft-free spot (the oven works well—don't turn it on!). This will double in approximately 30 minutes. Transfer to bread mixer. Add an additional 2¼ cups flour and a little over ¾ cups water. Knead with dough hook until shiny, slightly sticky, not a tight or stiff dough. Transfer to a floured counter and roll to ½ inch thick, roughly large pizza size. Put on a large baking sheet and lay cooked roast on top. Rub the top and sides of roast with the sage-garlic rub.

Sage-garlic Rub

1 ounce sage, stems removed
4 large cloves garlic, minced in food processor
3 tablespoons butter

Sauté sage and garlic in butter for 5 minutes and set aside. Salt and pepper roast well. Pull dough over top of roast and pinch edges to enclose. Bake at 400° for 15 to 18 minutes, till dough is a light golden brown. Take out and brush with melted butter. Can dust with paprika if desired.

Au Jus

While cooking the dough-wrapped ham, reduce reserved liquid by at least half. Salt and pepper to taste and serve on the side.

PAM TILLIS' OPRY INDUCTION PARTY MENU
August 26, 2000

Domestic and imported cheeses garnished with fresh fruit, bread
   sticks, lavash, and gourmet crackers
Assorted finger sandwiches
Lobster medallions with tarragon honey mustard mayonnaise
Pepper beef and Boursin cheese on sourdough crouton
Tomato-basil crostini
Toasted five-cheese ravioli
Vegetable spring rolls with English mustard
Mini chicken Oscar
Chocolate cake with raspberry filling
Assorted truffles and chocolate-covered strawberries

Brad Paisley.

Brad Paisley

Joined the Opry cast in 2001

When Brad Paisley was inducted into the Grand Ole Opry on February 17, 2001, he wore his heart on the sleeve of the bright yellow jacket that the late Buck Owens wore to perform at Carnegie Hall in 1966, as captured on the cover of the acclaimed *Live at Carnegie Hall* album. Paisley's reverence for traditional country music and its iconic artists is well known and utterly genuine, nurtured at a young age, first by his grandfather, a fan of masterful guitarists Merle Travis, Chet Atkins, and Les Paul. Paisley got his first guitar from his grandfather—a picker himself—when he was just eight years old. A quick study, he began performing in public two years later, and writing songs when he was twelve, which led to his participation as a regular on the famed Saturday night Jamboree USA radio show at nearby Wheeling's WWVA radio station. It was there that he was first exposed to Grand Ole Opry members and legends, opening shows for his personal heroes, including Roy Clark, Jack Greene, and Little Jimmy Dickens.

Paisley came to Nashville to attend Belmont University's noted music business program, but it was a week *after* graduation that he received the diploma he craved, signing a songwriting deal at EMI Music Publishing. His unique vocals on the song demos he was cutting led to his deal with Arista Records, which in 1999 resulted in his first number 1 single as an artist and a writer. "He Didn't Have to Be" was co-written with close friend Kelley Lovelace, whom he met at Belmont. The song helped drive his first album, *Who Needs Pictures,* to platinum.

It also gave him access to the stage of the Grand Ole Opry, where he made his debut on May 28, 1999. There, he renewed friendships with old buddies Jack Greene and Little Jimmy Dickens, and forged new relationships with other members of the Opry. He had logged more than forty appearances there when he was inducted in 2001; a letter from George Jones that was read during his introduction as the newest Opry member said, "I am counting on you to carry on the tradition."

Paisley has done just that, personally and professionally honoring those who came before him, by blending traditional influences into the new songs he writes; reintroducing old classics like the Vern Gosdin hit "Is It Raining at Your House"; recording, with fellow Opry member Alison Krauss, "Whiskey Lullaby," a song co-written by longtime Opry member Bill Anderson; and following that up with the duet "When I Get Where I'm Going" with another traditionalist, Dolly Parton.

And then there's his relationship with the Opry's longest-tenured member, Little Jimmy Dickens, who has played roles in multiple Paisley videos, as well as taped appearances on Paisley's concert tours. It is a friendship that bonded at a pond in Alabama, at the end of three fishing poles.

When I first came to Nashville, I wanted to go fishing with Little Jimmy. I have always been a big fan of his, and I knew he liked fishing. I was brand-new as a singer in town then, but I figured it wouldn't hurt to ask, all he could say was no, so when I met him backstage at the Opry, I did, and he said, "Well, yes, I'd like that. Why don't you call me?" And gave me his number. My friend Kelley's in-laws, Faye and Dub Smith, live just over the Tennessee border in Alabama, and have a farm pond. That's where we go a lot; you can catch hundreds of fish 'cause it's so well stocked, it's almost cheating. So I called Jimmy and asked him if he wanted to take a ride down there with us, and he said sure, how about Monday morning. We said fine, we'd pick him up at seven. So Kelley and I are driving out to his place in the truck and it's about five to seven, and there he is, standing out by his mailbox, with two fishing poles in one hand and a tackle box in the other. He was wearing an orange cap and he looked just like Elmer Fudd. Kelley says, "Well I'll be, there he is." We pulled up, he got in the truck and we talked all the way down. He was real nice and so funny.

There were two reasons I wanted to do this. One was 'cause I really wanted to go fishing with him, and two, so Faye and Dub could meet him. They are just real nice, country people and have always been Opry fans. Their absolute favorite is Little Jimmy; they had their picture taken with him backstage one time. Kelley and I decided to surprise them and not let them know we were bringing him with us. We just called and told them we were coming down to fish.

Every time we go down there to fish, Faye just goes to town, mak-ing us the most wonderful food, everything you can imagine. It's like a holiday spread. Most of the stuff we eat they grow right there.

When we pulled up they both came out of the house and he got out of the truck and it was so great to see their faces. Dub just says, "It's Little Jimmy Dickens!" So we go fishing like we always do. The pond is within sight of the house. What always happens is Faye comes out on the porch and calls down to the pond, "Kelley, it's ready. Y'all want to come eat?" It's the greatest day in the world. You fish all day, you eat twice, and then you take leftovers home.

There is a lot of truth to Paisley's wry song, "I'm Gonna Miss Her (The Fishing Song)"; the hobby is his passion. "It's about being on a boat with someone you like doing something you love. A bad day fishing is still a good day. Fishing with Little Jimmy Dickens is always a good day."

Faye and Dub (short for the initials of his given name, D.W.) Smith live on a farm atop Sand Mountain, Alabama, and from Faye Smith's kitchen come some of his favorite meals. "When Brad and Kelley are com-ing down to fish, Brad always wants to know if Faye has the pork chops ready," Dub says. "That's his favorite thing. She really puts out a spread, pork chops with gravy, corn, mashed potatoes, slaw, green beans, macaroni and cheese, and of course, banana pudding."

Faye Smith's Fried Pork Chops and Gravy
Brad's favorite fishin' supper

2 or 3 pounds pork chops, bone in	Pepper
Flour	Shortening
Salt	Two 10½-ounce cans cream of chicken soup

Melt shortening in cast-iron skillet to cover bottom. Dredge pork chops through flour, salt, and pepper. Fry in shortening until golden brown, turn to brown other side, cook until done. Remove chops from skillet. Drain shortening from pan, but do not rinse. Pour cream of chicken soup into skillet; fill both cans with water and add. Bring to a boil, stirring with a wire whisk until smooth. Return chops to pan; lower heat and simmer all until chops are tender. Serve with pan gravy.

BRAD PAISLEY'S OPRY INDUCTION PARTY MENU
February 17, 2001

Because Brad Paisley was inducted during the winter season of the Opry, when it is staged at the Ryman Auditorium, Brad's party was held just across the back alley at Jack's Bar-B-Cue where there was more room.

Pork, turkey, and beef barbecue with buns, hot and mild sauces
Baked beans
Potato salad
Coleslaw
Fountain drinks, coffee, sweet and unsweetened tea
Chess and chocolate fudge pies
Decorated cake

Trace Adkins

Joined the Opry cast in 2003

Trace Adkins has torn it up on the football field, lost a finger in an industrial accident, was a pipe fitter on an offshore oil rig, received severe facial injuries in an auto accident, had his leg crushed by an exploding four-hundred-barrel oil tank, and survived a bullet through his heart and lungs. But the six-foot-six iron man is such a big softie that on the night in 1996 that he made his debut on the Grand Ole Opry, he brought his girlfriend Rhonda onstage, got down on one knee, and made a very public and heartfelt proposal. To the delight of the crowd, she said yes, and one year later, they were wed on the lush green grounds of one of the South's most historic properties, Nashville's Belle Meade Plantation. After they exchanged vows and rings, Adkins serenaded his bride with "The Rest of Me," a tender tune he had just written with guitarist Kenny Beard.

On August 23, 2003, when he was inducted into the Grand Ole Opry by Ronnie Milsap, he and Rhonda had been married seven years, had two little girls, and a third on the way. Time for the seven-year itch? Hardly. Once again, Adkins wore his heart on his sleeve, singing "Then They Do," the poignant tale of children growing up and going off in the blink of an eye. The doting dad of five daughters (two grown girls from his first marriage) admits the song tore him up the first time he heard it, and that it took several takes in the studio for him to make it through the recording without breaking down. As members of the audience wiped tears from their eyes, Adkins flipped the script; he and his band kicked into "Hot Mama," the wink-and-a-nod tip of the hat to moms with a sassy side. On that night, he told the Opry audience, "Don't look to me to be the guy that's going to carry the torch for traditional country music, 'cause that ain't gonna happen. If you expect that, I'm going to disappoint you."

Adkins knows something about disappointment, though for a long time, he was on the receiving end. He grew up in Sarepta, Louisiana, and in high school joined a

Trace Adkins.	gospel quartet, the New Commitments. While his resonate baritone perfectly fit into the four-part harmonies that define that genre of music, his larger-than-life, no-holds-barred personality was better suited to the rough-and-ready honky-tonks of Louisiana and Texas where he performed when he wasn't working on offshore oil rigs. After about ten years of knocking around, and knocking on doors with no response, Adkins put away his guitar and his dreams and called it a day. Though he tried to quit music, music wouldn't quit him, and in 1992, he moved to Nashville to give it his last best shot. He worked construction by day and played bars at night, and finally a Music Row producer wandered into one of those bars and heard Adkins sing. He signed him almost on the spot, and in 1996, Capitol Records released Adkins' debut album, *Dreamin' Out Loud.* That record delivered a one-two-three punch: "Every Light in the House," went to number 3; "I Left Something Turned on at Home" hit number 2; and "(This Ain't) No Thinkin' Thing" became his first number 1 hit. Oddly it would be his last number 1 hit for some time, as his next two albums disappointed on airplay and sales charts. Adkins may have been down, but the big guy wasn't out; in 2001, he got back up to speed with *Chrome* and has been on a roll since. Adkins' powerful voice carries well beyond country radio and concert stages; he's a frequent guest—in cartoon form—on the animated show *King of the Hill,* has been national spokesman for KFC, done ads for trucks and jeans, and narrated music and Western documentaries. He is also frequently on the hot seat as a regular guest on Bill Maher's *Politically Incorrect;* the unabashed right-wing Republican says what he means and means what he says. He isn't afraid to raise the ire of left-leaning thinkers, nor is he adverse to raising eyebrows of social conservatives with the sexually suggestive lyrics and overtly sexual images of one of his biggest—and most unexpected—songs and videos to date, "Honky Tonk Badonkadonk." As audacious as he may appear, Adkins knows there's a time and a place for everything, and he won't be repeating his 2006 ACM Awards show no-holds-barred performance of the hit—surrounded by sixteen gyrating Las Vegas showgirls—on the stage of the Grand Ole Opry. But there's no doubt that every time he performs on the Opry, the audience can expect the unexpected.

On the sweltering August night that he joined the cast of the Grand Ole Opry, his segment was hosted by a true hot mama, Lorrie Morgan. Afterwards, Adkins, Opry members, family, and friends celebrated backstage between shows with a surf and turf buffet prepared by the Wildhorse Saloon catering crew.

Marinated Grilled Vegetable Skewers with Lemon Thyme Dressing

Recipe by Michael E. Swann, Executive Chef, Gaylord Opryland Resort and Convention Center

Skewers

1 cup zucchini cut into 1-inch squares

1 cup red bell pepper cut into 1-inch squares

12 large cherry tomatoes

12 medium shiitake mushroom caps

1 cup Japanese eggplant cut into 1-inch squares

Twelve 10-inch bamboo skewers, soaked in water for 1 hour

Lemon Thyme dressing

½ cup grapeseed oil

¼ cup extra virgin olive oil

⅓ cup white balsamic vinegar

¼ cup fresh chopped thyme

2 tablespoons chopped curly parsley

¼ cup kosher salt

1 teaspoon ground black pepper

Juice of two lemons

Juice of one lime

Mix all dressing ingredients together and blend with an immersion blender until emulsified, or whisk together briskly with small whisk or fork. Let set up for 1 hour.

Place vegetables on skewers in the order listed above. Place skewers into half of the dressing and marinade for 15 minutes. Grill on open fire grill until brown on all sides. Baste with remaining dressing and serve immediately.

TRACE ADKINS' OPRY INDUCTION PARTY MENU

Vegetable crudité's served with house-made dips

Seasonal and tropical sliced fruits

Imported and domestic cheeses with gourmet crackers

Chips and salsa

Grilled shrimp skewers with chili and cilantro

Marinated, grilled seasonal vegetable skewers with lemon thyme
    dressing

Smoked prime rib of beef, au jus, with creamed horseradish

Onion, French, and seven-grain rolls

Soft drinks and bottled waters

Decorated cake

The Del McCoury Band. L to R: Ronnie McCoury, Jason Carter, Rob McCoury, Del McCoury, and Alan Bartram.

Del McCoury

Joined the Opry cast in 2003

Del McCoury was born in Bakersville, North Carolina, but his family moved to York County, Pennsylvania, when he was a child. Jean Campbell was also born in North Carolina, and when she was just a year old, her family moved to Maryland. In 1960, Jean went to see her uncle, a bluegrass musician, perform at a show in Baltimore and caught the eye of the young banjo player in that band, who asked her uncle if he could drive his niece home. The next night, Del McCoury showed up at Jean's front door, and though her parents were not initially keen on the idea of their daughter dating a musician, four years later, they were married. The newlyweds moved to California in 1964, but didn't find the lifestyle to their liking, and came back home to York County about six months later. "I guess you could say we're both half Yankee," Jean admits. That might be true, but the McCoury family is pedigree bluegrass, through and through.

McCoury's family was musical, particularly fond of old-time music, and tuned in regularly to the Grand Ole Opry. In 1950, older brother G.C. brought home some 78s recorded by Flatt and Scruggs, and Del McCoury was hooked from the first time he heard "Rolling in My Sweet Baby's Arms." With help from his brother, he learned to play banjo; when he couldn't find anyone to teach him the three-finger style, he taught himself by listening to Scruggs over and over on record, and practicing until he got it right.

McCoury hooked up with Keith Daniels, another North Carolina refugee who was living in Baltimore, and he began performing with Keith Daniels and the Blue Ridge Partners in 1958, then later with younger brother Jerry with the Franklin County Boys, and finally with Jack Cooke's Virginia Playboys. It was through Cooke that McCoury came to play with Bill Monroe in 1963 as a member of the Blue Grass Boys. Monroe already had a banjo player, so he asked McCoury to audition to be his guitar player. Though he hadn't played guitar seriously since he was a child, he got the guitarist job and the role of lead singer to boot, singing in the high lonesome style Monroe popularized. He was a Blue Grass Boy for a year, appearing several times on the Opry, until he moved to California to join the Golden State Boys.

When he and Jean returned to York County, he took jobs doing construction and logging, while immersing himself in the bluegrass scene that thrived in the Maryland, Pennsylvania, and Virginia area. He and Blue Grass Boy alumnus Billy Baker formed the Shady Valley Boys, and then Del started his own band, Del McCoury and the Dixie Pals. Bluegrass wasn't a particularly lucrative genre of the music industry in the sixties and seventies, so the members of most bluegrass acts moved in and out of bands frequently. Even though he could only devote himself part-time to music, McCoury recorded some albums and established a good reputation on the circuit. When he traveled—weekends doing bluegrass festivals as far as a thousand miles away—Jean was at home with their three children, Rhonda, Ronnie, and Rob.

At one of his father's shows in New York's Lincoln Center, Bill Monroe let Ronnie play his mandolin, and it made such an impression that he devoted himself to the instrument, becoming good enough that in 1981, when he was just thirteen, he began playing with the band on a part-time basis. Rob McCoury joined his dad and brother onstage in 1987, first on bass before moving on to banjo. With both his boys by his side, Del changed the name of the Dixie Pals to the Del McCoury Band.

In 1992, having two albums under their belt, the family moved to Nashville and the Del McCoury Band moved to the forefront of the bluegrass world, beginning their remarkable collection of awards from the International Bluegrass Music Association.

On October 25, 2003, McCoury became a member of the Grand Ole Opry, inducted by Patty Loveless, with whom he sang "Workin' on a Building."

He and the band have not confined themselves to bluegrass, performing and recording with Steve Earle, Phish, and the String Cheese Incident; covering songs by Tom Petty as well as the Lovin' Spoonful; and appearing at internationally known music festivals like Bonnaroo, High Sierra, and Newport Folk Festival.

In 2006, Del McCoury finally realized a project he began twenty-five years before with the release of his first gospel album, *The Promised Land*, recording seven songs from the late Albert Brumley's catalogue, as well as "Gold Under My Feet," written by fellow Opry member Billy Walker, who had pitched it to McCoury one night at the Opry's winter home in the Ryman. Though Walker tragically died in a traffic accident in May 2006, he did get to hear McCoury's recording of his song before he passed. Another, "Ain't Nothing Gonna Come Up Today," was co-written by McCoury and Jerry Salley, inspired by the motto on the door of Roy Acuff's dressing room at the Grand Ole Opry House, which reads, "Ain't Nothin Gonna Come Up Today That Me And The Lord Can't Handle."

According to Jean, her husband would have a hard time handling anything very complicated in the kitchen, as he's not much of a cook. "Well, he could probably cook an egg if he had to, but he doesn't really ever have to." Jean is the cook in the family, and when her husband was still playing in bands up north, she recalls many get-togethers with other musicians and their families. "They would come over to the house with their wives and children. I would cook some main dishes, and the other women would bring sides and desserts. We'd eat and the guys would play and sing. The kids were little then. It was just so much fun; those were really special times."

Though the McCourys lived above the Mason-Dixon for most of their lives, she considers herself a Southern cook. "I'm the oldest of three girls, and I guess I learned to cook watching my mother, and she was raised in the South. Now I don't do a lot of frying anymore, but on weekends when Del's home, I make a big breakfast—eggs, bacon, sausage, biscuits, and gravy. Back when we lived in York County, I worked for about ten years, usually on the second shift. I always made supper before I went to work at night and left it on the stove, so if they came home from a show while I was at work, they had something good to eat."

Though Rob and Ronnie are both married, they still love Mama's cooking, and the entire McCoury family gathers at Jean and Del's for holidays—turkey for Thanksgiving, ham for Christmas and Easter—and anniversaries and birthdays. One thing they count on is Jean's Black Cake. "I've been making this cake forever. I can hardly read the recipe card anymore it's got so many stains on it and the writing is so faded, but I know it by heart I've made it so many times. We have this cake at every holiday, and it's a tradition for anniversaries and of course birthdays. I don't know if it's Southern or Yankee—maybe it's half of each, like Del and I—but it's good and everybody in the family loves it."

Jean McCoury's Half-Yankee Black Cake

2 cups flour	2 cups sugar
¾ cup cocoa	2 eggs
¾ cup vegetable or canola oil	1 teaspoon baking powder
2 teaspoons baking soda	2 teaspoons vanilla
½ teaspoon salt	2 teaspoons instant coffee

Beat flour, cocoa, oil, baking soda, salt, sugar, eggs, baking powder, and vanilla together in electric mixer for two minutes. Dissolve instant coffee in 1 cup warm water, and add to batter. Mix until completely blended. Pour batter in greased 9-by-13-inch baking pan. Bake at 350° for 30 to 35 minutes. Cool before frosting.

Frosting

1 cup milk	1 cup sugar
2 tablespoons cornstarch	1 teaspoon vanilla
1 cup Crisco	Creamy peanut butter

In a saucepan over medium heat, stir together milk and cornstarch until thick, remove from heat, and set aside to cool. In bowl, vigorously beat Crisco, sugar, and vanilla until fluffy and soft. Add cooled cornstarch mixture and mix well. Add creamy peanut butter by the tablespoon to personal taste. Frost cake. (This recipe makes more frosting than you will need.)

Terri Clark

Joined the Opry cast in 2004

In the western part of Canada, country music is tremendously popular, and it provided the soundtrack to Terri Clark's youth in Medicine Hat, Alberta, about twenty-five hundred miles away from Nashville. Her grandparents, Betty and Ray Gauthier, were musicians who worked the Canadian country music circuit, opening shows for Opry legends and country stars like Johnny Cash, George Jones, and Little Jimmy Dickens. Though they retired before Clark was born, many of her early childhood memories are of informal jam sessions with their musician friends in their living room. Terri's mother, Linda, a folksinger, sang her daughter to sleep, and when she was nine, taught her three chords on an acoustic guitar. The instrument rarely left her hands until her sixteenth birthday, when her father gave her a Martin D-28 guitar. Bands and public performances ensued, and shortly after her high school graduation, girl and guitar headed to Nashville at age nineteen.

First stop, Tootsies Orchid Lounge, where she talked her way into a job singing for tips. She played three days a week, making about twenty-five to thirty dollars a day, supplementing that with odd jobs around town. As Grand Ole Opry announcer Hairl Hensley says when he kicks off the Tootsies segment of the show, the world-famous nightclub is "just thirty-seven steps to Tootsies from the Grand Ole Opry, seventy-four for Little Jimmy Dickens!" But the challenge for hundreds of aspiring entertainers who flock to Music City and haunt the honky-tonks of Lower Broad hoping for their big chance is getting from the stage of Tootsies to the stage of the Grand Ole Opry.

For Terri Clark, progress was measured in two-year increments. In 1989, just two years after her arrival, she met her future manager, who sent the raw, young talent to professional finishing school, teaming her up with a vocal coach and a veteran publisher. Two years after that, a five-song demo secured her a publishing deal with Sony/Tree, which offered a $350 weekly advance, a sign to Clark that she was on the

Terri Clark.

right path. One thing led to another, and in 1993, she was signed to Mercury Records. In July 1995, her first single, "Better Things to Do," hit country radio. Clark and her band hit the road, and by the end of the year, *Billboard* magazine named her Top New Female Country Artist.

While she counts Loretta Lynn, Patsy Cline, Barbara Mandrell, and Reba McEntire as musical influences and career role models, her look was more George Strait and Clint Black: blue jeans, boots, and an artfully shaped Stetson tagged her Nashville's first female hat act. Her confident presence, bold personality, outspoken opinions, sassy material, and imposing physical presence—she's five feet eleven inches without the boots and hat—made Terri Clark one of the most distinctive female artists in contemporary country music.

In 2004, she added another distinction to her list of career achievements: the first female Canadian artist—and only the third Canuck after members Hank Snow and Stu Phillips—to join the cast of the Grand Ole Opry. The surprise invitation was extended during an Opry performance. At the close of her song "Girls Lie Too," Steve Wariner joined her at the mike and, noting how much the Opry loved surprises, told her there was one waiting in the wings for her. At that cue, her mother, who had been flown in from Alberta, walked onto the stage with a sign that read simply, "Grand Ole Opry, June 12."

It was as close to an engraved invitation as would come, and her response was immediate and effusive. "Ever since I was a little girl, I dreamed of being on the Grand Ole Opry. It was enough for me just to stand onstage with those people, but to get invited to be a member is incredible."

On June 12, 2004, Marty Stuart, Pam Tillis, and Patty Loveless welcomed Terri Clark to the cast. Standing on the circle of wood taken from the stage of the old Ryman Auditorium—thirty-seven steps and seventeen years from where she got her start in Nashville—Clark sang her hits "I Wanna Do It All" and "Girls Lie Too," and closed out the segment with "Walkin' After Midnight," paying tribute to a Grand Ole Opry legend.

Terri Clark might hail from the far north, but at her request, her induction party menu was pure south of the border.

TERRI CLARK'S OPRY INDUCTION PARTY MENU
June 12, 2004

Chips and salsa

Vegetable crudités with Mexican dip

Taco and fajita station with spicy ground beef, spicy chicken strips, onions, peppers, taco shells, and flour tortillas

Black beans

Sour cream, guacamole, diced tomatoes, shredded cheese, black olives, and salsa

Coffee, tea, and soft drinks

Decorated cake

Dierks Bentley.

Dierks Bentley

Joined the Opry cast in 2005

While it wasn't necessarily a shotgun wedding, Dierks Bentley and the Grand Ole Opry had a very short engagement. And Marty Stuart, who extended the proposal, didn't exactly get on one knee. Bentley was about an hour into his show at the House of Blues in Los Angeles in late July 2005 when Stuart walked out onstage and popped the question to the confused Bentley and a puzzled audience. Taking the mike, he said, "Dierks, will you marry the Grand Ole Opry?"

Two months later, the ceremony was performed on the Grand Ole Opry stage, a career milestone on a very long and winding road trip.

A DNA profile on Bentley would hardly have predicted a future as a hard-core country music singer. He was born and raised in a totally nonmusical family in Phoenix, Arizona. Frustrated by fruitless attempts as a young teen to learn the rock and roll guitar licks all his peers were playing, his direction abruptly changed course when a friend played him a Hank Williams, Jr., song, "Man to Man." He connected with country, and there was no looking back. At nineteen, Phoenix was in his rearview mirror, and his destination was Nashville. In Music City, armed with a fake ID, he enrolled in Country Clubbing 101, taking classes in local bars from seasoned professors working the live music scene. He embedded himself in the front row of the Station Inn, Nashville's bluegrass institution, studying house band the Sidemen every Tuesday night, taking tips from lead singer Terry Eldredge, who told the aspiring artist, "Hear it in your head, process it through your heart, and let it come out of your mouth."

He got a regular gig at the city's most notorious dive bar, the Springwater, a venue so proudly rundown that fixing the leaky roof wasn't considered; instead, when it rained, musicians simply sidestepped the puddles onstage to avoid electrocution. Bentley set a goal that before his twenty-third birthday, he would play the songwriter's citadel, the Bluebird Cafe, and with just a few weeks to spare, he crossed that one off his list.

His day job was carefully chosen to further his education; like Alan Jackson, he snagged a position at The Nashville Network, but rather than the mail room, where Alan toiled, Bentley was assigned to the tape library. Researching old music footage for the network for a country music documentary, he began making his own textbooks, compiling lists of classic and obscure songs that caught his eye and ear.

Bentley eschewed industry functions and parties for the honky-tonks of Lower Broad, where he continued to hone his stage performance and try out the songs he was writing. The next step was cutting his own album; using rock, country, and bluegrass musicians, his sound was a unique blend of all three genres, distinguished by his clean, fresh vocals. The project led to a writing deal with Sony/Tree, an iconic Nashville publishing company whose roster of greats includes Nashville Songwriting Hall of Famers like Harlan Howard and Hank Cochran. Bentley was paired up with another Tree writer, Brett Beavers, and when the voice on their demos piqued the interest of label executives in town, he did a showcase and ended up signing with Capitol Records. In short order, an album was made, a single released, and Bentley hit the road with his band.

In his first full year on a major label, Bentley spent three hundred days on the road, a grueling—though he maintains exhilarating and inspirational—schedule that was not dissimilar to the ones experienced by charter members of the Grand Ole Opry and the country and bluegrass legends who influenced him. His debut self-titled album turned out three chart-busting hits—the instantly recognized "What Was I Thinkin'" foremost—and set the stage for his onstage invitation to join the Grand Ole Opry.

On October 1, 2005, Dierks Bentley became the youngest member of the Grand Ole Opry at that time, his induction fittingly taking place during the segment sponsored by one of his old haunts, Tootsies Orchid Lounge. After performing "Come a Little Closer," he was joined onstage by the man who first extended the invitation, Marty Stuart. Presenting Bentley to the audience, he said, "As country music has changed and grown through the years, the one thing that has remained steady is the Grand Ole Opry. I am proud to introduce the newest member . . . Dierks Bentley."

During the induction, Opry general manager Pete Fisher presented Bentley with the Opry Member Award, a fourteen-inch bronze and oak wood replica of the Opry's vintage microphone stand designed by renowned sculptor Bill Rains. A portion of the trophy's wooden base recreates the famed circle of wood taken from the stage of the Ryman Auditorium, home of the Opry from 1943 to 1974, and placed in the stage at the Grand Ole Opry House. The wood used, taken from old Ryman pews, became available following the Ryman's restoration in 1994. Holding up the coveted trophy that has been presented to each current and new cast member since 2000, Bentley said, "This here is the ultimate backstage pass. I share this honor with these guys behind me who ride the bus. Thanks!"

Between shows, members of the Opry cast, management, crew, friends, and family joined Bentley and his band backstage for the reception catered by Gaylord Opryland Resort.

Tennessee Smoky Mountain Paella

Recipe by Michael E. Swann, Executive Chef, Gaylord Opryland Resort and Convention Center

With chicken apple sausage, white fish, scallops, and shrimp. Served with Tennessee Hoppin' John risotto.

Paella

1 pound Aidells of San Francisco chicken apple sausage, cut into 1-inch cubes
1 pound whitefish, cod, or halibut, cut into 1-ounce pieces
1 pound (10 to 20 count) sea scallops, with straps removed
1 pound (16 to 20 count) shrimp, peeled and deveined
½ cup basil pesto

Rub all sausage and seafood down with the pesto and let rest for 2 hours. Roast in 350° oven for 12 to 15 minutes, and let rest.

Rice

½ cup extra virgin olive oil

1 medium onion, diced

½ cup red chile pepper, diced

2 cups arborio rice

2 quarts chicken broth

¼ pound Parmesan cheese, shredded

½ cup curly parsley, chopped

½ cup kosher salt

⅛ cup ground black pepper

¾ cup cooked black-eyed peas

2 cups fresh turnip or mustard greens, washed and stemmed, cut into 2-by-2-inch pieces

In a 16-inch paella pan, add 2 ounces of olive oil and heat until it smokes. Add the onions, pepper, and raw rice; cook until the rice slightly browns. Gradually add the chicken broth in 1 cup increments until all stock is absorbed. Add cheese, parsley, salt, pepper, black-eyed peas, stir with a wooden spoon until smooth and rice has no crunch, approximately 20 minutes. Add sausage, seafood, greens, and remaining olive oil to the paella pan. Serve immediately with a glass of sangria. Serves six 8-ounce portions.

Sangria Wine

Twelve 7.5 milliliter bottles merlot or zinfandel wine

4 oranges, cut into wedges

4 limes, cut into wedges

4 lemons, cut into wedges

1 pineapple, cut into wedges

3 Granny Smith apples, cut into wedges

2 Anjou pears, cut into wedges

¼ cup sugar

3 cinnamon sticks

Pour all wine into a large glass container. Wash and cut all fruit and marinate in wine for 2 hours in refrigerator. Strain, add sugar and stir well to dissolve. Add cinnamon sticks and serve cold.

DIERKS BENTLEY'S OPRY INDUCTION PARTY MENU

October 1, 2005

Corn Bread Panzanella (diced corn bread tossed with diced tomatoes, cucumbers, red onion, garlic, and fresh herbs) with marinated asparagus

Antipasto tray of Parma ham and imported provolone cheese, salami and mortadella, marinated peppers and mushrooms, grilled artichokes and eggplant, Greek and Italian olives, artisan breads and bread sticks

Tennessee Paella (roasted chicken apple sausage, whitefish, scallops, and shrimp) served with Tennessee Hoppin' John risotto, black beans, and organic local greens

Fried green tomatoes with a tomato coulis

Fried pickles with chipotle aioli

Chocolate picture collage of Dierks and Jake the Dog

Chocolate cake from Sweet 16th bakery

Iced tea, lemonade, and coffee

Recipe Index

Bibliography

In addition to numerous personal interviews with Opry members and staff, and firsthand knowledge, the author relied upon publicity materials from record labels, management firms, and sponsor corporate offices, as well as the following published works, Web sites, and electronic material from the Internet.

Reference List, Print Material:

Bufwak, Mary A., and Robert K. Oermann. *Finding Her Voice: Women in Country Music 1800–2000.* Nashville: Vanderbilt University Press and the Country Music Foundation Press, 2003.

Eng, Steve. *A Satisfied Mind: The Country Music Life of Porter Wagoner.* Nashville: Rutledge Hill Press, 1992.

Schlappi, Elizabeth. *Roy Acuff: The Smokey Mountain Boy.* Gretna, LA: Pelican Publishing Company, 1978, 1993.

All Music Guide to Country: The Definitive Guide to Country Music. 2nd edition. San Francisco: Backbeat Books, 2003.

The Encyclopedia of Country Music: The Ultimate Guide to the Music. New York: Oxford University Press, 1998.

Grand Ole Opry 80th Anniversary Picture History Book. Nashville: Gaylord Entertainment Company, 2005.

Martha White's Southern Sampler: Ninety Years of Baking Tradition. Nashville: Rutledge Hill Press, 1989.

Pickers, Slickers, Cheatin' Hearts & Superstars: Country the Music and the Musicians. New York: Abbeville Press, 1988.

Reference List, Internet sources:

Alabama Music Hall of Fame, www.alamhof.org/index.html

Ankeny, Jason; Brennan, Sandra; Bush, John; Cooper, Peter; Davis, Hank; Erlewine, Michael; Erlewine, Stephen Thomas; Huey, Steve; Kurutz, Steve; Manheim, James; Vinopol, David. All Music Guide, www.allmusic.com

Birthplace of Country Music Alliance, www.birthplaceofcountrymusic.org

Country Music Hall of Fame, Hall of Fame Inductees, www.countrymusic halloffame.com/site/inductees

Country Music Television, Inc., www.cmt.com/artists/

The Grand Ole Opry, www.opry.com

Hillbilly-Music.com, www.hillbilly-music.com/index.php

International Bluegrass Music Museum, Hall of Honor, www.bluegrass-museum.org/hallofhonor.html

Nashville Songwriters Foundation, Nashville Songwriters Hall of Fame, www.nashvillesongwritersfoundation.com

The National Academy of Popular Music, Songwriters Hall of Fame, songhall.org/index.php/splash

Neal, Chris, *The Nashville Scene,* "The Quiet Man," www.nashvillescene .com/Stories/Arts/2005/08/04/The_Quiet_Man/index.shtml

Rock and Roll Hall of Fame, www.rockhall.com

Uncle Dave Macon Days, www.uncledavemacondays.com

Permissions

Books:

Cash, June Carter. *Mother Maybelle's Cookbook: A Kitchen Visit with America's First Family of Country Song.* New York: Wynwood Press, 1989. Used by permission.

Cash, Mrs. Ray. *Recipes and Memories from Mama Cash's Kitchen.* Goodletsville, TN: Southern Post Card Co., 1981. Used by permission.

Parton, Willadeene. *All-Day Singing & Dinner on the Ground.* Nashville: Rutledge Hill Press, 1997. Used by permission. Thanks to Willadeene Parton.

Pearl, Minnie. *Minnie Pearl Cooks.* Nashville: Aurora Publishers, 1970. Used by permission.

Pruett, Jeanne. *Feedin' Friends.* Vol. 1. Franklin, TN: Harris Press, 1986. Used by permission. "I love feedin' my music friends," Jeanne Pruett.

Wells, Kitty. *Kitty Wells Country Kitchen Cookbook.* Madison, TN: Kitty's Cook Book Co., 1964. Used by permission.

Song Lyrics:

"Candy Kisses" Words and Music by GEORGE MORGAN © 1948 (Renewed) UNICHAPPELL MUSIC, INC. All Rights Reserved. Used by Permission of ALFRED PUBLISHING CO., INC.

"I Like Beer" Words and Music by TOM T. HALL © SONY/ATV ACUFF ROSE MUSIC. All Rights Reserved. Used by Permission of SONY/ATV MUSIC PUBLISHING.

"Jambalaya" Words and Music by HANK WILLIAMS © 1952 (Renewed) SONY/ATV ACUFF ROSE MUSIC and HIRIAM MUSIC for U.S.A. World outside U.S.A. controlled by SONY/ATV ACUFF ROSE MUSIC. All Rights Reserved. Used by Permission of SONY/ATV MUSIC PUBLISHING and ALFRED PUBLISHING

Photo Credits

From the Grand Ole Opry Archives: pp. xx, 4, 7, 8, 12, 14, 22, 28, 48, 53, 62, 66, 77, 80, 84, 192

Additional Sources:
Alan Mayor: p. 112; Charles Small: p. 200; Chris Hollo: pp. 56, 89, 94, 104, 110, 114, 121, 122, 124, 130, 142, 146, 152, 154, 172, 174, 176, 188, 194, 198, 209, 214, 218, 226, 232, 236, 243, 246, 252, 258, 262, 268, 270, 275; Curtis Hilburn: pp. 220, 238; Donnie Beauchamp: pp. 23, 26, 38; Gaylord Entertainment: p. 160 (bottom photo); Gordon Gillingham: pp. 32, 71, 76, 88, 108; James M. Clymer, Jr.: p. 46; John Hood: p. 40; Les Leverett: pp. 138, 139, 159, 160 (top photo), 166, 179, 182, 215; Marvin Cartwright: p. 98; Philip Hight: p. 265; Sid O'Berry: p. 132

All other illustrations and photographs are unattributed and from the Grand Ole Opry archives.